AF174163

Luminos is the Open Access monograph publishing program from UC Press. Luminos provides a framework for preserving and reinvigorating monograph publishing for the future and increases the reach and visibility of important scholarly work. Titles published in the UC Press Luminos model are published with the same high standards for selection, peer review, production, and marketing as those in our traditional program. www.luminosoa.org

The Suburban Frontier

The publisher and the University of California Press Foundation
gratefully acknowledge the generous support of the
Ahmanson Foundation Endowment Fund in Humanities.

The Suburban Frontier

Middle-Class Construction in Dar es Salaam

Claire Mercer

UNIVERSITY OF CALIFORNIA PRESS

University of California Press
Oakland, California

© 2024 by Claire Mercer

ORCID profile: Claire Mercer https://orcid.org/0000-0003-0991-3693

Suggested citation: Mercer, C. *The Suburban Frontier: Middle-Class Construction in Dar es Salaam*. Oakland: University of California Press, 2024. DOI: https://doi.org/10.1525/luminos.199

Library of Congress Cataloging-in-Publication Data

Names: Mercer, Claire, author.
Title: The suburban frontier : middle-class construction in Dar es Salaam / Claire Mercer.
Description: Oakland, California : University of California Press, [2024] | Includes bibliographical references and index.
Identifiers: LCCN 2024008350 | ISBN 9780520402386 (paperback) | ISBN 9780520402393 (ebook)
Subjects: LCSH: Middle class—Tanzania—Dar es Salaam. | Urbanization—Tanzania—Dar es Salaam. | Suburbs—Tanzania—Dar es Salaam. | Real estate investment—Tanzania—Dar es Salaam.
Classification: LCC HT384.A35 D37 2024 | DDC 307.7409678/232—dc23/eng/20240412

LC record available at https://lccn.loc.gov/2024008350

33 32 31 30 29 28 27 26 25 24
10 9 8 7 6 5 4 3 2 1

For Adam

CONTENTS

ILLUSTRATIONS

FIGURES

MAPS

TABLES

ACKNOWLEDGMENTS

This book is the outcome of many long-term relationships for which I am deeply grateful. In Tanzania, this book project started in the home of Clement and Frediel Kwayu, into which I have always been so generously invited. Aililya introduced me to house-builders and Aikande has deepened my understanding of Tanzania. The support and friendship of Angellah Swai and of Perfect, Queen, and Pudensiana has sustained me in Tanzania since we first met in 1996. Thank you to Claudia and (the late) Conrad Mtui and their family for welcoming me into their wonderful home in Dar es Salaam.

Fieldwork in Tanzania was conducted with the permission of the Tanzania Commission for Science and Technology, which I gratefully acknowledge here. This book would not have been possible without the generosity of the numerous people with whom I spoke in Salasala, to whom I am indebted. At the University of Dar es Salaam, I have benefited from the support and insights of Opportuna Kweka and Bashiru Ally, and from the assistance of Hysinta Antony, Bernard Dedas, and Dickson Kikoti. Thank you to John Lupala, Sarah Kyessi, Danny Mwasandube, Aisa Solomon, and Marygrace Webber for their time and expertise, and to Wilbard Kombe, Faustin Maganga, Cosmas Msoka, and Daniel Msangi for sharing insights from their research. I have also learned a great deal from my current coresearchers Isaac Arthur, Tony Asare, Thomas Gillespie, Maia Green, Iddy Mayumana, Diana Mitlin, George Owusu, and George Temba. Joseph Kironde and Shaaban Sheuya deserve special mention for their enormous insight into housing in Tanzania, which they have so generously shared. Thank you to Lisa Richey and the Everyday Humanitarianism in Tanzania team for all the generative conversations—Line Engbo Gissel, Herbert Hambati, Lucas Kitula, Peter Kragelund, Hamudi Majamba, Esther Mlingwa, Rosemary Msoka, Daudi Mukangara, Innocent Pantaleo, Mogens

Kamp Justesen, Yvette Ruzibiza, Consolata Sulley, and Simon Turner. In Dar es Salaam I always look forward to seeing Peter Bofin and Elector Kilusungu, Elise Rupiah, Ramadhani Mongi, Sakina Mwinyimkuu and Antony Mwendemaka, Aluta and Zubeda Kweka, Emmanuel Tayari and Resty Gombo and Omari Mbura. Thank you all for your friendship and support over the years.

At the London School of Economics and Political Science I am extremely lucky to work with a wonderful group of scholars and students. I am especially grateful to Ryan Centner, Julia Corwin, Alicia Lazzarini, Kasia Paprocki, Megan Ryburn, and Austin Zeiderman, who read and commented on multiple chapters. Thank you also to the past and present regular participants in the Writing the World seminar in the Department of Geography and Environment for the stimulating and supportive intellectual community that you helped to build over the years I was writing this book: Laura Antona, Emmanuel Awohouedji, Mattie Cox, Kate Dawson, Pooya Ghoddousi, Yoonai Han, Martina Manara, Sandiswa Mapukata, Tanya Matthan, Carwyn Morris, Billy Ndengeyingoma, Gabriela Neves de Lima, Mara Nogueira-Teixiera, Morgan Olive-Carmellini, Erica Pani, Harry Pettit, Vishnu Prasad, Niranjana Ramesh, Line Relisieux, Fizzah Sajjad, Deen Sharp, Sraman Sircar, Jessie Speer, Vittoria Sottini, Frida Timan, Ran Wei, and Melissa Weihmayer. Thank you also to my colleagues Nancy Holman, Gareth Jones, Murray Low, Alan Mace, Romola Sanyal, Hyun Bang Shin, and Michael Storper. Special thanks to the late Sylvia Chant, whose enthusiasm, care, and incisive commentary is greatly missed. At LSE I have also learned much from conversations with Catherine Allerton, Catherine Boone, Ernestina Coast, Carolin Dieterle, Suzi Hall, Deborah James, David Lewis, Kate Meagher, and Alpa Shah.

The book has been vastly improved after close reading of all or parts of it by Marco di Nunzio, Claudia Gastrow, Garth Myers, Ben Page, Lisa Richey, and Jason Sumich. I have long benefited from the friendship and scholarship of Jim Brennan, Dan Brockington, Helen Dancer, Mike Degani, Hazel Gray, Andy Ivaska, Irmelin Joelson, Alexandra Panman, Matteo Rizzo, and Stina Møldrup Wolff, and especially of the 1990s TYCS crowd—Ned Bertz, Dan Brockington, Laura Edmondson, Jim Igoe, Tim Kelsall, Kathleen Mulligan Hansel, Stefano Ponte, and Lisa Richey. I am also grateful for the many conversations I have had over the years about geography, African cities, and the middle classes with Julie Archambault, Chloe Buiré, Corentin Chanet, Sharad Chari, SJ Cooper-Knock, Tom Cowan, Owen Crankshaw, Patricia Daley, Jason Dittmer, Alastair Fraser, Tom Goodfellow, Zoe Groves, Branwen Gruffydd Jones, Tariq Jazeel, Lena Kroeker, Charlotte Lemanski, Carola Lentz, Zoe Marks, Colin McFarlane, JoAnn McGregor, Paula Meth, Morten Nielsen, Joël Noret, Sasha Newell, David O'Kane, Sue Parnell, Jenny Robinson, Tabia Scharrer, Jonathan Silver, AbdouMaliq Simone, Rachel Spronk, Tatiana Thieme, and Katie Willis.

Funding for the research on which the book is based was awarded by the LSE Department of Geography and Environment Seed Fund, LSE STICERD and the

Economic and Social Research Council (grant ES/V002759/1). I am also grateful to the Department of Geography and Environment at LSE for the two terms of sabbatical that I was granted in 2020–21, during which I wrote a large part of the book.

At the University of California Press, I am grateful to have worked first with Kim Robinson and then with Naja Pulliam Collins. Naja has skillfully and enthusiastically guided me through the book production process. A huge thank-you to Line Relisieux for her help in the final stages of preparing the book manuscript, and to Elise Rupiah for help with Swahili. The original maps in the book were expertly drawn by Mina Moshkeri (formerly of the LSE Design Unit) and Kelvin Kamnde (of the Department of Geography at the University of Dar es Salaam). I am particularly grateful to Joseph Kironde for tracking down a map of Dar es Salaam's squatter areas in the 1980s that originally appeared in his magisterial doctoral thesis on the history of land and housing in Dar es Salaam. Thank you as well to Manja Hoppe Andreasen for permitting me to use her excellent maps of Dar es Salaam as the basis to draw new ones. I am also grateful to Ohio University Press for allowing me to redraw a map of the 1920s urban planning zones that appeared in James Brennan's book *Taifa: Making Nation and Race in Urban Tanzania* (2012: 30). Maps 1 and 2 were previously published in: Claire Mercer, "Boundary Work: Becoming Middle Class in Suburban Dar es Salaam," *International Journal of Urban and Regional Research* 44, no. 3 (2020): 521–36. Parts of chapter 4 are published in: Claire Mercer, "The Coloniality of Space: Landscape, Aesthetics and the Middle Classes in Dar es Salaam," *Antipode* (forthcoming).

Finally, this book has been deeply shaped by my long-term research collaborations with Ben Page and Maia Green. Ben Page has shared every step of this intellectual and emotional journey: thank you. Maia Green has always made me see things differently: *asante dada*. Thank you to Mike and Lynne Clitheroe for their encouragement and for asking difficult questions about class formation while we were walking the dog. I am sorry that Mike didn't get to add the final product to his extensive library. Special thanks to Mum and Pippa for their boundless support, and for *not* asking difficult questions about class formation. Adam and Caspar stoically bore my absence while I was away doing fieldwork. Thank you both for all the joy you bring. This book is for Adam, who has been there all along. He has always said the title of the book should be *Sofas of Distinction*. I didn't follow his advice, but thank you, Adam, for everything else.

ABBREVIATIONS

AA	African Association
CCM	*Chama Cha Mapinduzi*, Party of the Revolution
DLHT	District Land and Housing Tribunal
DAWASCO	Dar es Salaam Water and Sewerage Corporation
GDP	Gross Domestic Product
IPTL	Independent Power Tanzania Ltd.
JKT	*Jeshi la Kujenga Taifa*, National Service Army
MKURABITA	*Mratibu wa Mpango wa Kurasimisha Rasilimali na Biashara za Wanyonge Tanzania*, Property and Business Formalization Program
MLHHSD	Ministry of Lands, Housing and Human Settlements Development
NHC	National Housing Corporation
OPEC	Organization of Petroleum Exporting Countries
SACODEA	Salasala Community Development Association
TANESCO	Tanzania Electricity Supply Company
TANU	Tanganyika African National Union
Tsh	Tanzanian Shilling
TTACSA	Tanganyika Territory African Civil Servants Association
URT	United Republic of Tanzania
WSG	Wazo Social Group

A NOTE ON EXCHANGE RATES

The Tanzanian shilling (TSh) has depreciated against other currencies over the time period covered in this book. According to the World Bank's data on average annual exchange rates, the equivalent value of $1 has changed from TSh9 (1982), to TSh575 (1995), to TSh1396 (2010), to TSh2294 (2020). Where possible, I have indicated the dollar equivalent for every value given in Tanzanian shillings. Where a specific year for the Tanzanian shilling value is not available, I have not provided a dollar equivalent.

Source: World Bank, "Official Exchange Rate (LCU per US$, period average—Tanzania," accessed November 12, 2023, https://data.worldbank.org/indicator /PA.NUS.FCRF?end=2021&locations=TZ&start=1982.

A NOTE ON PSEUDONYMS AND PLACE NAMES

I have used pseudonyms for all interviewees and social groups. Public servants and locally elected officials are referred to by the title of their office. Registered organizations are referred to by their real names. All place names are real.

Introduction

Middle-Class Construction on Dar es Salaam's Suburban Frontier

The house stirs at five a.m. on a Monday morning. There is noise and clatter as doors are banged on to wake those still asleep, bathing water is heated in the kettle in the kitchen, milk with spices is warmed for tea, breakfasts are hastily thrown together from the remains of last night's dinner, shirts are ironed, and school books are collected. Godwin corrals his nephew and his two children with a sense of increasing urgency. One by one the family members get into the car parked outside the house. On a good day they manage to leave by six a.m. Sammy, one of the domestic workers, pulls open the metal gate to let the car out. Headlights on: it's dark on the bumpy drive down the earth road that twists through the neighborhood to the smooth tarmac, where suddenly everything speeds up as you join the line of cars heading towards the city center. If you're not on the tarmac road by six a.m. you won't reach the city center until nine a.m., that's what they say.[1] Godwin, who works as a civil servant in a government office in the city center, takes a short detour from the tarmac road to drop his children at their private English-medium primary school. Later he drops his nephew, who has just started work with a state-owned bank on the other side of the city center. If all goes smoothly Godwin can get to his office, twenty kilometers from the smart house he built with his wife in Salasala, in the city's northern suburbs, by half past seven. His wife Gilda, who is self-employed, leaves the house later on in her smaller, older car, having instructed the two members of the domestic staff on their duties for the day. She runs a couple of small pharmacies and beauty parlors that she and Godwin have built in nearby suburban neighborhoods.

In the afternoon, the school bus brings the children back home. They watch television, play on the PlayStation, and maybe do some homework. Mercy, one of the domestic workers, starts preparing the evening meal based on instructions she has received on her mobile phone from Gilda, who is still at work supervising the repair of a hood hair dryer in one of her salons. She comes home at eight p.m. and quickly fries some fresh fish that she bought from a roadside vendor on the way home, to accompany the potatoes and vegetables that Mercy has prepared. Godwin comes in at half past eight, having mostly sat in traffic jams snaking out of the city since he left the office two-and-a-half hours previously. The household eats, some sitting in the open-plan kitchen/diner/living room, some in front of the large flat-screen television mounted on the wall in the living room, which is showing the national news. The headline is a story about a group of poor urban residents who are complaining about a government scheme to relocate them thirty kilometers from the city center after their makeshift homes in Dar es Salaam's Msimbazi Valley were destroyed by floods. Godwin grumbles, "But they know they shouldn't have been in there [the Valley] in the first place." His nephew arrives later on a *bodaboda* (motorcycle taxi) that he picked up at the nearby junction with the tarmac road, having reached there from the city center by bus. He has been to evening class after work to study for a graduate accountancy qualification.

By ten p.m. the front door and grille are locked and everyone is resting in their bedrooms, except for Gilda, who sits in front of the television, flicking between a US Christian television channel, a Nigerian Pentecostal channel, and her Whats-App groups on her smart phone—one each for her family members, her husband's family, the church committee, one for parents at the children's school, a group of neighbors, and one for a group of women entrepreneurs in Dar es Salaam. At five a.m. the next morning they start again.

This is a typical day for an upper-middle-class family in twenty-first-century Dar es Salaam, and I begin with it because it is both spectacular and ordinary. It is spectacular because the land on which Godwin and Gilda now live, in their self-built bungalow surrounded by a high wall, was farmland until the turn of the twenty-first century. As recently as the 1990s the city's northern hinterland was sparsely populated by a patchwork of extensive farms owned by indigenous Zaramo, who tended cashew and coconut trees, and some farms of various sizes owned by in-migrants and urbanites who grew fruit and vegetables for local markets, the larger of which grew for export.[2] In between were scattered small settlements, a couple of large stone quarries, some abandoned sisal plantations, and a cement factory. Just two decades later, the transformation of this hinterland into low-density, desirable residential neighborhoods was well underway as urbanites sought affordable land on which to build the house to which they aspired. It is also ordinary: middle-class suburban life centered on so many unremarkable dwellings that seem to embody a global suburban ideal: close enough to benefit from the city's economic and social life, but far enough not to have to deal with the everyday hubbub and hassle.[3]

These suburban neighborhoods have much in common with a globalized suburban model, but they are also distinctive in significant ways. Perhaps most

FIGURE 1. A house in the early stages of construction, Salasala, September 2012. Photo by author.

FIGURE 2. The same house in April 2015. Photo by author.

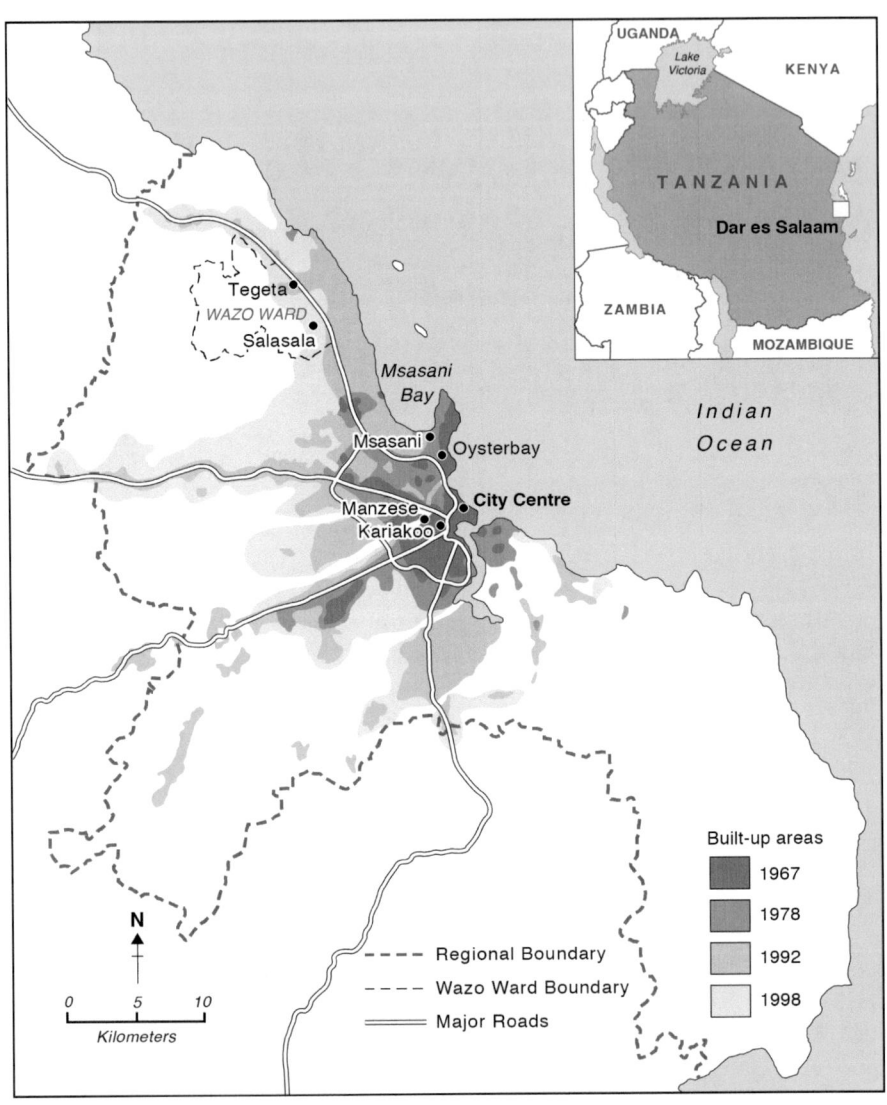

MAP 1. Dar es Salaam, showing growth of the city over time and the location of Wazo Ward and Salasala. Drawn by Mina Moshkeri 2018, based on Briggs and Mwamfupe (2000) and Andreasen (2013).

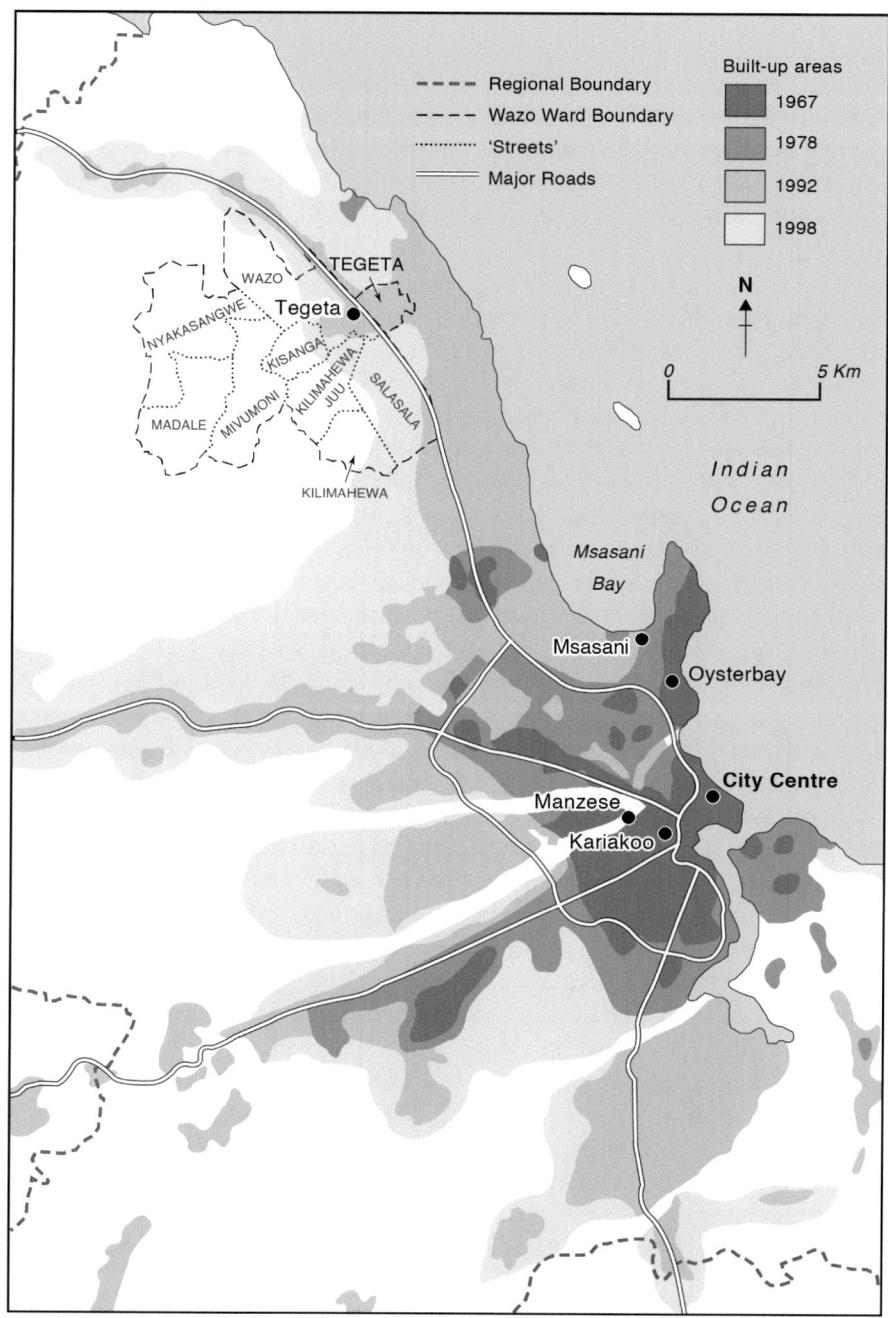

MAP 2. Subwards (*mitaa*) in Wazo Ward in 2018. Drawn by Mina Moshkeri 2018, based on Briggs and Mwamfupe (2000) and Andreasen (2013).

importantly, they are being developed through the repetition of thousands of individual cash-based domestic building projects rather than through large-scale financialized property development. The long history of land use and settlement that precedes the more recent self-building boom has given rise to a socially and spatially heterogenous suburban zone, much of it lacking tarmac roads, sanitation, and running water. These are, in fact, mostly informal settlements, but not as they have been commonly represented in African cities. Most residents may lack formal legal titles to the land they occupy, but that has not stopped many of them from making substantial investments in their suburban property. It is not uncommon to walk past coconut trees down an earthen lane to discover a recently completed two-storey house, smartly painted in the latest pastel colors and roofed with the most up-to-date aluminum roofing sheets, just visible behind an elaborately decorated concrete wall topped with shards of broken glass. Over the last two decades people like Godwin and Gilda have increasingly congregated at, and transformed, the city's edge. Who is building these houses here, how, and why? What kind of urban space is under construction? What is it like to live here? And what does this mass autoconstruction on the city's former periurban edge tell us about the contemporary reshaping of African cities?

This book addresses these questions. It examines the transformation of Dar es Salaam's periphery since the late nineteenth century from rural hinterland, to periurban fringe, to suburban frontier, from the vantage point of the neighborhood of Salasala. The land on the present suburban frontier, which curves around the city twenty kilometers from the center, has been transformed from a zone of shifting cultivation sparsely populated by the Zaramo into residential neighborhoods containing some of the most sought-after property in the city. Starting from the last third of the nineteenth century, land was enclosed, alienated, nationalized, enclosed again, and commodified as it was claimed by Arab and European investors, then colonial and postcolonial governments, and then farmers and urban residents. By the early 2000s most remaining Zaramo had been dispossessed through hundreds of individual informal market transactions. In their place, a mosaic of the urban poor, lower-middle, and upper-middle classes had transformed this formerly rural hinterland into a residential suburban frontier. By the mid-2010s, as land prices climbed ever higher, savvy suburban residents were anticipating where the next suburban frontier might develop beyond places like Salasala. They were buying land close to Dar es Salaam in the neighboring districts of Kibaha and Bagamoyo in the expectation that the suburb would come to them.

There is more to this story than a narrative about changing land use on the urban periphery. The central aim of this book is to examine the suburban frontier as *the* place where Africa's middle classes are shaped. Drawing on the long tradition of sociospatial dialectical thinking in human geography,[4] I argue that Dar es Salaam's middle classes are building distinctive suburban landscapes, and that those landscapes in turn shape what middle-classness is. Suburban space is neither an inert backdrop for the ready-made middle-class lives that are to be the subject of analysis, nor an inevitable step on a linear and universal path of urban development. Thinking with sociospatial dialectics enables us to see space and society as dynamically coconstituted in a particular time and place. By spatializing our understanding of the dynamics of middle-class formation, I show how investment in property—land, houses, and landscape—is central to middle-class formation and urban futures in Africa.

If suburbanization is a defining feature of contemporary global urban change,[5] then Africa's urban peripheries are a key site where that process will unfold. Africa's urban population is projected to triple between 2018 and 2050 to 1.5 billion people, or 22 percent of the world's urban population.[6] Most of these urban residents will make their lives in extensive neighborhoods beyond the central city, in "the peripheral city that is the real city."[7] In Dar es Salaam, a city that is projected to grow from just over six million inhabitants in 2018 to over ten million by 2030 to become one of Africa's five megacities, this process is already underway, as the population residing in peripheral areas is growing faster than in central areas.[8] Much of this urban extension is residential in character and peppered with many small businesses, industries, and retail outlets, often located in people's homes.[9] This is organic suburbanization, constructed, extended, and improved incrementally as thousands of individual cash-based domestic building projects take shape. It is also highly unequal. The majority of peripheral residents will have to build their own homes, but only a minority will be able to build a comfortable house like Godwin and Gilda's. As Africa's urban peripheries are slowly transformed, new ways of being middle class become possible and new forms of sociospatial inequality emerge. Understanding how these processes are unfolding on the suburban frontier is vital for thinking about the future of African cities and urban inequality.

THE COLONIALITY OF SPACE

The new urban forms that are taking shape on African urban peripheries defy easy characterization.[10] Recent work in urban studies has generated productive ways of thinking about the dynamics of urban expansion in cities of the Global South such as insurgent and incremental change, and peripheral, plotting, piecemeal, extensive, and massive urbanization.[11] Yet none of these characterizations fully captures the dynamics that have shaped Dar es Salaam's urban periphery. This is a space that does not fit existing theoretical or vernacular ways of thinking about cities.[12] It is not quite the suburb of Euro-American urban theory, with its mixed population and spontaneous land use. Nor is it the *maeneo yasiopangwa* (unplanned areas) or the *makazi yasio rasmi* (unofficial residencies/residential areas) that government officials and planners refer to when talking about the greater part of the city's informally built environment. These terms corral very different kinds of urban space (suburbs, informal settlements, slum areas) into one single negative category, even though the differences between them are significant. The lack of a vernacular term for the urban residential periphery also suggests that these new spaces do not fit an established, collective geographic imagination among Dar es Salaam's residents.

The dynamics of land are central to an understanding of African urbanization. We need to know more about how land—and property more widely—is being accessed, made, and used, and by whom, in Africa's urban peripheries.[13] In recent years, investment in high-end urban real estate and satellite cities has been fueled by elite and international capital,[14] but the actors and instruments involved in these developments are very different from the small-scale, cash-based transactions that shape the vernacular land markets through which urban populations access and use land in most African cities.[15] To better grasp these processes, I draw on recent scholarship that has explored the significance of land as a key driver of urban dynamics in cities of the Global South,[16] as well as work on land in rural Africa and agrarian change more broadly. This work draws attention to the political and economic dimensions of land: to the specific mechanisms of dispossession, enclosure, and commodification; to the enduring colonial legacies on land tenure and recent attempts at land reform; to the relationship between property and authority; and to the consequences of all this for social differentiation and class formation.[17]

The first residential suburbs to be built in many African towns and cities were constructed by colonial governments in their attempts to racially segregate urban space.[18] In former British colonies such as Kenya, Nigeria, South Africa, Tanzania, Zambia, and Zimbabwe, for example, suburbs were planned as exclusive residential enclaves for Europeans, and continue to be seen as relatively exclusive, well-serviced residential zones. Colonial urban planning—however patchy and incomplete—enframed African cities, leaving its imprint not only on the city's material form, but also on how people thought about urban space and their place in it.[19] The coloniality of space lingers in the built environment and the visceral experience of the city's landscapes.[20] The colonial is not the only logic of the production of urban space, but it remains as the spatial residue of the coloniality of power.[21] It endures in colonial land tenure regimes that render the majority of urban residents as squatters without access to decent housing. It endures in residents' ideas about the aesthetics of good urban space in terms of topography, planning, and architecture. It endures in a hierarchical way of thinking about urban space in which some places are better than others and people higher up the social hierarchy deserve to live in better places. As I show in this book, it is central to middle-class urban imaginaries and urban spatial practices.

In Tanzania, popular representations of urban space are saturated with the residue of the coloniality of space. The tripartite colonial enframing of Dar es Salaam divided the city into three zones distinguished by building regulations, which became known in Swahili as *uzunguni* (the place of the European), *uhindini* (the place of the Indian), and *uswahilini* (the place of the Swahili, referring to the coastal African urban culture but in this context meaning "African").[22] There are other, more localized terms that refer to specific neighborhoods. Yet this colonial enframing is nevertheless persistent and pervasive as a typology of postcolonial urban space that is used to refer to upscale planned neighborhoods (*uzunguni*), commercial districts historically dominated by the Indian community (*uhindini*), and unplanned, unserviced neighborhoods containing densely packed housing (*uswahilini*). This framing is regularly deployed in everyday life in cities across the country even if, as I explore in chapter 4, the newly constructed suburban landscapes of the urban periphery do not quite fit this geographical imagination.[23] They may be more desirable residential neighborhoods, but they do not quite approximate *uzunguni*, the original suburbs built and serviced for Europeans by the colonial state; and they are not like *uswahilini* either, since the lower density and larger scale of houses on the suburban periphery produce very different landscapes. The fear that these new suburban areas might eventually degenerate into *uswahilini* drives middle-class residents to seek land further out, where they plan to build again. In the process, they push the suburban frontier further outward.

THE SUBURBAN FRONTIER

The making of Dar es Salaam's suburban frontier has been far from a smooth and linear trajectory. Alienation, dispossession, and enclosure have stalked the city's hinterland through the years of colonialism, socialism, and liberalization. These processes have produced distinctive trajectories in and around Salasala, such that enclosures were later undone by nationalization, and socialist policies paved the way for further dispossession and enclosure. Land has remained alienated since the advent of German colonial rule, but the processes of dispossession, enclosure, and property-making in the city's hinterland have been slow and incomplete.

The suburban frontier emerged when the first spacious and well-serviced suburbs—the original *uzunguni*—were laid out for Europeans at Oysterbay in the 1930s. Located five kilometers north of the city center, Oysterbay was designed as an exclusive European enclave from which Africans, apart from those who worked as domestic staff, were excluded.[24] The rest of the urban population was left to fend for itself in terms of housing provision. The houses that were built from local materials to accommodate Africans in the city center, known as Swahili houses, constituted valuable urban property from which a new class of African landlords profited, but supply was always outstripped by demand.[25] In the late colonial period the state belatedly invested in a small number of housing schemes for Africans, opening up new suburbs in Ilala, Magomeni, Temeke, and Kinondoni, where an emergent elite, most of whom were salaried government workers, could live in improved conditions with formal, secure tenure. By the eve of Independence in 1961 a state-built suburban frontier, characterized by better-quality housing and planned layouts, was beginning to emerge in archipelagic form on the city's edge from Oysterbay in the north to Temeke in the southwest.

In the 1970s and 1980s the suburban frontier was pushed slowly outwards towards the city's rural hinterland, away from the original inner suburbs, which began to densify. This shift was prompted by limited government attempts at urban housing provision. These included a large-scale urban planning scheme in Mbezi; Sites and Services schemes in Sinza, Kijitonyama, and Mikocheni in the late 1970s; and Sites and Services schemes in Tegeta and Tabata in the early 1980s. These schemes planted new suburban oases of formally planned land with secure tenure to the west and north of the city. The majority of these schemes were located in the north, consolidating Kinondoni's position as the most desirable part of the suburban frontier. Plots were allocated or passed on to an emerging upper-middle class, most of whom were state employees.[26] The Sites and Services schemes drove demand for adjacent unplanned land, such that by the end of the 1980s land on the suburban frontier had become a "hotcake."[27]

During this time the periurban and rural areas that lay beyond the suburban frontier underwent significant, if imperceptible, change. After independence and the shift to socialism heralded by the Arusha Declaration in 1967, most of the plantations, estates, and other properties that had been privately enclosed during the precolonial and colonial eras were nationalized. Villagization was carried out in the rural parts of Dar es Salaam and Coast regions in the mid-1970s, forcing Zaramo scattered throughout the city's hinterland to leave their farms and move to communal *ujamaa* villages.[28] Since claims to land outside of the city rested on customary land tenure, there was great uncertainty over people's control and use of land, which paved the way for new enclosures and dispossession. Relocated farmers were allotted plots and farms in the *ujamaa* villages, sometimes on land previously owned by others. Some farmers abandoned their former farms located far from the *ujamaa* village.[29]

As agricultural production declined and a food crisis unfolded, urbanites were directed to farm on the city's edge through a series of government "operations" in the late 1970s and early 1980s, setting in motion land commodification and further enclosure, and entrenching Zaramo dispossession. Unused land that fell within village boundaries was allocated to city dwellers by village authorities; land was also acquired by urbanites from Zaramo and other farmers, who sold their land or parcels of it for a small fee. Others claimed land or were resettled on the nationalized estates and plantations. Although land itself could not legally be bought and sold at this time, "secret sales" became increasingly common in the 1980s on the pretext of paying for trees and other improvements on the land such as buildings.[30]

In the 1990s a combination of economic liberalization, population growth, and housing demand pushed more urbanites into the city's periurban and rural hinterland in search of a piece of land on which to build or farm. Among the urban middle classes, many of whom were government workers in receipt of perquisites for housing and travel, the suburban frontier became a favored location in which to invest in land to support small-scale farming and livestock activities to provide additional income streams.[31] By the time Tanzania's new Land Acts were published in 1999, permitting the sale of bare land, there was already a thriving land market. Demand for land grew, land prices increased, and former farmland was subdivided and sold off. Newcomers fenced in their plots and began to build large modern houses using the newest building materials. This book is concerned with what, and who, was constructed in the process.

The book develops the concept of the self-built suburban frontier as a zone of commodification, dispossession, accumulation, risk, aspiration, and experimentation that is especially productive for middle-class formation.[32] The middle classes have been the principal beneficiaries of the commodification of land and the enclosure of plots on the suburban frontier, accumulating assets in the form of land that can be built on, loaned, or sold, and houses that can be lived in or rented out. Yet their property is also at risk in this suburban gray zone where the statutory land tenure of the city bleeds into the customary land tenure that prevails in the formerly rural hinterland.[33] Middle-class experience on the suburban frontier is thus shaped by the twin possibilities for accumulation and loss. Property is always open to contestation from neighbors or strangers, or reclamation by the state under eminent domain. The suburban frontier is also a zone of aspiration where the middle classes seek to consolidate their social position through the aesthetic value of the architecture and landscapes they have created.[34] In building desirable residential space that has pushed into the city's rural hinterland, the middle classes have transformed the landscape from scattered farms and bush into a sea of small-scale self-built houses on individual plots. The relative size, quality, and lower densities of these buildings, together with the attention paid to architectural design and the use of new building materials, has produced what residents consider to be a desirable suburban landscape when compared with both the congested inner-city neighborhoods and the scattered, poorer-quality housing of the periurban fringe that lies beyond the suburban zone. Finally, the suburban frontier is also a social and cultural frontier.[35] Here the new middle classes are pioneering suburban lifestyles built around new consumption practices and privatized leisure, transport, and social services. By way of the private car, food is purchased, children are schooled, family is visited, religious services are attended, and weddings are celebrated without one's having to enter the city's historic core. For the middle classes, life is increasingly lived on the suburban frontier.

TANZANIA'S MIDDLE CLASSES

Amidst the enthusiasm for "Africa rising," in 2011 the African Development Bank produced estimates of the size of the middle class in forty-four African countries.[36] At an estimated 5.2 million people, Tanzania had one of the smallest middle classes on the continent.[37] The country was placed eighth from the bottom of the African Development Bank's table, with 2.9 percent of the population categorized as "middle class" (with a daily per capita expenditure between US$4 and US$20) and 12.1 percent categorized as the "middle and floating classes" (with a daily per capita expenditure between US$2 and US$20).[38] Despite its small size, the apparent emergence of this middle class fitted well with international financial institutions' and consultancy firms' narrative of African economic successes that had resulted from their policy prescriptions. In Tanzania macroeconomic trends were strong from the 2000s, with growth rates hovering between 5 and 7 percent.[39] The country reached Lower Middle Income Country status in July 2020.[40] Poverty rates also fell. Between 2007 and 2017–18 the percentage of the population living in extreme poverty, as measured by the national food poverty line, dropped from 11.8 percent to 8 percent, and the percentage of the population falling below the national basic needs poverty line fell from 34.4 percent to 26.4 percent.[41]

A cursory glance beyond these positive macroeconomic indicators shows that the headline trends have not translated into fewer people living in poverty, and that inequality is on the rise.[42] The World Bank, for example, notes that about 49 percent of the population still live below the international poverty line of US$1.90 per person per day, and that despite reductions in the proportion of the population living below the poverty line, population growth has meant that the absolute number of those living in poverty has increased.[43] The vastly different experiences of Tanzania's recent macroeconomic growth are captured in the Gini coefficient, which has grown countrywide from 0.34 in 1991–92 to 0.38 in 2017–18, and has grown even more in Dar es Salaam (from 0.30 in 1991–92 to 0.42 in 2017–18).[44] Despite this polarizing picture, there is also evidence that the livelihoods of some have been slowly improving over time as a result of modest household or individual investments in agriculture, land, and livestock.[45] In Dar es Salaam, that evidence is writ large on the urban landscape. Housing conditions have improved.[46] Investments in small properties have provided opportunities for income and modest accumulation. A third of homeowners in the city rent out rooms in their own house.[47] In 2012, rental of business and residential property provided a quarter of disposable income in Dar es Salaam households.[48] Dar es Salaam residents have also been investing in both urban and rural land. While this is difficult to quantify due to the lack of a reliable cadastre, especially at the city level, national data suggest a substantial increase in the proportion of medium-scale farms (over twenty hectares) owned by urban households, which was up from 17.2 percent in 2005 to 78.9 percent in 2010.[49] These households may not easily map onto the African Development Bank's measure of the middle class, but the evidence for incremental increases in property ownership points to a significant driver of socioeconomic differentiation across urban and rural space.

The "discovery" of Africa's middle classes has generated considerable debate about how they should be understood.[50] Critical voices have warned that the boosterist discourse around the middle classes suggests that neoliberal economic reform has reaped benefits. Others have questioned the consumption focus of research on the middle class at the cost of analyzing wealth, or whether these middling groups constitute a social class at all.[51] The middle classes have a longer history in Africa than their recent discovery suggests. Their emergence is not simply a recent and inevitable step along a universal trajectory of economic and political development. Given the changing ways in which social science has approached questions of class in Africa since the mid-twentieth century, the middle classes, in their true fashion, have not always been clearly discernible.

The actors in most accounts of Tanzania's political economic history are usually members of the elite, made up of top politicians in CCM and government bureaucrats;[52] their financial backers in the private sector, many of whom are Tanzanian Asians; and top military personnel; or they are the poor.[53] This is understandable in a country that embarked on one of Africa's most committed socialist projects, where the ruling party has held power since independence in 1961, and the majority of the population makes a living from small-scale agriculture or the informal economy. Yet the elite-poor binary does not capture the full spectrum of socioeconomic differentiation and social experience in Tanzania. I develop this point in more depth in relation to middle-class appropriation of property in Dar es Salaam in chapters 2 and 3, and provide a brief outline here.

During the German and British colonial periods interstitial classes began to emerge as a result of colonial policies around commodity production, education, and housing.[54] In Dar es Salaam government jobs were only available to those who had attended the elite government Tabora School or one of the Christian mission schools, which in 1933 amounted to 1.84 percent of the territory's African population.[55] Nevertheless a "middle stratum" emerged, formed of lower-level government clerks, traders, and landlords,[56] such that by the eve of independence a colonial report suggested that "a nucleus of an African middle class which enjoys a relatively comfortable standard of living and regards itself as a different and superior stratum of African society" was discernible.[57] Yet this was a very small group, particularly in comparison to other African countries with much longer histories of development in the professions, trade, or landownership.[58] The class relations of the independence period have been most thoroughly laid out by Issa

Shivji, who argued that this small middle stratum of clerks, traders, and teachers solidified into a petty bourgeoisie during the independence struggle, out of which a "bureaucratic bourgeoisie" or ruling class finally emerged and took control of the state and the economy.[59] The shift to socialism and the associated nationalization of productive assets, trade, and property enabled the bureaucratic bourgeoisie to wrest control of the economy from the commercial bourgeoisie, most of whom were Asian, though they were still subordinated to the international bourgeoisie. The bureaucratic bourgeoisie was formed of the top echelons in politics, the administration, economy, and military and constituted about 0.1 percent of the labor force in the 1970s.[60] Below it, Shivji parsed the petty bourgeoisie into three strata based on occupation and position in the party-state bureaucracy: an upper stratum of intellectuals, headteachers, higher civil servants, professionals, prosperous traders, farmers, transporters, businessmen, and private executives; a middle stratum of employees in mid-level government and parastatal positions, teachers, salaried employees, rich farmers, soldiers, police, security and military personnel; and a lower stratum of small shop-owners, craftsmen, and lower-salaried workers. Despite laying out these different strata, Shivji's analysis was mostly concerned with the class dynamics of the bureaucratic bourgeoisie, and he had less to say about the petty bourgeoisie.

Subsequent work on the socialist period has taken this middling group more seriously, underlining the relationship between these groups and the politics of urban space. Joseph Kironde and James Brennan have examined how elites and middle classes accessed and profited from urban space through landlordism and housing schemes (see chapters 2 and 3).[61] Dar es Salaam's rentier class of the 1960s and 1970s was made up of landlords "of varying means and all colours."[62] Control over urban property was central to the race and class dimensions of national politics. It also underpinned livelihood strategies for many urbanites beyond the urban elite and shaped the popular politics of the time for the urban majority. For example, landlords, as well as traders, shopkeepers, and civil servants, came under increasing scrutiny in the 1970s, their socialist credentials subject to suspicion. In the popular discourse of the time, this group was often referred to as *naizisheni* or *naizi* (from "Africanization," the move to replace colonial and Indian control of the economy, property, and the state after independence).[63] At the same time, the educated middle classes asserted their symbolic capital more quietly, as for example through the production and dissemination by urban Christian women of advice literature for young women who had recently arrived in the city.[64]

As *ujamaa*-era controls on accumulation were dismantled in the 1980s, those who could do so embraced the opportunities that came with liberalization and the opportunity to acquire, trade, build, and consume. Those with less access to economic resources and fewer political and bureaucratic connections were more likely to cleave to socialist ideology and modest living.[65] As liberalization

proceeded through the 1980s and 1990s, the possibilities for middle-class reproduction began to diversify away from the state. There were limited employment
opportunities in the private sector, and in business,[66] the land market developed
and private schools were established at the same time as structural adjustment took
hold and inequality began to increase.[67] The changing social fabric was captured
in local social commentary on the emergence of the *wakubwa* ("bigshots") the
matajiri ("the rich"), as well as the *deiwaka* ("day labourer"), *walalahoi* ("those
who sleep heavily after hard labor"), and *wanyonge* ("the oppressed").[68] No moni-
ker entered the popular consciousness that readily identified the middle classes,
who became "the unmarked carriers of the moral status quo" and who saw themselves as educated, hard-working, altruistic, and modest.[69] They stood in contrast
to the *wakubwa* and *matajiri*, who were widely held to have benefited from liberalization through corrupt practices and who were viewed with a mixture of envy
and suspicion as a result.[70] They also stood in contrast to the poor, a position most
commonly expressed through the ideology and practices of *maendeleo* ("development"). *Maendeleo*, on a personal level, indicated the achievement of a certain
level of education and an ability to plan and improve one's life. People who demonstrated personal *maendeleo* undertook activities such as membership in wom-
en's groups or investment in modest long-term projects such as new-breed dairy
cows, new crops, houses, and rental properties.[71] They patronized the respectable
performing arts and avoided those they considered *ya ushenzi* ("uncivilized").[72]
Others saw it as their responsibility to "develop" the poor through NGO or social
protection work.[73]

By the time the African Development Bank discovered the middle classes in
the 2010s, they were already a socioeconomic and cultural force in Tanzania, even
if they were difficult to pin down. Macroeconomic growth in the 2000s was not
accompanied by structural change in the economy. The lack of industrialization
has meant that the middle classes are not precisely defined by the relations of
production and have historically been more dependent on the state for their economic and social reproduction. Agriculture is the largest sector of employment
(tables 1 and 2).[74] Manufacturing and construction offer higher incomes than
agriculture but employ smaller proportions of the population (4.6 percent and
2.5 percent respectively in 2020–21).[75] Foreign Direct Investment has been skewed
towards extractive industries and has not generated large numbers of jobs.

The middle classes are difficult to grasp in this macroeconomic picture, not
least because many of them have developed a portfolio of economic activity to
maximize possibilities and minimize risk. Those I have spoken with include high-
and low-level state employees, salaried workers in international companies and
the banking, insurance, and legal professions, sales managers, employees of religious institutions and universities, business owners, the self-employed, and those
retired from public service. Most rely on a combination of formal employment
with a business or self-employed activities. Many of them are also homeowners,

TABLE 1 Percentage distribution of employed
persons aged 15+ by sector, United Republic
of Tanzania 2020–21

Sector	Percentage
Agriculture	58.4
Private	25.8
Household activities	13.0
Public	2.8

SOURCE: National Bureau of Statistics (Tanzania) 2022: 36.

TABLE 2 Percentage distribution of employed persons aged 15+ by occupation,
United Republic of Tanzania 2020–21

Occupation	Percentage
Skilled agricultural and fishery workers	59.8
Elementary occupations[a]	13.8
Service workers and shop sales workers	11.7
Craft and related workers	8.1
Plant and machine operators and assemblers	2.6
Technicians and associated professionals	2.1
Professionals	0.9
Clerks	0.6
Legislators, administrators, and managers	0.4

SOURCE: National Bureau of Statistics (Tanzania) 2022: 34.

[a] Street vending, shoe cleaning, domestic work, building caretaking and watching, refuse collection, and laboring in agriculture, forestry, and fisheries, mining, construction, transport, manufacturing.

landlords, and landowners. For this reason, I suggest it is worth paying more attention to property in order to understand the position of the middle classes in Africa.

MIDDLE-CLASS PROPERTIES

The approach taken in this book is to see middle-class formation as a process that takes place over time as property is accumulated. Property, understood here as land, houses, and landscapes, slowly accretes into economic and cultural capital that is passed on within families. This approach retains the understanding from Karl Marx that class is a social relation generated by the social dynamics of unequal ownership of capital and property. It also recognizes, with Max Weber and later with Pierre Bourdieu, that unequal class relations are reproduced through culture.[76] In this book, cultural capital is explored through the aesthetic power of domestic architecture, suburban landscapes, and lifestyles. Finally, the focus on class formation follows E.P. Thompson's insistence that class is neither a structure nor a category, but "something which in fact happens (and can be shown to have happened) in human relationships."[77] The book examines how this process is spatialized through the dialectical formation of the middle classes and the suburban frontier.

Marx, Weber, Bourdieu, and Thompson were theorizing the dynamics of European societies in historical conditions very different from those that have structured African societies and economies. Recent anthropological writing on the emergence of the "global middle classes" has developed our understanding of class dynamics beyond Europe and America. In this work social classes are not categories into which people fit based on their relation to the means of production, occupation, or measurements of income or expenditure, which is all but impossible to do in contexts where there has been limited industrialization, where much economic activity takes place informally and most people simultaneously manage several projects that generate income. Rather, social classes are formed over time by conjunctural processes that shape economies, societies, and cultures.[78] Rachel Heiman, Carla Freeman, and Mark Leichty have gone the farthest in elaborating a practice approach to class that is cognizant of broader political economic structures but also attendant to the everyday repetition of actions that form the basis of social classes and the distinctiveness, or antagonisms, between them.[79] The focus on practices is useful in the context of Tanzania. The middle classes, as noted above, may be "unmarked" in the vernacular, but the lack of a collective noun for middling types does not mean that they do not exist in practice. Social classes are also shaped by the things that people do, perhaps unconsciously, in the course of their everyday lives.[80] In this book, I pay attention to the dispersed yet repeated practices related to property on the suburban frontier: how people acquire, secure, and develop plots of land; how they slowly build a house over time; how they decorate their homes; how they represent the landscape; how they plan for the future; how they spend their leisure time. Land acquisition, landscape formation, house-building, and lifestyle are distinctive repertoires of property practice through which middle-classness emerges on the suburban frontier.

The middle classes have a long history in Africa. Class dynamics in Africa have been shaped by the impact of colonialism, globalization, and limited industrialization; the significance of the state for accessing power and controlling resources; overlapping social and political configurations of authority, community, and identity; and different frameworks of land tenure and property rights. Although the conditions of middle-class formation are specific to particular times and places, education and formal employment are significant factors that have shaped middle-class trajectories over time across the continent and were often interrelated. Early access to formal education during the colonial period, available only to a minority via mission stations, offered the main route to a salaried, if junior, post in a colonial government administration. This laid the foundations for social inequality as many government employees passed their economic and cultural capital on to the next generation through formal education.[81]

Alongside these "conditions of possibility"[82] for middle-class formation, we must add property. Property in Africa has been examined in relation to the social organization of access, use, and control of productive resources such as people, land, livestock, and natural resources.[83] Unequal access to and control over these resources has been central to the dynamics of social inequality over time and is at the heart of class analyses of the agrarian question in Africa.[84] Property has also been analyzed in relation to the construction and exercise of political authority, citizenship, and inheritance.[85] Yet, with the notable exception of the work of Nkululeko Mabandla, who shows that land acquired over three generations formed the basis of the relative wealth of the middle-class families that he interviewed in Transkei in 2010,[86] property has received less attention in discussions of Africa's middle classes.

Property is multidimensional. In much of Africa, land and houses are significant economic assets. Land can be an input to agricultural production, market gardening, or small-scale business, a vehicle for speculation, a means of saving cash, a source of patrimony when gifted or of income when sold. Land also provides valuable space to build a house. Self-built houses provide relief from the vagaries of the rental market and opportunities for home-based businesses or for renting rooms and houses to others.

Property also stores symbolic capital. Houses and neighborhoods are rich sites for making statements about personhood, status, and taste.[87] As I show in chapter 4, the new self-built suburbs in northern Dar es Salaam are desirable because they are considered to be neighborhoods of lower-density, higher-quality housing. The symbolic capital of middle-class houses and suburban landscapes can be traced back to colonial land law and urban planning. In British colonies, English land laws imported ideologies of land use and "improvement" in which the capacity to use land in ways considered by the colonizers to be productive was linked to the supposed inherent nature of persons and justified what Bhandar has called a "racial regime of ownership."[88] In British colonial Africa, the system of indirect rule was developed to govern Africans through what the British thought were the natural tribal units in the countryside to which Africans belonged. In urban areas colonial land laws and urban planning were used to distribute access to urban space and infrastructure unequally among racial groups.[89] Well-laid-out and serviced suburbs were developed for Europeans while the housing and urban infrastructure needs of Africans were neglected on the basis that Africans were urban sojourners who would return to their rural tribal areas where they naturally belonged. Cemented in the built environment and scaffolded by colonial land law and urban planning, the coloniality of urban space was not dismantled in the postcolonial period.[90] In many postcolonial African cities, the ideologies of appropriate land use have seeped into urban culture and continue to shape ideas about the aesthetics of urban space and who belongs where in the city. Middle-class identities are built on the apparent order of well-laid-out suburban landscapes. The ordered and civilized use of urban space is taken to reflect the educated and rational properties of middle-class persons, whose symbolic capital appears to justify their natural belonging in larger houses on bigger plots in better neighborhoods.

Finally, property is a disposition and set of practices that has come to characterize middle-class experience on the suburban frontier. Acquiring, securing, and developing land occupies a great deal of time and emotional labor, from the hunt for an affordable and secure plot, the labyrinthine negotiations and transactions with vendors, neighbors and government officials, to the months and years of incremental building. The middle classes invest much time, money, and energy securing their land and making themselves legible to the state in order to obtain insurance against alienation or other unwanted encroachments. As we will see, such efforts have rarely resulted in the successful procurement of legal title to date. Nevertheless, the financial, physical, and emotional investment required to claim a plot and build a house that matches one's sense of social standing incubates a sense of possession and private property.[91] The middle classes think of themselves as developing the land. They build bespoke homes for their families, clear and maintain access roads, plant or erect and maintain boundaries, and bring water and electricity to their plots. They are not simply "occupiers" or "users" of land parcels, as designated in Tanzanian land law—they have found, bought, staked out, enclosed, built, maintained, and developed their own private property. Property has become a "state of mind,"[92] an embodied practice and a shared set of experiences and interests among the middle classes. Middle-classness is deeply implicated in the making of property on the suburban frontier.

OUTLINE OF THE BOOK

The book examines the development of suburban space in Dar es Salaam by zooming in on three adjacent *mitaa* (subwards) in Wazo Ward in the north of Kinondoni District (map 2): Salasala, Kilimahewa, and Kilimahewa Juu.[93] The area has been progressively subdivided into smaller administrative units over time, and so for simplicity I refer to the three *mitaa* as Salasala unless there is a specificity to note. This also reflects the way in which many residents refer to their neighborhood. Fieldwork was conducted through repeat research visits to Dar es Salaam between 2012 and 2018, and is informed by research in Tanzania carried out over the previous fifteen years. There is little reliable formal data to be collected on land use and property ownership over time in informally developed neighborhoods such as Salasala: only formally owned property appears in the land register, which is in the minority in Dar es Salaam, and even these entries can be erroneous. Recent drives to formalize property ownership in informal neighborhoods through offering interim property rights have not had much success in making property ownership more legible.[94] The methods used to gather the data for this book have relied on qualitative and ethnographic approaches. I have switched between ethnographic methods with five key interlocutors, all of whom have built houses in the three *mitaa*, and 210 qualitative interviews with a broad range of suburban residents of different social classes; local, municipal, and national officials; community groups, planners, and local politicians.

Chapters 1 and 2 examine the development of Dar es Salaam's suburban frontier through the relationship between class formation and property. In chapter 1, "Groundwork: The Coloniality of Space," I examine how, since the establishment of the city in the last third of the nineteenth century, those in better-off positions have reproduced their relative privilege through property. From the German and British colonial officials who alienated land to suit their interests, to the Arab, Indian, and African landlords who built and rented urban property, to the post-colonial elite members of party and government who manipulated state housing schemes, those who could claimed and invested in property. In so doing they shaped the city and laid the foundations of social differentiation on the basis of race and class. Yet at the same time African urban residents have a long history of finding space for themselves in the city, however small, and despite property laws being stacked against them. The chapter ends in the late 1970s as the city was convulsed by economic problems, the urban population had almost tripled in just over a decade, and self-built, informal settlements had begun to seep into the peri-urban and rural hinterland as the expanding population sought to find their own solutions to the city's chronic housing shortage.

Chapter 2, "The Suburban Frontier," analyzes the consolidation of the suburban frontier from the 1980s, when Ali Hassan Mwinyi became president. Known as *Mzee Ruksa* or "Mr. Permission," his name is synonymous with the period of economic liberalization and opportunity for the *wabenzi* (those who drove expensive imported cars such as Mercedes Benz). While much has been written on the political and economic elite during this period, less has been said about the middle classes, who also took the opportunity to shore up their position by investing in land and buildings, transforming the city as they did so. From the mid-1980s the period of *mageuzi* (reforms) brought significant economic, political, and sociocultural change and forms the context for much of what follows in this book. These reforms opened up the land market, enabled access to imported consumer goods from bottled beer to everyday plastic homeware items to building materials and cars, and eventually saw the increasing popularity of new lifestyle trends such as baby showers and school graduation parties (explored in chapter 6). Yet while *mageuzi* brought significant change, this period is also characterized by stark continuities with the processes outlined in chapter 1, including socioeconomic inequality and the unequal possession of property. The chapter examines how this played out on the city's northern edge, as the suburban frontier was pushed north through Kinondoni as more people sought urban land to invest in. A slow-motion land grab unfolded through multiple small-scale instances of dispossession, commodification, and enclosure. By the time of my fieldwork in the mid-2010s, I neither encountered nor learned of any Zaramo who continued to live in Salasala. In their place emerged a periurban economy of farms and homes, many of which were owned by elite and middle-class urbanites who supplemented their incomes with proceeds from their periurban farms. During the 1990s and the 2000s, Kinondoni's periurban zone was transformed into a suburban frontier of investment and enclosure. Plots and houses were enveloped by walls and fences, ever smaller pieces of land were claimed and built on, and the unique self-built suburban landscape took shape.

Chapters 3, 4, 5, and 6 flesh out life on the contemporary suburban frontier in Salasala. I start with land, which is foundational to the analysis developed in this book about the suburban frontier, property, and middle-class reproduction. Land enabled the investment of earnings, opened up future income streams (for example through renting or conducting business from the property), projected social status, and ensured social reproduction. But land was also unstable: most suburban residents had built on unplanned land in informal settlements. In this uncertain environment, buyers can be duped by brokers, neighbors can encroach on boundaries, strangers can invade unguarded land, family members can feud over a plot, and government agencies can demolish unauthorized constructions to accommodate official changes in land use. Chapter 3, "Land," explores the ways in which the middle classes are better placed than the urban poor to navigate these challenges, given their generally higher levels of education, their connections to strategically useful individuals, and their experience of and confidence in dealing with government bureaucracy: indeed, many in the middle classes are themselves part of the bureaucracy. The chapter discusses how unplanned land is transacted outside of formal land allocation procedures, and describes the measures that those with knowledge and experience of urban land markets take to secure their investments, including in the local courts. I discuss my interlocutors' experiences with the formal planning and land administration system in their attempts to get their unplanned plots surveyed and titled. Though the middle classes have more resources and networks at their disposal than do the urban poor, they rarely succeed in gaining state recognition of their land ownership and must therefore make do with other strategies to secure their asset. A fine-grained hierarchy of options emerges in which middle-class residents make their property private by placing beacons around their boundaries, building walls, surveying their land, or obtaining an "offer" of a formal title from the Ministry of Lands, Housing and Human Settlements Development. Herein lies a key difference between the middle classes and the elite, who rarely struggle to obtain state recognition of their property.

Chapter 4, "Landscape," turns to the relationship between the aesthetic qualities of the suburban frontier and the pursuit of middle-class distinction. In Dar es Salaam, landscape aesthetics are not only a matter of taste and social judgment, but are also deeply informed by colonial attempts to enframe African urban space and the ensuing coloniality of space.[95] I show how colonial Dar es Salaam was shaped through planning regulations into three racially distinct zones that came to represent separate and distinctive types of urban landscape: *uzunguni*, *uhindini*, and *uswahilini* (the place of the European, the Indian, and the Swahili [African], respectively). Drawing on Frantz Fanon and Ngũgĩ wa Thiong'o's insistence on the psychological and visceral impact on the colonized of the colonial enframing of urban space, I analyze middle-class suburban residents' references to this colonial enframing as they make and represent suburban space. Just as the colonizers' self-representation relied on the integral presence of the colonized, so too does middle-class suburban self-representation rely on the presence of *uswahilini*. Middle-class suburban residents in Salasala continue to reproduce the coloniality of space, enframing *uswahilini* as a chaotic, disorderly space, and to distance themselves from it. Yet this enframing strategy, this projection of power, is only partial, as the material landscape falls between *uswahilini* (because it is unplanned and lacks services) and *uzunguni* (because of the relatively low-density, high-quality buildings). While the suburban middle classes can build walls around their houses, they cannot protect the suburban landscape from insurgent house-building by the less well-off. It is difficult to assert authority over the landscape amidst the cacophony of claims in the autoconstructed city.

Chapter 5, "Domestic Architecture," turns to the scale of the home and examines the house-building projects of suburban residents as they attempt to build the home to which they aspire. Houses are significant because, it seems, everyone has a building project. Houses consume time, money, imagination, and emotions. They are also unambiguously visible on the suburban landscape. In a political context in which accumulation and conspicuous consumption are often viewed with suspicion, these houses index the growing inequality that has characterized the postliberalization era in Tanzania. In this chapter I explore the politics of domestic architecture on Dar es Salaam's suburban frontier, in which the size, style, and speed of a building project are read by family, friends, and neighbors as a statement on how the builders view themselves, their place in Tanzania and in the world. Drawing on the projects of five suburban residents, I examine the ways in which building, decorating, extending, repairing, and living in a house are central to middle-classness. These five residents and their building projects capture a range of similarities and divergencies in terms of socioeconomic position and family configuration, building stage, taste, and aesthetic orientation. This allows us to grasp something of what holds the middle classes together as a social group while also appreciating the differences among them. Houses make a clear statement about the middle-classness of their builders. To the extent that building is an open-ended process, the capacity to build is key to being middle class. But in their not-quite-as-imagined state, these houses capture both the desires and the frustrated aspirations that characterize middle-classness in Dar es Salaam.

Chapter 6, "Lifestyle," asks what all this house-building and suburban investment means for everyday life in these neighborhoods. How do people spend their time in suburban space? What new lifestyle practices are possible, and how are existing social practices being reconfigured? The chapter examines how Dar es Salaam's new suburban neighborhoods are oriented to leisure activities and sites of consumption that have become central to middle-classness. Two things are notable: the expansion of the range of social events that now warrant conspicuous celebration to include new rituals; and the increasing privatization of those celebrations, by withdrawing either into the private space of the home or to an exclusive space in one of the newly constructed suburban private-hire function halls. The chapter first discusses the home as a site of both work and leisure and as a space for the cultivation of distinctive habits, activities, and tastes. I then turn to consider key suburban sites where the middle classes congregate—the private-hire hall, the English-medium private school, and the bar. The suburban neighborhoods that are under construction are increasingly oriented to the sites and services of consumption central to middle-class reproduction.

The conclusion draws the empirical material together to show how residents build and use the suburban frontier to reproduce middle-classness in Dar es Salaam. The suburb is a key site of middle-class reproduction, where property can be invested in and lives can be lived at some remove from the urban poor. Yet the stability of this strategy for middle-class reproduction is threatened by a contradiction at the heart of this sociospatial configuration. For all their efforts to secure land and to build new urban neighborhoods, the middle classes cannot enclave themselves on the suburban frontier. People continue to sell off ever smaller plots of land, and newcomers continue to buy and build whatever they can on it. The threat of *uswahilini* is never far away. And so the middle classes plan their next move. They scope out opportunities in adjacent periurban and rural districts, they buy land, and they plan their next building project. The suburban frontier will move on.

The sociospatial dynamics of the suburban frontier described here challenge contemporary claims about what drives urbanization in Africa. Urbanization is indeed taking place without industrialization, but the processes of accumulation and class formation that drive urbanization are not limited to large-scale, financialized flows or the investments and deals of elites. Part of what drives urbanization in predominantly cash-based economies where housing stock is insufficient are the everyday investments that people make in land and buildings. People's unequal ability to do so produces not only the poor and the elite: the middle classes have also been constituted through this process. In Dar es Salaam and beyond, they are reshaping the city.

Groundwork

The Coloniality of Space

Abeid's half-acre plot was located on a gentle slope near the tarmac road that wound through the center of Salasala. On it he had built a modest concrete block, three-bedroomed house and a couple of exterior structures. The interior of his house was finished with white painted walls and shiny white floor tiles, and was sparsely furnished. Now that he had retired from his government clerical job, he preferred to invest his time and money in the project he ran from the other structures he had put up on his plot: a row of modern pens for raising chickens, which he sold to local bars and at local markets. Abeid was a relatively early arriver in Salasala, having bought land in 1995 for TSh150,000 ($260). When I met him in 2015 he estimated that his plot would sell for around TSh50 million ($25,108). The huge rise in the value of Abeid's land was not unusual in Salasala. According to one local broker, the going rate for a half-acre plot in a premium location on the tarmac road in Salasala in 2015 was TSh400 million ($200,865), while a similarly well-located plot of just one-quarter of an acre could expect to fetch TSh250 million ($125,540). Small plots (a quarter of an acre or less) farther from the tarmac road could be bought for TSh10–20 million ($5,022–$10,043). The demand for land in and around Salasala had transformed the city's former rural hinterland into desirable residential neighborhoods, despite the fact that they were mostly unplanned, informal settlements that lacked piped water and sanitation. Nevertheless, Salasala had become a highly sought-after place to build a house by the 2010s, especially among Dar es Salaam's middle classes.

These first two chapters examine how this transformation from rural hinterland to sought-after suburb took place from the end of the nineteenth century.

Inspired by James Brennan's appeal for accounts of urban Africa to pay attention to "the rents of the dead"—long-term patterns and processes of property creation, rentier activity, and accumulation—this study places the emergence of the contemporary suburban frontier at Salasala in a broader account of the dialectical sociospatial development of Dar es Salaam in which the making of property and social differentiation are deeply entwined.[1] The wider story begins in familiar territory among Africa's colonial capitals.[2] The colonial state's alienation of land and the legal bifurcation of urban and rural land, the hostility to Africans residing in urban areas, the policies and practices of urban racial segregation, and the neglect of urban housing and services for Africans resonate beyond Dar es Salaam, particularly in those cities that were established in the context of colonial rule.[3] The initial reluctance of Belgian, British, French, German, and Portuguese colonial states and employers to provide African housing, and the partial reversal of this position from the 1940s in an attempt to stabilize and appease urban labor forces, have been documented in cities such as Abidjan, Accra, Dakar, Conakry, Kinshasa, Lusaka, Maputo, Mombasa, Nairobi, and Zanzibar.[4] Various forms of colonial urban property—from European suburbs to housing estates to subsidized finance to workers' accommodations—laid down significant urban resources that transformed urban space and laid the groundwork for social differentiation.

In order to explore how this played out and the consequences for sociospatial differentiation in Dar es Salaam, this chapter examines the groundwork that established the coloniality of space and the middle classes in the city. I first discuss the legal frameworks and administrative practices that were developed to manage land and urban planning during the German and British colonial periods. Law and bureaucratic practice relating to land, urban and rural space, and housing provided the conditions in which the original suburban frontier—an exclusive, well-serviced enclave for Europeans—was initially constructed in Kinondoni at Oysterbay. By the end of the colonial period a handful of housing estates had been developed by the colonial state for an emerging class of educated, employed Africans in the north and west of the township, establishing those areas as the city's most aspirational residential neighborhoods. Chapter 2 examines how this small state-built suburban frontier grew after Independence, as first the new elite and then the middle classes scrambled for land and housing in Kinondoni. What marks out the Tanzanian urban experience as unique is the state's twin disavowal of both the city and the middle class during the socialist, and to some extent the postsocialist, periods. Yet, while the state oscillated between hostility and ambivalence towards the suburban frontier, many of its bureaucrats, officials, and employees were among those busily investing in suburban property: transforming land into a commodity, building houses, and pushing the frontier outwards. They were constructing both the city and the middle classes.

MAKING COLONIAL SPACE: LAND

Lying twenty kilometers to the north of Dar es Salaam's city center, the area in which Salasala is located today constituted part of the city's rural hinterland until the 1970s. It is likely that Salasala originated among the slave- and wage-labor plantations established by the Shomvi around the end of the nineteenth century. This part of the Swahili coast between Bagamoyo and Dar es Salaam, the Mrima Coast, was settled between the seventeenth and nineteenth centuries. The Mrima Coast was populated by indigenous Shaha and Shirazi, and by Shomvi, who were elite members of Swahili society of mixed African and Persian descent who dominated long-distance trade networks between the Swahili Coast, the hinterland, and the Indian Ocean.[5] Throughout the nineteenth century a combination of the caravan trade and up-country famine brought large numbers of people to settle at the coast, particularly around Bagamoyo and other smaller coastal settlements such as Kunduchi and Dar es Salaam itself, then a small village known as Mzizima. These settlers, many of them from the Uluguru Mountains two hundred kilometers to the west, became known as a distinct ethnic group, the Zaramo. They farmed the land, replaced the Shaha as the indigenous peoples, and formed the largest ethnic group in what became the Dar es Salaam region.[6] By the advent of the German colonial period in the mid-1880s, the rural hinterland of Dar es Salaam was known as *Uzaramo* (place of the Zaramo).

It is difficult to be precise about authority over land on this part of the Mrima Coast during this period. Glassman notes that there was "no Swahili concept of private land ownership."[7] Land in the coastal settlements such as Pangani, Bagamoyo, and Kunduchi was generally under the control of local leaders (whether Shomvi or Shirazi, or Zaramo leaders known as *mapazi*), who had rights to lease, gift, or sell land to newcomers.[8] Outside of the coastal settlements, Zaramo shifting cultivators occupied scattered farmsteads, where they grew cassava, grains, fruit, and vegetables interspersed by uncultivated bushland. Ownership of planted trees conferred use and inheritance rights on the descent group, and individuals could loan land to newcomers on a sharecropping basis.[9] With the rise of Omani power centered on Zanzibar from the 1830s and the alienation of land for Zanzibari-Omani rice and coconut plantations, the existing systems of land use and authority came under strain. This perhaps explains why some Shomvi elites retreated a few kilometers inland to establish plantations at places like Salasala and Goba towards the end of the nineteenth century.[10]

The periods of German (1885–1916) and then British (1919–61) colonial rule brought sweeping changes to the organization and control of land across the territory. The German Imperial Decree on Land Matters of 1895 and its subsequent clarifications and amendments established the basic principles of authority over land and land rights that underpin the coloniality of space in the present day: the alienation of land by the colonial state, the centralization of authority over land allocation and transfer in the state, the introduction of the concept of private property, and the bifurcation of land rights along racial and spatial lines.[11] Yet these powers were not absolute: as we shall see, despite German and British intentions to monopolize power over land, laws and rules were navigated or ignored by Dar es Salaam's residents as they bought, sold, built, sublet, and squatted in and around the township. These too are the hallmarks of the coloniality of space.

The Imperial Decree alienated all land in the territory by declaring it *Herrenlos Kronland* (unowned Crown land) vested in the German Empire. Land that could be proven to be held privately, customarily, or communally was exempted. A further circular in 1896 differentiated documented ownership claims that conveyed security of tenure from permissive rights of occupation as evidenced by cultivation.[12] The native population was granted permissive rights of occupation in accordance with native law and custom, yet these rights were never considered equivalent to the private property rights afforded to settlers.[13] The bifurcation of land ownership was therefore racial and spatial. European and Indian settlers and planters claimed land in the towns and the most fertile agricultural areas as individuals with private property rights, but natives lacked the requisite documentary evidence to prove their property ownership, particularly in the towns.[14] These processes intersected to dispossess the majority of the native population from the land they had occupied in urban spaces and to lay the groundwork for an urban-rural bifurcation of land rights that was consolidated during the British colonial period.

In Dar es Salaam township there were no recorded African property owners left by the turn of the twentieth century.[15] The German colonial government negotiated purchases of Arab-, Indian-, and European-owned land; natives, on the other hand, could simply be compensated—or intimidated—and removed.[16] The 1903 Land Registration Ordinance provided for the registration of natives' land in towns, but this had little effect on natives' landownership in practice. By the outbreak of the First World War the authorities in Dar es Salaam township had only dealt with registering the property of Europeans and Indians, and few Africans could produce the documents required by the German administrators to substantiate their land claims.[17] Outside of the township along the coastal strip dominated by Zanzibari-Omani plantations, land acquisitions and transfers took on a frontier-like quality. Arab claims to their plantations established during the period of Zanzibari hegemony were recognized by the Germans. Colonial officials further alienated large tracts of land for German and Indian settlers' plantations.[18] In Kunduchi, close to present-day Salasala, the German district officer owned a plantation of thirty square miles that stretched from Tegeta to Africana.[19] Local populations also participated in this land market, taking advantage of loopholes in German land law through which it was possible to obtain title by prescription (the principle on which established, long-term use of land begets continued use of that land).[20] This loophole enabled "land-hungry investors and savvy coastal leaders" to buy and sell land along the coastal strip.[21] By the end of the German colonial period speculative practices, particularly outside of the township, and the dispossession of Africans of urban land were well underway.

MAKING COLONIAL SPACE:
THE URBAN AND THE RURAL

The British colonial administration reaffirmed the alienation of land by the colonial state and the inferiority of Africans' land rights that had been established during the German colonial period.[22] The 1923 Land Ordinance declared all occupied and unoccupied land as public land under the control of the governor, save for preexisting freeholds. The German district officer's plantation at Kunduchi, for example, was parceled out to Arab, Greek, and Indian investors.[23] The occupation of public land was permitted, according to the terms of Britain's mandate,[24] via a granted statutory right of occupancy issued by the governor for up to ninety-nine years "for the use and common benefit, direct or indirect, of the natives."[25] A 1928 amendment to the 1923 ordinance extended statutory recognition to native occupation of land under customary law, but this deemed right of occupancy remained inferior to both a granted right of occupancy and government control over public lands into the postcolonial period.[26]

The racial and spatial bifurcation of land rights introduced by the German colonial administration paved the way for a dual system of land tenure that was fleshed out under British indirect rule. Indirect rule functioned as a form of decentralized despotism in which European settlers were governed by, and had rights as citizens enshrined in, imported European law, while native subjects were administered according to customary law overseen by a native authority.[27] The dual system rested on the racial and spatial assumptions that Europeans belonged in towns while Africans were members of territorialized rural tribes.[28] In the first two decades of British colonial rule in Tanganyika, Africans were not thought to be adaptable to urban areas and their permanent residence in towns was resisted by the colonial administration.[29] These assumptions were coded into British colonial land law and administrative practices, such that the British colonial state did not consider customary law applicable in townships.[30] Secure land tenure (a granted right of occupancy) was available in planned urban zones and on German-era freeholds, but in practice this excluded the majority of Africans from holding title to urban land as few could compete in the land market with Europeans and Indians.[31] Africans were granted only deemed rights of occupancy under customary law outside of the township boundaries. Throughout the British colonial period officials argued against expanding freehold tenure to Africans on the basis that they would not make productive use of their land: they would sell it, or collateralize and lose it, and end up drifting to the towns, becoming "detribalized" and placing undue burdens on government.[32]

This apparently neat bifurcation of land rights into native/rural/customary and nonnative/urban/statutory provided the parameters within which land could be legally occupied, but it could not fully contain the reality on the ground. This was most apparent in Dar es Salaam's periurban and rural hinterland, which increasingly served to accommodate rural migrants and urban workers. From the turn of the century Dar es Salaam had been surrounded by Zaramo villages located beyond the (then) town boundary where migrants to the town settled: at Buguruni, Tabata, and Ubungo; the Sukuma villages at Msasani and Magogoni; the Nyamwezi settlements at Kinondoni and along the Msimbazi Valley; the Ngoni settlements at Keko and Kijitonyama; and the Sudanese settlements at Gerezani.[33] What were the land rights of those who had migrated from their up-country native territories where they held communal land rights but who now occupied land in the Uzaramo native authority? What were the land rights of natives residing in Dar es Salaam's hinterland as their villages were swallowed up by the growing township? What were the land rights of those who bought or sold land outside of the township? These ambiguities, together with the tension between the recognition of customary land rights in law and their inferior status in practice, would become hallmarks of the coloniality of space, fomenting chronic ambiguity in land rights and tenure security that would last into the next century. This was nowhere more evident than in the hinterland of the expanding town and on the suburban frontier that developed there.

In tandem with colonial land law, colonial urban planning laid the groundwork for the development of the suburban frontier. Urban racial segregation by building type was introduced with two sets of *Bauordnung* (building regulations) in 1891 and 1914, and further developed by the British in 1924 when their plan for the town comprised three zones with different building and planning regulations that effectively segregated the town along racial lines (map 3). Zone One was reserved exclusively for European-style residential buildings and stretched from the harbor, through the government district to the well-laid-out suburban housing provided for Europeans along Sea View. In the 1930s Zone One was extended to the newly constructed European suburb of Oysterbay, where plot sizes permitted large houses and landscaped gardens and residents enjoyed flush toilets and surfaced roads. The construction of Sea View and, later, Oysterbay planted an exclusive suburban frontier on Dar es Salaam's northern periphery—an oasis of space, services, and security of tenure amidst the official neglect and underinvestment in urban housing that characterized urban space for the rest of the township's residents. Zone Two was for mixed residential and business use and corresponded with the growing commercial area to the west of the European zone dominated by the Indian community. Buildings in both Zones One and Two were to be constructed with permanent materials, which effectively excluded the majority

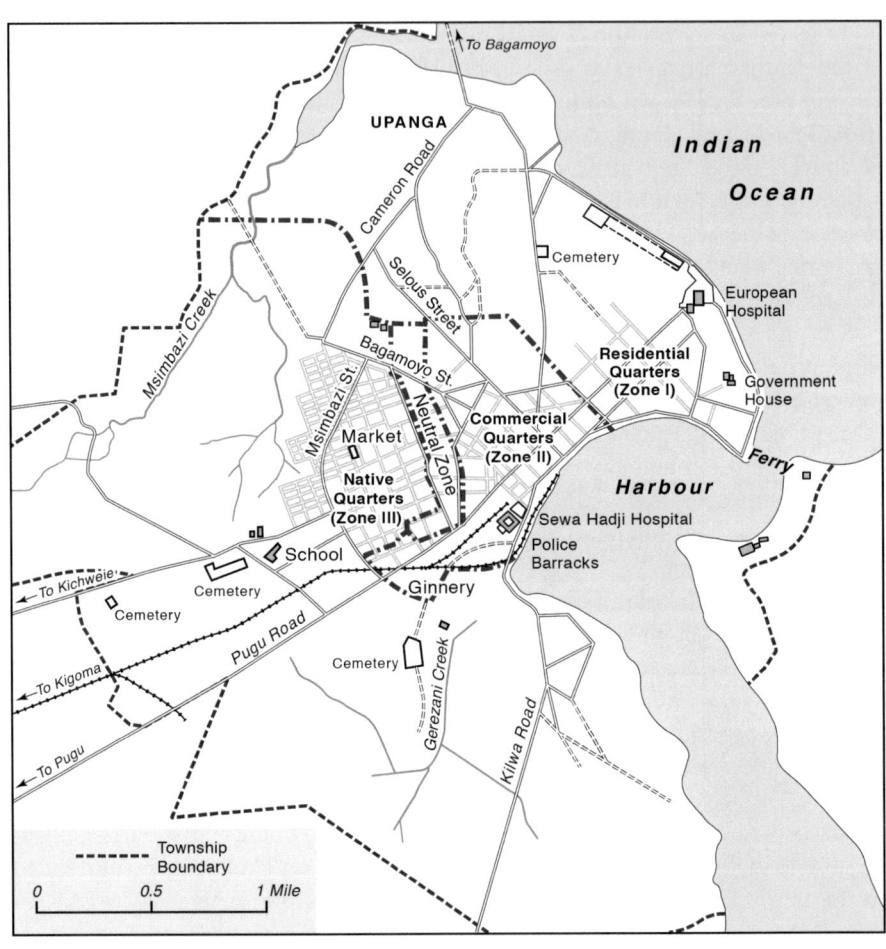

To Bagamoyo

UPANGA

Indian

Ocean

Cameron Road

Selous Street

Cemetery

European
Hospital

Bagamoyo St.

Residential
Quarters
(Zone I)

Government
House

Msimbazi Creek

Msimbazi St.

Neutral Zone

Market

Commercial
Quarters
(Zone II)

Ferry

Native
Quarters
(Zone III)

Harbour

Sewa Hadji Hospital

School

Police
Barracks

To Kichwëie

Cemetery

Cemetery

Ginnery

To Kigoma

Pugu Road

Cemetery

Gerezani Creek

Kilwa Road

To Pugu

Township
Boundary

0   0.5   1 Mile

MAP 3. Zones I, II, and III in Dar es Salaam in the 1920s. Drawn by Mina Moshkeri 2023, based on 1925 map of Land, Survey and Mines Department, TNA 12589/I, in Brennan (2012). Reproduced with permission of Ohio University Press.

of Africans, who were relegated to Zone Three at the far west of the township where construction in local materials was permitted. The zones were somewhat porous—380 native huts still stood in Zones One and Two in 1931, and the city's central market was relocated to Kariakoo in 1923, bringing with it many Indian traders who subsequently built and rented property in Zone Three.[34] But over time property was increasingly made to fit the zones, for example by refusing permits to Africans to build or repair buildings in Zones One and Two, enabling the authorities to demolish native buildings on health and safety grounds as at Gerezani and Kisutu. The three zones became known by their Swahili names: *uzunguni* (place of the European), *uhindini* (place of the Indian), and *uswahilini* (place of the Swahili, in this context meaning "African").[35] Each of these became associated with a specific type of urban landscape in a relational hierarchy of urban space, as we shall see in chapter 4.

MAKING COLONIAL SPACE: HOUSING

Social differentiation among the African population during the colonial period was tied in part to the creation and control of urban property.[36] Much urban property—land and housing—was generated by those navigating or ignoring colonial legal frameworks. People squatted, sublet, built, and rented space in and around the township and profited in the process. Opportunities for accumulation also presented themselves via the colonial state's meager efforts to provide urban accommodation for Africans, as we shall see, but these were only accessible to a select few in employment during the British colonial period.

The reticence to permit Africans rights to urban space during the colonial period was as evident in the realm of housing as it was enshrined in land law and urban planning. Government housing provision during the British period was woefully inadequate, never even attempting to keep pace with the town's African population. This was partly due to official neglect—the Tanganyika government was low on the list of the British government's colonial priorities—but local officials were also reluctant to waste money on what they thought were temporary African town dwellers.[37] Yet the urban population, and demand for urban housing, continued to grow. Following the high population growth rates of the late nineteenth century, the town grew at a much slower rate after the First World War, from 24,600 in 1921 to 34,300 by 1931, reaching 45,100 by 1943. Thereafter the rate of population growth substantially increased with in-migration, such that the town's population reached 69,277 by 1948 and then 128,742 by 1957.[38] According to the 1931 population census the township's African population included domestic servants (2,873), casual laborers (2,425), dock workers (1,642), traders (583), cooks (566), those of "no occupation" (530), and clerks (454). The Public Works Department hired a daily average of two thousand laborers, and approximately two thousand laborers worked on the sisal estates in the township's hinterland, including in and around Kunduchi and Salasala.[39]

Limited government efforts to accommodate Africans in the town were initially focused on Zone Three. This consisted of Kariakoo from the 1900s and was extended to Ilala from the 1930s to accommodate Africans evicted from other parts of the township. A total of 2,084 building plots were laid out in Kariakoo and Ilala for Africans to lease and build their own housing. Until the 1940s, this was the extent of authorized urban land provided for African self-built houses in the township. Minimal services were available. By 1932 Ilala had sixteen hundred residents, one standpipe, one public toilet, and no waste collection, street lighting, or police patrol. In 1939, Africans—who constituted three-quarters of the township's population—paid £9,000 in taxes, yet only £4,331 was spent in Zone Three from a district budget of £18,235.[40]

Conditions in the township also suffered as a result of the depression and the Second World War. In 1931, 40 percent of those usually in work in the town were unemployed,[41] and by 1939, thirty thousand natives were living in three thousand huts with no access to authorized land on which to settle in the township.[42] Matters in Zone Three were exacerbated by the high rents in Zone Two, which pushed many Indians to build or rent accommodation in Zone Three. Since Indians in Kariakoo tended to rent to other Indians who could afford to pay more for rooms, the overall effect was to limit available accommodation and push up rental prices for Africans in the native quarter of the town.[43] A colonial government report in 1942 found that 87 percent of African junior government employees could not afford to live on their wages. In-migration increased, there was a shortage of building materials, and rents doubled between 1943 and 1947.[44] The scarcity and cost of housing, along with the paucity of "starvation wages" and generally poor urban conditions, prompted three strikes between 1939 and 1947 led by the township's dockworkers,[45] the last of which escalated into a general strike that shut down the township for a week and spread up-country.[46]

Forced to respond, the colonial government developed a limited "urban entitlement" for those it considered bona fide urban residents, graded according to official racial category, which included food and clothing rations, rent controls, and various housing initiatives.[47] Unauthorized urban dwellers, on the other hand, were to be removed. *Wahuni* (a term for "undesirables," referring to the un- and underemployed) were considered unproductive idlers who fomented disorder. Starting in the late 1930s, attempts to round up tax defaulters morphed into raids. Between March and December 1947, 904 "undesirable persons" were repatriated to their rural home areas; by 1954 this had risen to 2314. In 1957–58, over 2 percent of the population of the town was forcibly removed annually in an attempt to stem the tide of unemployed "drifters" coming to the town, and to clamp down on what the colonial government identified as law-and-order problems.[48]

Despite these attempts, the colonial government began to accept that (some) Africans were indeed staying in the towns. As in other colonies, the Tanganyika government undertook to support the development of a small African middle class that would, it was hoped, become a settled urban workforce reproduced in stable nuclear families.[49] Housing was central to this goal. In fact, housing schemes for government workers had been proposed two decades previously by salaried Africans. As early as the 1920s, the Tanganyika Territory African Civil Servants Association (TTACSA) had lobbied the colonial government for preferential access to plots on which they could build, but at the time the authorities did not wish to appear to be favoring government workers.[50]

While the government housing schemes of the 1940s and 1950s were pivotal to the emergence of a middle class, this episode demonstrates that an emerging class consciousness had earlier roots among the territory's mission- and government-schooled, English-speaking Africans who were employees in the colonial service, teachers, doctors, and traders.[51] This was a relatively "new" social group compared to the existing Islamic coastal elite, being mostly Christian and coming from rural areas.[52] It was also very small: in the late 1930s Africans in the colonial secretariat, for example, numbered 4 (out of 18), 2 in the Treasury (out of 39), and 14 in customs (out of 114).[53] TTACSA was formed in Tanga in 1922 and subsequently established branches in Dar es Salaam and Tukuyu; in the northwest the Bukoba Bahaya Union was formed in 1924.[54] The Tanga branch ran a library, a football team, and evening classes in English, geography, and history. Between 1925 and 1927 the Dar es Salaam branch had seventy members. They petitioned the colonial government for housing allowances, better salaries, and leave; Iliffe describes TTACSA's purpose as "a combination of mutual improvement and elite unity" for those who saw themselves as "the vanguard of civilisation" who needed to "earn enough to lead suitably respectable lives." In 1927 the Dar es Salaam branch of TTACSA demanded employment terms equal to those of Africans in colonial service in Kenya and Zanzibar but was met with "a curt reply" from the Colonial Office.[55]

Leaders of TTACSA went on to become leaders in the African Association (AA), formed in Dar es Salaam in 1929 as the representative organization for Africans in the territory. The forerunner of the Tanganyika African National Union (TANU), which pushed for independence, the politics of the AA was a mix of class concerns and African unity that struggled in the 1930s and 1940s to bring together an alliance of educated civil servants, traders, property owners, and urban notables.[56] In the early 1930s, for example, members of the AA in Dar es Salaam protested the colonial authority's ban on Africans' admission to certain films, but their objection was on behalf of AA members only, who they argued were more educated and civilized than most Africans. Similarly in the 1950s, educated Africans were writing to local newspapers to decry the lack of suitable, separate housing for educated, "civilized" Africans, at a time when only 2 percent of the city's African population could write in English and fewer were able to read English-language newspapers.[57] Government clerks did not want to mix with the uneducated and unpropertied, and certainly not with *wahuni*.[58] Colonial newspapers played a crucial role in shaping a "bourgeois culture" among this small group of employed Africans, creating space for discussion of what ideas such as "progress" and "civilization" might mean, and providing a means by which an emerging middle class could participate in a discourse of modernity that foregrounded self-help, associational life, and respectability.[59] Appropriate housing, necessary for living "respectable lives," was a constant concern for this small but emerging group of educated urban employees.

By the 1940s the colonial government effectively agreed with them. They now saw the incubation of an urban middle class—most of whom were government workers—as crucial to maintaining consent to colonial rule and to containing the "radical potential" of the urban masses.[60] However, colonial policy on class formation among urban Africans in Tanganyika pulled in different directions, denying an independent African bourgeoisie an economic base on which it could build itself while simultaneously providing access to a government-controlled asset—a limited amount of relatively high-quality housing—as the basis for the formation of a middle class dependent on the colonial state.

The passing of the Colonial Development and Welfare Act (1940) in Britain provided access to much-needed funding for a more coherent approach to urban development. The colonial government set out the first town and country planning legislation, gave Dar es Salaam municipal status, earmarked public funds for urban infrastructure, and set out various urban planning schemes in which plots would be demarcated for self-construction.[61] The 1950 Ten-Year Development Plan for Tanganyika, with a budget of £24.5 million,[62] set aside £1.2 million for African housing and £3 million for European housing. Despite colonial anxieties about the political implications of poor-quality African urban housing conditions, the racial hierarchy of urban entitlement was nevertheless evident in the different resources made available for housing: £1,500–3,000 per house for Europeans, £1,000 per house for Asians, and £216 per house for Africans.[63] Between 1946 and 1950, the colonial government constructed 261 two-room houses for rent to Africans at Ilala and 242 houses at Temeke (map 4), and a further 3,000 plots were demarcated there by 1960. During the 1950s there were further houses (450) and plots (3,107) demarcated at Magomeni, 700 plots provided at Kinondoni and 1,000 plots demarcated in Kigamboni.

These initiatives were paltry compared to the housing needs in the township, but they were explicitly aimed at nurturing an African middle class.[64] The Temeke housing scheme, for example, was only available to Africans earning top salaries.[65] In the Magomeni scheme government clerks, the wealthiest group of Africans, were the largest group of allottees; in addition, 30 percent of the house builders in the scheme already owned another house.[66] Financing for house-building was

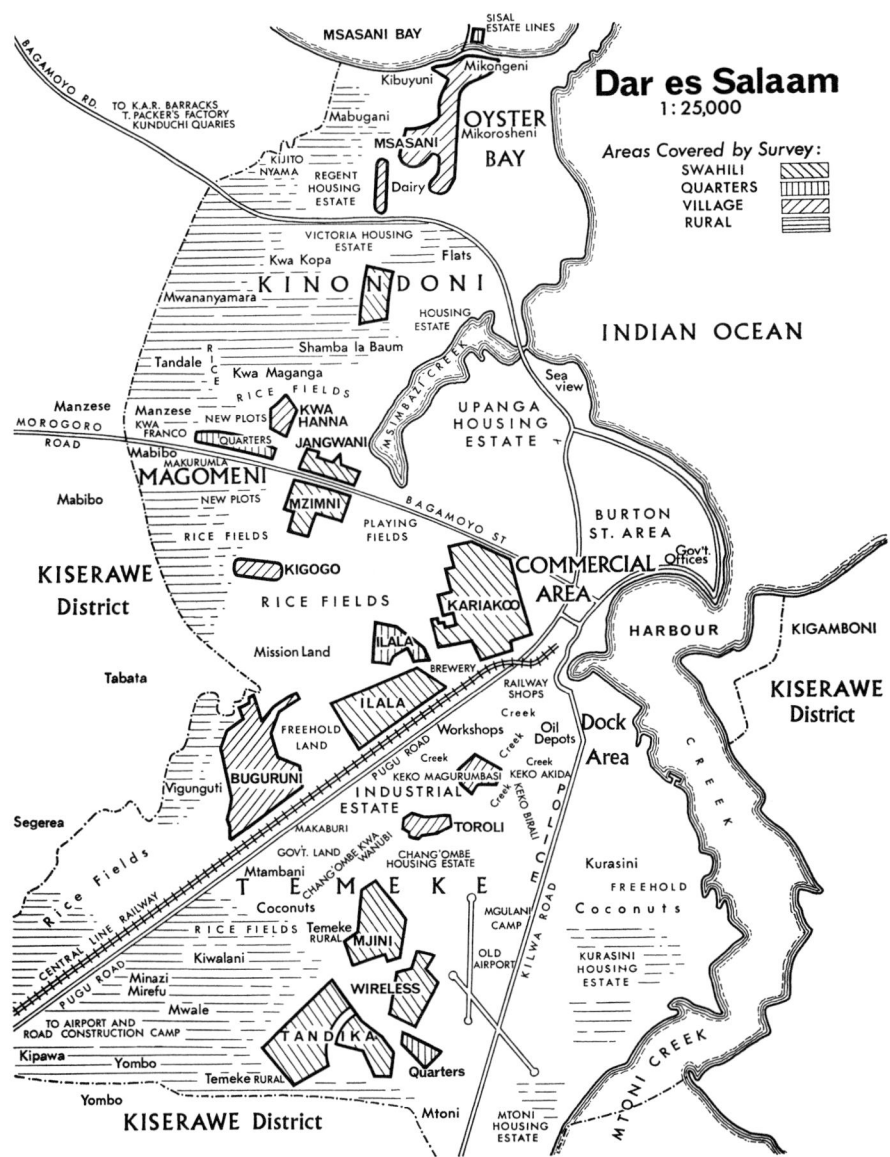

MAP 4. J. A. K. Leslie's map of Dar es Salaam township in the late 1950s (East African Institute of Social Research 1963).

made available to those with sufficient funds. A deposit of £75 unlocked a £500 house-building loan from the government's African Urban Housing Loan Fund, which after a slow start in 1953 was oversubscribed by 1960.[67] In both rental and self-build schemes, only Africans who were employed on the highest salaries could access colonial housing. By planting small oases of valuable property amidst the township's poor-quality housing stock, the colonial authorities laid the groundwork for both class differentiation and the next wave of the suburban frontier. As we shall see, after independence, Africans in top government roles continued to use their position to gain access to sought-after government urban property schemes, breathing life into the suburban frontier as they did so.

It was not only government-built enclaves that generated opportunities in the housing sector. The African response to Dar es Salaam's housing problem came from an emerging class of enterprising landlords. Many of the buildings constructed in Zone Three and beyond were Swahili houses built for residential and rental use. The Swahili house was relatively cheap to build and was constructed from mangrove-pole frames, mud walls, and palm-frond roofs. It was built around a central corridor that provided direct access to single rooms that could be rented out individually. The corridor was entered from an open veranda at the front, where people could sit or sell charcoal and firewood, and led to a private courtyard at the back that provided communal space for latrines, cooking, and washing clothes. The architectural style proved popular as the house could be extended over time as resources allowed; tenants could also be accommodated without much disturbance to the owners (many of whom lived in the house themselves). In 1939 there were roughly three thousand African homeowners in Dar es Salaam (about 20 percent of the town's African population) who had constructed Swahili houses for rental. Women were among them, having invested profits from beer-brewing and prostitution into property: by 1952 women constituted 20 percent of all taxpaying African homeowners.[68] By the time of his 1956 survey of Dar es Salaam, J. A. K. Leslie noted that the township contained over twelve thousand African-owned houses and over eight thousand landlords, and that three-quarters of the town's population were tenants. He estimated that landlords could make up to 25 percent profit on rents.[69] African homeowners constituted "the core of urban capitalists . . . and they formed the middle stratum of the African population."[70]

Much of this property was not formally recognized by the colonial government. The lack of authorized space on which to build in the township meant that many Africans had no choice other than to build in what were referred to by the colonial authorities as "unplanned" locations, mostly agricultural villages inside or just beyond the township boundary. According to the Township Rules of 1923, residential construction within the township was only permitted within the requisite zone and on receipt of a permit from the colonial authorities. Since there was insufficient space in locations zoned for Africans' residential use (Zone Three), many simply squatted, occupying land without permission in places such as Buguruni,

Chang'ombe, Gerezani, Keko, Kigogo, Kinondoni, Magomeni, Mikoroshoni, Msa-sani, Segerea, and Temeke. In one of the clearest instances of the coloniality of space in the contemporary city, all of these places have become popular neighborhoods in which a large proportion of residents still lack secure title.[71] Whether the construction of unauthorized buildings warranted tolerance or removal depended on their proximity to government or European property. At Gerezani, for example, 132 native homes that had been constructed close to European railway employees' housing were removed in 1929. Of those 132 homes, 37 were compensated at a very low rate, on the basis that they were the only "huts" that had been constructed before the passing of the 1923 Township Rules. However, the construction by Africans of a similar number of buildings at Keko, close to the docks but further away from nonnative buildings, was undisturbed. Unplanned settlements continued to grow during the 1930s, 1940s, and 1950s, outpacing the colonial government's capacity to respond. By 1960 the Land Office estimated there were 5,000 homes built in such areas.[72]

Those who could neither build, find, nor afford a room in the township settled outside of its boundaries. Dar es Salaam township's rural hinterland was a thinly populated patchwork of plantations, villages, farms, and bush, but it offered opportunities for renters and landlords beyond the authorities' capacity for oversight. Despite the fact that this was Uzaramo territory, where land was supposed to be governed by communal use and customary law, in practice there was intense speculation and frontier-like activity, as had been the case during the German colonial period. Land was bought, sold, rented, and squatted. Land was purchased by "nonnatives," sold to them by Africans and Arabs who themselves were able to navigate loopholes in colonial land law in order to sell ostensibly communal lands to which they claimed long-standing ownership; and Africans squatted on landlords' coconut plantations, paying rent and guarding trees in exchange for residence and cultivation rights.[73] Some even sublet or hired laborers themselves.

SOCIALISM AND SOCIAL CLASS
IN THE POSTCOLONIAL CITY

During the 1960s and 1970s the independent government grappled with the contradictions of urban development. After independence in 1961 and the Arusha Declaration in 1967, the political instincts of the government towards redressing the spatial distortions of colonialism rubbed up against the interests of the "bureaucratic bourgeoisie" and an emerging middle class, many of whom lived in Dar es Salaam.[74] These were social classes in formation, and their contours were neither clearly demarcated nor fixed.

In terms of land there was much continuity with the colonial period. The Tanzanian government maintained existing British land laws.[75] All occupied and unoccupied land became public land under the control of the president.[76] Freehold titles were abolished:[77] existing (German-era) titles were converted to government

leases in 1963, and then to granted rights of occupancy in 1969. The effective nationalization of land streamlined the land tenure system, in which rights of occupancy
were either directly granted or deemed granted in the case of customary tenure.
Private individual ownership of land, its purchase, sale, or rent was prohibited. In
urban areas the government had the sole right to alienate public land, for example
by declaring a planning area, and to allocate plots to individuals with a granted
right of occupancy for thirty-three or ninety-nine years. It was assumed—by land
administrators, following their colonial forebears—that customary rights did not
exist in urban areas because land in towns could only be legally acquired with a
granted right of occupancy.[78] Since urban land was public land, those not in possession of a granted right of occupancy could be dispossessed of their land. They
were entitled to compensation for "unexhausted improvements" only (buildings,
trees), since the land itself had no value.

The party of the independence struggle, TANU, consolidated its control of the
state under the leadership of President Julius Nyerere, and in 1976 it merged with
the Zanzibari Afro-Shirazi Party to become the *Chama Cha Mapinduzi* (CCM;
Party of the Revolution). Between 1962 and 1965 the country became a one-party
state, party organs were established from the National Executive Committee down
to the *balozi* (ten-household cell), the army and trade unions were brought into
the party structure, native authorities were abolished, and civil servants and police
were required to join the party.[79] State control of the economy was extended over the
second half of the 1960s and 1970s as Tanzania turned to socialism. This included
the disbanding of the cooperatives and the formation of state trading companies
and marketing boards, the establishment of industrial parastatals, and, with the
Arusha Declaration in 1967, the nationalization of foreign enterprise, including
financial institutions. The leadership of these institutions—ministers, politicians,
the civil service, the judiciary, the military, and the parastatals—formed a ruling
class or "bureaucratic bourgeoisie" that wrested control of the economy from the
"commercial bourgeoisie" that had formed during the colonial period, although
the assets of those connected to the party mostly remained intact.[80] The central
contradiction of Tanzanian socialism lay in the fact that it was the bureaucratic
bourgeoisie who took control of the economy in their own interests, rather than
in the interests of workers and peasants.[81] As we shall see, they also created and
then monopolized urban residential property on Dar es Salaam's suburban frontier, finally attaining the desired respectability and separation from the rest of the
city's residents.

Between the bureaucratic bourgeoisie and the workers and peasants, an interstitial group began to take shape during the 1960s and 1970s. The expansion of
the civil service and industrial production created opportunities for those who
had completed secondary education, including in skilled factory work and lower-
level civil service jobs such as agricultural extension workers, teachers, and techni-
cians. The civil service alone expanded rapidly during the 1970s at about 11 percent
a year.[82] Many of those who moved to take advantage of opportunities in the city

in the 1960s had completed secondary education up-country. This emerging middle class enjoyed state employment, rising salaries and promotion opportunities, access to public housing and government health facilities, affordable consumer goods, and subsidized food staples.[83] They also enjoyed new modern leisure facilities such as the city's drive-in cinema, one of only a handful on the continent, which opened in 1966.[84] Hugely popular, the drive-in epitomized the promise of socialist modernity in an independent Tanzania and provided the emerging middle classes in the city with Sunday afternoon leisure entertainment. It was a mostly middle-class pursuit, since most patrons had cars (although it was also possible to catch the film from outside). In 1963, half of mid-grade civil servants in Dar es Salaam owned cars, supported by state-financed loans.[85] Yet the drive-in—or more specifically the cars in which patrons sat—also symbolized the contradictory position of the middle classes in the 1960s: on the one hand their lifestyles proved that Tanzanians could now enjoy the fruits of independence, while on the other their conspicuous consumption was seen to come at the cost of national development. Nyerere himself railed against wasteful expenditure on imported vehicles by government workers, and particularly by graduates "whose education had been financed by revenue raised from the sweat of peasants."[86] Better to buy a bicycle, or to walk.[87] Yet there was a difference between the elite—exemplified by the minister who ordered seventeen Mercedes Benzes for regional commissioners "despite being told not to,"[88] and most government employees who were importing cheaper, used vehicles.[89] At the same time, workers who were waiting for unreliable state-owned buses or who had to walk to work could see their bosses driving cars.[90]

The emerging middle classes occupied an uneasy position in political ideology and national culture as espoused by President Nyerere and TANU. Nyerere's *ujamaa* philosophy of socialism was to be built on national self-reliance and rural communal production, the latter to be achieved in a countryside reorganized around collective villages. This would require hard work and sacrifice from all citizens in the pursuit of national development.[91] After the relative buoyancy of Dar es Salaam's economy in the 1960s, the 1967 Arusha Declaration signaled a political, economic, and cultural turn away from the cities and from Dar es Salaam—the colonial capital—in particular. According to TANU's socialist ideology, cities contained the highest concentration of exploitative activity and benefited from services provided at rural peasants' expense.[92] They were a drag on national progress. In government-owned newspapers, radio broadcasts, and in political speeches, the decadent, unproductive, and immoral city-dweller became the foil for the frugal and hard-working rural peasant who symbolized national citizenship and development.[93] Nationalist discourse approved of the *wananchi* (citizens) as long as they were productive *wakulima* (farmers) or *wafanyakazi* (workers). *Wanyonyaji* (exploiters) and *wahuni* (the urban un- and underemployed), on the other hand, were cast as threats to the project of nation-building, being idlers, loiterers, or both. Of particular concern were the urban exploiters or *makupe* (ticks), the *bwanyenye* (bourgeoisie), and the *makabaila* (landlords), many of whom owned property in Dar es Salaam.[94] In popular discourse these tensions were captured in the figures of the *kabwela*, the poor urbanite who was exploited and oppressed by the *naizisheni* or *naizi*, the privileged city dweller, usually a civil servant, landlord, shopkeeper, or employer, who lived off the hard work of others and who had prospered from nationalization without qualifications or effort.[95] *Wanyonyaji, makabaila*, and *wahuni* were urban caricatures who lived off unearned urban rents or unproductive street hawking while failing to add value to the national economy.[96]

Nyerere sought to tackle urban landlordism and conspicuous consumption among government officials with the Leadership Code, the most controversial element of the Arusha Declaration, at least within the party.[97] It forbade government officials and their spouses from "capitalist activities" including landlordism, owning shares, directing companies, or receiving more than one salary.[98] Then in 1971 the government passed the Acquisition of Buildings Act, which nationalized all buildings worth more than TSh100,000. They were given to the National Housing Corporation to rent out, though few Africans ended up renting these properties: some ended up in the control of well-placed civil servants and politicians.[99] The Acquisition of Buildings Act and rent restriction legislation were partly driven by an attempt to protect Tanzanians from exploitative landlords. In addition, the Acquisition of Buildings Act was also an attempt to intervene in the property market on behalf of urban Africans, effectively nationalizing many Indian-built constructions in *uhindini*.[100] Yet none of these interventions struck a decisive blow against urban landlords, and although the Leadership Code made profiting from residential property more difficult, it did not entirely stop government officials, or others connected to the Party, from so doing.

Against this backdrop, the middle classes found ways to justify their presence in Dar es Salaam—they were part of the educated, productive group showing others the way to national development.[101] They were respectable, morally upstanding citizens who deserved their position in the city as a result of their education, discipline, and hard work. They had foils of their own: they were not among the city's *wahuni*, prostitutes, or sexual predators; their personal comportment and their domestic arrangements were modest and respectable; and they refrained from conspicuous consumption.[102] They were also not the elite, who used their positions to capture high-value residential property in the postcolonial period.

THE COLONIALITY OF SPACE—ELITE CAPTURE
OF THE SUBURBAN FRONTIER

Despite the government's efforts to prevent class differentiation in the 1960s and 1970s, an elite group dominated by senior government employees, politicians, and party and military officials nevertheless managed to prosper in the postcolonial period, not least through their acquisition of the most secure residential property in the best locations in Dar es Salaam. In the years leading up to and following independence, Tanganyika's governing elite availed themselves of the newfound opportunities to acquire residential property in and around the former European enclave areas of the city, most of it in the city's northern suburbs. They effectively set in motion a scramble for the suburban frontier. As early as 1959, senior civil servants and ministers moved into properties or were allocated plots for construction in the European suburbs of Oysterbay and Msasani Village.[103] In Zanzibar a similar process took place after the 1964 revolution, where "one of the Revolutionary Council's first official acts was the acquisition of the 'eight ministerial houses at Mazizini', the beachfront villas of the upper crust of colonial officers."[104]

As Africanization of the civil service gathered pace, the state both created urban residential property and supplied the financial means for employees to access it. In the early 1960s a Revolving Loan Fund was set up to enable senior officials to purchase plots and build houses in Kinondoni's inner and outer suburbs of Upanga, Kurasini, and Magomeni. The fund lent TSh16.3 million to 230 borrowers between 1963 and 1968.[105] At Magomeni, plots in the low-density area were distributed to ministers, high-ranking civil servants, and politicians.[106] The small number of housing initiatives that were undertaken reinforced unequal access to property rather than responding to the urgent housing needs of Dar es Salaam's growing population. The National Housing Corporation (NHC), founded in 1962, pursued a number of initiatives in its first decade, including slum clearance and the construction of new homes, but suffered from a lack of funding and was abandoned by central government a decade later, having built just 8,209 housing units in the city, most of which were sold or rented to civil servants.[107] Between 1970 and 1973 alone the NHC's Dar es Salaam office received 5,500 housing applications.[108] Other initiatives aimed at easing the housing supply problem for urban employees included the launch in 1973 of the Tanzania Housing Bank. Despite its mandate to provide financing for low-cost housing, its loans were nevertheless captured by the better-off.[109] In the mid-1970s the bank was dispensing loans averaging TSh32,300, three times the cost of building a six-room Swahili house.[110]

The 1970s World Bank–sponsored Sites and Services schemes in Kinondoni consolidated the suburban frontier as a zone of promise and speculation for those with resources. Located in the then periurban areas of Kijitonyama, Sinza, and Mikocheni, all three sites were close to the Bagamoyo Road and the former European residential suburbs. Although Sites and Services schemes were supposed to provide serviced plots on which the poor could complete their own construction, they became much more mixed areas in the 1980s as original allottees transferred land to better-off households and others maneuvered to have "creations" (additional plots) added to the neighborhoods.[111] In 1980 only 15 percent of the plots had completed houses on them, while 29 percent of plots were empty, suggesting a high degree of speculation.[112] In Mikocheni, high-ranking government officials were conspicuously overrepresented among the plot allottees, as they had been previously in the allocation of low-density plots in Magomeni. Following the World Bank's withdrawal of support from further Sites and Services schemes in Tanzania, the government went ahead with its own large-scale urban planning scheme in Mbezi in the late 1970s and further Sites and Services schemes in Tegeta and Tabata in the early 1980s. These schemes unleashed a frenzy of speculative activity—at a time when the Leadership Code was in place—as well-placed bureaucrats scrambled to secure plot allocations for themselves or others in their social network. Investigating the allocation of plots in Mbezi, Joseph Kironde found a maze of double allocations, random changes to plot numbers, "creations," and instructions from highly ranked civil servants, including the principal secretary in the Ministry of Lands, for plots to be allocated to particular individuals.[113] Similarly, although the Tegeta and Tabata Sites and Services schemes were planned to provide resettlement sites for residents of inner-city areas slated for demolition, plenty of plots were allocated to civil servants and politicians in those schemes as well.

With these new oases of state-planned urban land in Kinondoni, the new suburban frontier began to take shape, offering security of tenure in areas laid out by government in formal planning schemes. By the 1970s and early 1980s an emerging middle class made up of mid-grade civil servants had joined the elite on the expanding suburban frontier. If they had the right connections they could live in a good location in a rented NHC flat, use their networks to access a plot in a planning scheme, and access a loan to build a house, which could then be rented out. The particularly savvy sublet all or part of their NHC flat. The NHC was reluctant to evict such tenants as they were important in the party structure.[114]

The majority of people living in Dar es Salaam, however, did not have access to planned plots in desirable locations with security of tenure in the form of a granted right of occupancy. This did not only apply to the urban poor: plenty of employees failed to obtain housing on the suburban frontier.[115] In 1975, a third of the ninety thousand residents of Manzese, one of the city's largest unplanned neighborhoods, had full-time jobs, including in manufacturing and the civil service.[116] The longstanding problem of the supply of surveyed land zoned for residential use continued. In 1972 the Lands Division provided 6,331 planned plots across the country at a time when the waiting list for high-density plots in Dar es Salaam alone was 15,000.[117] But the problem was also a bureaucratic one. There was an "implicit class bias" in the planning and administration of urban space that valued bureaucratic procedure and technical expertise above the interests of the urban poor.[118] In other words, government officials did not simply use their positions and their networks to gain control of prime residential land in the city for their own benefit, but they also did little to help those who found the procedure difficult to navigate and who lacked the right connections. Pursuing a formal plot was, in the words of one observer:

> a tedious procedure which an applicant has to forbear with patience and more often than not expense; if the frustration of waiting for long hours in unfriendly office corridors is to be ignored. Expenses on the part of the applicant due to this tedious

procedure can be more in the form of the numerous fares in the course of chasing the elusive Certificate of Occupancy or in attempts by applicants to get moving a certificate which for some unaccountable reason has decided to 'sit' in one of the offices for an unnecessarily long time. We can note here that it is those from the middle and upper strata of the petty-bourgeoisie who are best suited to bureaucratic wrangles in contrast with the workers who may be exasperated and overwhelmed or even repulsed by officious obstructionism.[119]

In the early 1970s the fees to acquire a planned plot added up to almost two months' average salary.[120] An application could take up to 280 days, assuming the application went smoothly. In fact it often took much longer, with applications for a plot having to wait months or years for a plot allocation committee to convene, before even starting the application for a right of occupancy for that plot. The procedure also assumed that the various officials spread across the understaffed departments involved in the administration of urban land (lands, surveys, valuation, town planning) interacted efficiently with one another. Breakdowns in the procedure were all too common, and yet the procedure had to be followed unless one knew how to successfully navigate the bureaucracy. As Richard Stren noted, "The aggressive, well-educated and better paid urban dweller will be much more capable of getting a plot for himself than low-income, rural migrants."[121] The belief in technocratic expertise was central to the class culture of high-ranking government officials, and it ensured that those lacking the requisite combination of money, experience, and connections were excluded from accessing prime planned land on the suburban frontier.

THE COLONIALITY OF SPACE—SQUATTING

The class bias of urban officials was also in evidence in the regular purges of *wahuni*, who were un- or underemployed in the city. These roundups and repatriations were a continuation of the colonial practice and were decried by those who saw the persecution of the urban poor as contradictory to socialism.[122] Their removal was officially justified on the grounds that they were being unproductive in the city. Yet their unruly presence in the city also unnerved the urban propertied classes who had invested in the idea of the modern, ordered city, in which the "growth of shanties and proliferation of itinerant traders were a blot on the landscape."[123]

The independent government found itself having to deal with unplanned, informal settlements early on. Land in unplanned settlements was not gazetted, surveyed, demarcated, or issued with granted rights of occupancy. As early as 1962 local planning officials advocated measures to discourage unplanned land acquisition and development. They complained of squatters in Magomeni, Buguruni, and Temeke and worried that new plans to give out building numbers in order to facilitate the collection of property tax would condone such buildings, making it impossible to demolish them at some point in the future. Yet the Dar es Salaam City Council and its Land Department, as well as the central government, provided neither the resources nor the political will to actually remove squatters.[124] The removal of squatters exacted compensation (for trees and "unexhausted improvements" such as buildings), which made the acquisition of land for planning purposes expensive. Throughout the 1960s and 1970s, the only squatter removals that took place were at Makaburini, Keko Juu, and Temeke South in 1967, Mwananyamala in 1968, and at Buguruni and Kisutu in 1975. These squatter settlements were, as Kironde notes, the "tip of the iceberg," and unplanned settlements continued to develop apace.[125] The 5,000 "squatter houses" recorded in Dar es Salaam in 1960 grew to 7,000 by 1963, 27,981 in 1972, and 43,501 in 1979, by which time these areas were housing 60 percent of the city's population.[126] By the late 1980s unplanned settlements had fanned out across the city and stretched up to twenty-five kilometers along the main road arteries into the city's northern periurban and rural edges around Tegeta, Kimara, Ukonga, and Mbagala (map 5).

After the relative gains following independence in 1961, making a life in the city became increasingly hard in the 1970s, as Dar es Salaam was beset by a deteriorating economy and an urban administration in crisis. The expanded postindependence state apparatus struggled to manage the economy. Crop authorities and parastatals failed to boost agricultural and industrial production, there was prolonged nationwide drought in 1973–74, the trade balance went into deficit, there was a chronic shortage of foreign exchange and imports, and the country became increasingly reliant on foreign aid.[127] Agricultural production was disrupted by villagization, which became compulsory in 1973.[128] By 1977 about 70 percent of the rural population had been moved to communal villages.[129] These problems were compounded by the breakup of the East African Community in 1977, the OPEC oil price rises, deteriorating terms of trade, and the war with Idi Amin's Uganda in 1978–79. GDP growth fell from 2.1 percent in 1979–81 to 0.6 percent in 1982–84.[130]

The macroeconomic situation had a devastating effect on households. The nationalization of industries and financial services and the rise of parastatals meant that, in 1976, the government was responsible for 65 percent of waged employment and 70 percent of the wage bill. Between 1974 and 1988 real wages fell by 83 percent.[131] In Dar es Salaam, there were shortages of food and household items, including staple grains, soap, and cooking oil. Queueing became a standard part of everyday life. By 1980 low-income families were spending 85 percent of their household budget on food (up from 56 percent in 1965), and even high-income families were spending 40 percent (up from 31 percent in 1963).[132] The maize subsidy, which had been in place since 1974 to compensate for declining real wages, was scrapped in 1984.[133] Parastatals were apportioned farmland and urban workers were encouraged to take up farming in the city's periurban fringes as part of the government's *Kilimo cha Kufa na Kupona* ("Farming for survival") campaign, which was to have long-lasting implications for Dar es Salaam's hinterland, as we shall see in chapters 2 and 3.

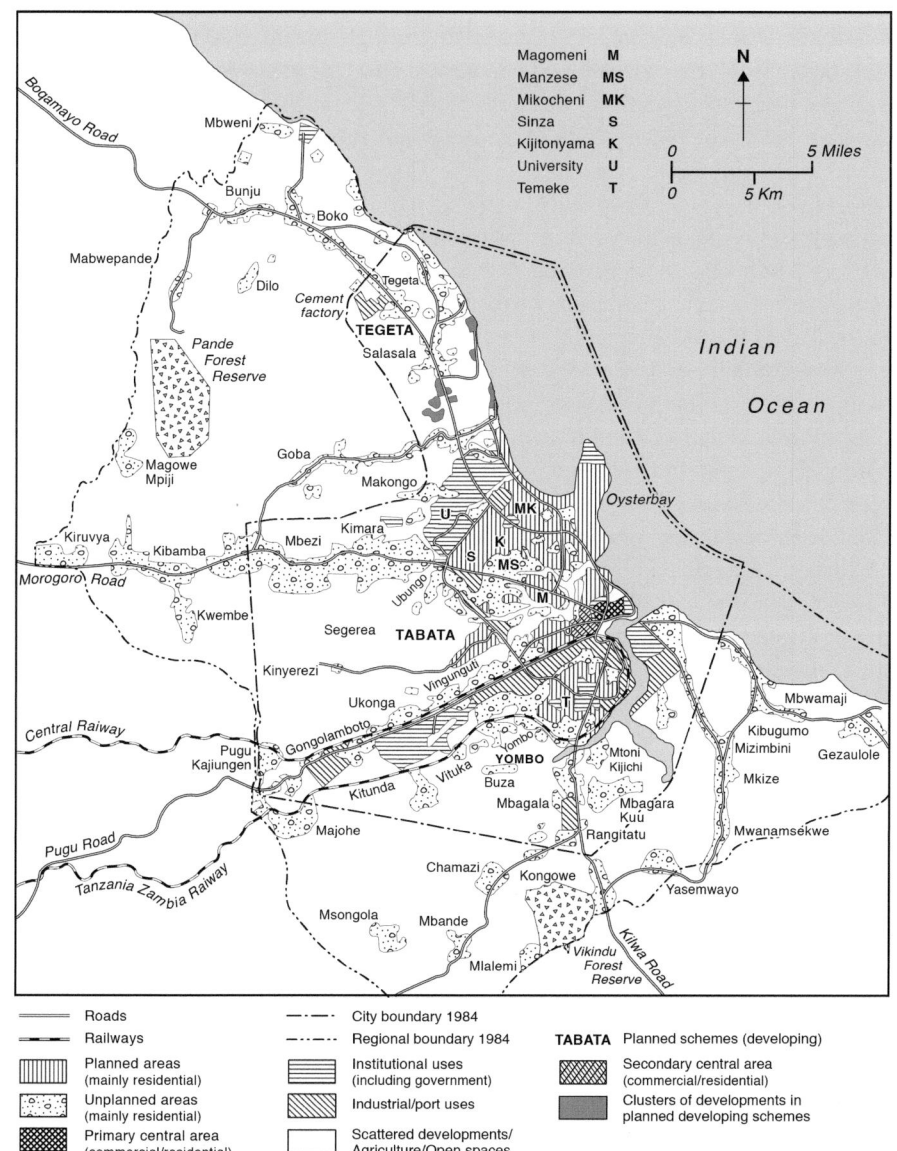

MAP 5. Dar es Salaam City and Region boundaries, and major squatter areas, 1984. Drawn by Mina Moshkeri 2023, based on Kironde (1994).

Compounding these problems was the decentralization policy of 1972, which abolished local governments. The Dar es Salaam City Council was dissolved in 1974. The city was divided into three districts (Ilala, Kinondoni, and Temeke) and managed directly by central government through the Dar es Salaam Regional Authority. With the government's focus on rural development, urban services declined and urban planning was neglected.[134] The passing of authority to central government made it very difficult to decentralize powers back to local governments when they were reinstated in 1978. This was particularly so in the case of land. Given the evident benefits of being able to control land allocation and use,[135] a long-standing struggle over the control of urban land emerged between the Ministry of Lands and the reinstated Dar es Salaam City Council. This exacerbated problems in the administration of urban land, as was seen in the allocation of plots in the Mbezi Planning Scheme.

The coloniality of space was writ large on the landscape as the city continued to grow. Between 1967 and 1978 the city's population almost tripled to 769,445,[136] but urban land delivery and housing could not keep pace. City master plans were approved in 1968 and 1979 but without the resources to implement them. The bureaucratic bourgeoisie had staked out their claim to the emerging suburban frontier through their manipulation of planning schemes in Kijitonyama, Sinza, Mikocheni, Tegeta, and Tabata. They also embarked on what Kironde drily calls "the struggle for Dar es Salaam's coastline" between the former European suburb at Oysterbay and Mbweni at the city's northernmost edge.[137] The vast majority of the city's dwellers had little choice other than to access land in unplanned settlements on which to build a house through purchase, inheritance, occupation, or allocation by local leaders. A process of in-filling and spreading out began, in which the various late colonial and postcolonial planning schemes were gradually surrounded by unplanned settlements. They were mostly tolerated by the government because it would have been politically difficult to evict the majority of urban dwellers from their homes. There was also little alternative. In the 1978 Dar es Salaam Master Plan all areas that had been squatted on were subsequently zoned for residential use.[138]

· · ·

The emergence of the middle class in Tanzania was both an intended and an unintended consequence of the colonial and then the postcolonial government's approaches to urban property. Initially anticipated to stabilize the colonial urban labor force and nurture respectable nuclear family households, the colonial state's belated investments in urban housing for employed Africans provided coveted economic and cultural assets for an emerging elite who also availed themselves of the colonizer's space on the eve of independence. The postcolonial state inherited a divided city in which sociospatial differentiation had already been etched into the landscape. The launching of the Arusha Declaration in 1967 heralded the country's

turn to socialism and a reorientation towards rural development and collective villages. The turn away from the towns was particularly marked in the case
of Dar es Salaam, which was stripped of its status as capital city in 1973 in favor of
Dodoma.[139] Yet many politicians and high-ranking civil servants continued to
invest in their daily lives in Dar es Salaam, where they made use of their positions
and networks to gain control of urban property. Below them an emerging class of
urban wage-earners, many of whom were in government employment, joined the
search for an urban plot that matched their employment status.

The coloniality of space does not only refer to the frameworks of colonial
law and the remnants of colonial administrative practice pertaining to land
rights and the management of space that lingered on after colonialism into the
socialist period. They provided the framework, but as we have seen they did not
fully contain the city and its inhabitants. Colonial and postcolonial land law
and administration provided the racial, then class-based ideologies that shaped
urban administrators' attitudes to how land should be used, by whom, and for
what. These were increasingly shared by Tanzania's elite and the small middle
class who had been able to mobilize their networks and know-how to establish
themselves on the most valuable urban land. But the coloniality of space also
provided opportunities for people to get by or to prosper by finding "unplanned"
space to rent or to build on, or to substitute income by renting rooms, subletting.
or farming at the city's edges. Over the next two decades, the growth of the city
would continue to exceed the colonial bifurcation of space between urban and
rural as more people looked to the suburban frontier as a place to make a life in
the city.

2

——

The Suburban Frontier

The suburban frontier that was established on Dar es Salaam's northern and western edges by colonial and postcolonial state planning schemes took on a life of its own in the 1980s and 1990s. The period of *mageuzi* (reforms) instigated by new president Ali Hassan Mwinyi, which saw Tanzania take steps towards economic and political liberalization, had profound implications for land use on the suburban frontier. Mwinyi negotiated the country's first Structural Adjustment Package with the IMF in 1986 and led the country to its first multiparty democratic election in 1995, which was won by CCM. Formerly proscribed "capitalist activities" such as landlordism, multiple salaries, shareholding, and directorships of private companies were openly tolerated after the Leadership Code was abandoned in 1991. The 1923 Land Ordinance of the colonial era was replaced by the Land Acts of 1999. The new land laws did not resolve the legal ambiguity in which most of Dar es Salaam's residents occupied land, but they did introduce significant changes, most notably the legal recognition that bare land could be bought and sold in its own right. More generally, *mageuzi* ushered in a period of economic, political, social, and cultural change that forms the context for what follows in this book.[1] While it is often noted that this was a period during which Tanzania's elite—the *vigogo* ("tree trunks")—took advantage of liberalization and enriched themselves through real estate investment, import-export activities, and the privatization of parastatals,[2] the middle classes were at the forefront of more subtle economic and social transformations. The scale of land transactions accelerated, imported consumer goods from bottled beer to everyday plastic homeware items to building materials and cars became available to those who could afford them, and new lifestyle trends such as baby showers and school graduation parties became increasingly popular (chapters 3 to 6). This was the age of *Mzee Ruksa* (Mr. Permission, meaning "things are now permitted"), as President Ali Hassan Mwinyi became known. With *mageuzi* there was, at least until the election of John Magufuli to the presidency in 2015, more conspicuous consumption and visible wealth compared to the recent past, evidenced by the imported cars that choked the city's streets, the imported goods on display in the small number of supermarkets, the gradual inflation in the size and cost of wedding celebrations, and the number of aspirational new houses that sprang up on the suburban frontier. Property and income generation projects no longer had to be concealed as they had been during the socialist period,[3] although the impulse not to reveal too much about one's assets remained. Yet while *mageuzi* signaled substantial changes, the period from the late 1980s was also characterized by continuities, most notably evident in the coloniality of space that continued to pervade land administration and land tenure.

Urban planning and land administration continued to be understaffed and underresourced,[4] and authority over the allocation of land continued to be a site of intense struggle between the central government and city administrations. In 1989 the Ministry of Lands issued a directive attempting to delineate the division of responsibilities between the ministry, regions, and districts, but it was hugely unpopular with local authorities and largely ignored. It required the formal advertisement of all available plots, the submission of applications for all allocations, and the filing of regular reports with the ministry. In Dar es Salaam the directive limited the City Council's responsibilities for plot allocation to high-density plots outside of the Sites and Services schemes. All other land in the city was to be allocated by the ministry. This was an attempt by ministry officials to claw back control over the most lucrative land allocations, but Dar es Salaam City Council officials continued to allocate land regardless. Chaos ensued as urban officials offered plots without the ministry's approval, the ministry withheld land title documents, official urban planning committees never met, and land deemed ineligible for urban planning such as open spaces, land reserved for public services, catchments, and conservation areas was allocated to individuals.[5]

Conducting background research for the new national land policy in the early 1990s, Issa Shivji collected detailed evidence of widespread malpractice in land administration, including the ad hoc allocation of plots by officials at all levels, double allocation, and the creation of additional plots in planning schemes.[6] Land allocation was opaque and dominated by social networks. As one Dar es Salaam city councilor who had served on a plot allocation committee commented, "Plots are allocated by *wakubwa*; we (the committee members) are often only asked to endorse allocations. After all, even without the committee endorsement, land offers are nonetheless granted. . . . It is not a question of 'first come first served' . . . now one has to know who and how."[7] More recent planning schemes seem to have suffered similar fates. For example, the 20,000 Plots Project that was launched in 2002 with the aim of providing clusters of planned plots across the city for self-builders and property investment firms ended up providing housing solutions for the salaried and the well-connected, but did little to address the city's acute hous-ing needs.[8] By 2003 an estimated 80 percent of the city's housing stock was located outside of formally planned state schemes in unplanned settlements.[9] While the quality of housing in unplanned settlements varied, all residents shared insecure legal status. They were trapped in the gray space created by the colonial bifurcation of land rights between the native/rural/customary and the nonnative/urban/statu-tory that continued to provide the framework for the interpretation and practice of Tanzanian land law.[10]

The new land legislation maintained several features of colonial land law and administration: the alienation of all land vested in the president on behalf of the people; the centralization of power over land in the Commissioner for Lands in the Ministry of Lands Housing and Human Settlements Development (MLHHSD); and the bifurcation of land tenure that distinguished granted rights of occupancy from deemed rights of occupancy.[11] This bifurcation was now mapped onto two new land categories: village land, which accounted for 70 percent of land in the country and was mostly held under customary rights of occupancy; and general land, which accounted for 2 percent of national land, mostly urban and estate land, and which could be held with granted rights of occupancy. A third category, reserved land (28 percent of national land) included all land set aside for forest reserves, national parks, public utilities and roads, hazardous land, and land designated under the Town and Country Planning Act.[12] One significant change was the legal recognition of customary rights of occupancy on village land as equal to granted rights.[13] Yet the distinction between customary and granted rights of occupancy remained, as did their primary association with rural and urban land respectively. The colonial bifurcation of land tenure thus remained a foundation of postcolonial land law and central to land administration practices. It has created significant problems for the large number of Dar es Salaam's resi-dents who have acquired land on the suburban frontier, a zone that confounds the neat administrative and legal bifurcation of space into urban/secure tenure and rural/customary tenure.

THE COLONIALITY OF SPACE
ON THE SUBURBAN FRONTIER

Dar es Salaam is surrounded by rural hinterland to the north, west, and south, with which it has been deeply entwined since its establishment as the capital city of the German colony. During the German and British colonial periods, the area under urban administration remained very small compared to the city's present dimensions, extending inland from the harbor along a five-mile, north-south radius by the time of independence in 1961. The Dar es Salaam District was much larger than the township, and until 1938 encompassed both the township and its hinterland as far north as Kunduchi, as far west as Ruvu, and as far south as Kisiju.

In 1938 the hinterland was separated from the township to form Temeke District; it was joined together with the township again to form Uzaramo District in 1942, which was renamed Kisarawe District in 1949. In the same year Dar es Salaam township was made a municipality, and in 1950 Dar es Salaam was made its own district (corresponding with the municipal boundaries). In 1960 the native administrations closest to the city—Kunduchi (where Salasala is located), Kigamboni, and Mbagalla—became part of the municipality under the Dar es Salaam District Office (map 6).[14] As is evident from the administrative bundling and unbundling of the township with its hinterland during both the German and British colonial administrations, the two were always treated differently. The bifurcation of land tenure that resulted from colonial racial ideologies about who could own what property in which location under what tenure also gave colonial authorities ample room to reconfigure the urban hinterland to suit their needs. One such example was the creation of a nine-and-a-half-mile-wide "zone of control" around Dar es Salaam township in the 1950s, which was to be preserved for planned satellite towns, villages, or agricultural use.[15] The principle that the colonial government could simply repurpose land held under customary tenure for planning purposes was subsequently backed up in law by the Town and Country Planning Act of 1956, which empowered government to declare any land as a "planning area," at which point existing customary rights would be extinguished. This established a precedent for insecure tenure in the city's former hinterland that has lived on into the postcolonial period.

Yet the city itself has always refused to be fully contained within the legal categories and administrative boundaries defined for it by colonial and postcolonial officials. This is most evident when it comes to land, as different land uses and practices of land tenure have long coexisted within the urban area. Colonial and postcolonial authorities found the constant churn of people between the township and the surrounding rural areas vexing. In fact, people were circulating between them as economic circumstances and farming rhythms dictated; or "going to ground," as Brownell notes.[16] As the township grew it encroached on surrounding rural areas. At independence the township contained villages in which residents held customary rights, as well as plantations and sisal estates, many of which were held as freehold land and were squatted by caretakers. They were mostly tolerated by the authorities, not least because of the power that had been enshrined in law to reclaim such land for planning purposes at any point in the future. Urban and industrial activities also spilled beyond the city boundary.[17] Since gaining city status at independence in 1961, Dar es Salaam has continued to outgrow its boundaries. In 1961 the city reached north to Msasani, west to Magomeni, and south to Temeke (map 6). By 1978 the city boundary was extended further into the periurban fringes where agricultural and residential land uses coexisted, incorporating Tegeta in the north, Mbezi Luis and Pugu in the west, and Rangi Tatu in the south. Dar es Salaam Region extended further still into

MAP 6. Dar es Salaam District and Municipality, and the Wakiliate of Kunduchi to the north, where present-day Salasala is located (in between Kunduchi and Goba). Drawn by Mina Moshkeri 2023, based on Molohan (1959).

the rural hinterland incorporating Bunju in the north, Kibamba in the west, and Kipara and Bandarini in the south, all of which were designated for agricultural use in the 1978 Master Plan. When the City Council was dissolved in 1974, the city was divided into three districts (Ilala, Kinondoni, and Temeke). The districts were subdivided into urban and rural wards; in Kinondoni the northern-most wards of Bunju, Goba, Kibamba, Kunduchi (where Salasala is located), and Mbweni were all categorized as rural in the 1978 and 1988 censuses. In 1988 the city officially contained fifty-two villages that had a combined population of 172,000 people (13 percent of the city's total population),[18] most of whom either were deemed to have customary rights or had evolved quasi-customary practices of land allocation and occupation, discussed below. However, the existing modes of land tenure were rendered deeply insecure with the publication in 1990 of the Town and Country Planning (Areas Ripe for Development) Order, which designated many of these villages as "planning areas" for the future expansion of formally planned urban space.[19] A further announcement by the Ministry of Lands in 1992 declared *all* periurban areas in Dar es Salaam to be planning areas. This meant that no further development should occur without planning consent. The designation of a "planning area" indicated that the land would be compulsorily alienated by the government in the future, compensation would be paid to sitting occupiers, town plans would be drawn up, and the land surveyed, parceled, and allocated. Four decades later this had not yet happened on a significant scale. Rather, these areas—most of which became part of the suburban frontier in the 1980s and 1990s—were developed organically by urban residents who acquired land and built houses themselves, regardless of any putative government plans.

The declaration of the land on which people came to build as planning areas in the early 1990s rendered it a legal gray zone. Land rights in the city's former rural hinterland, most of which was governed according to customary law by native administrations during the colonial period, continue to be ambiguous in Tanzanian law. Although customary rights were given statutory recognition in the new land legislation, in practice land administrators in urban areas reproduced the coloniality of space by treating customary rights as inferior to granted rights of occupancy. The British colonial administration had been of the firm opinion that "in a township all the land should be 'alienated' from tribal tenure,"[20] and Tanzanian land administrators in the postcolonial period appear to have been of the same view.[21] The designation of rural or periurban land as a planning area effectively overrode existing rights to land under customary tenure. Customary rights would be quashed on receipt of compensation by the state; alienated landowners could then apply for a plot in the subsequent new planning scheme and obtain a formal leasehold (granted right of occupancy). The principle that urban land should be transformed from customary tenure to formal leasehold was paramount. Yet, the relevant legislation (the Town and Country Planning Ordinance, Cap. 378) did not lay this principle down in law; moreover, in the Dar es Salaam case the government has never made any compensation payments to those whose land was gazetted by government notice in 1990 and 1992. No systematic cadastral records exist to prove to whom payments should be made, and there has never been a budget from which to make such payments.[22] This has rendered the legal basis on which most people who have accessed land informally in these formerly rural and periurban areas outside of the original township highly precarious. When tested in court in the 1980s, a number of judges upheld the view that customary rights could indeed be extinguished in declared planning areas without the payment of compensation, but the Court of Appeal took the opposite view on several occasions.[23] As we shall see in chapter 3, what has transpired in this legal gray zone is a generalized feeling of insecurity of tenure for those who hold quasi-customary tenure on formerly customary land. The majority of the city live with the coloniality of space on a daily basis.

DISPOSSESSION, COMMODIFICATION, AND ENCLOSURE ON THE SUBURBAN FRONTIER

The expansion of the city into its periurban and rural hinterlands that had begun during the colonial period picked up pace in the 1970s with a number of government campaigns designed to keep unproductive urbanites out of urban areas. Among the most significant was Operation Pwani, the regional villagization directive in Dar es Salaam, which required people living in scattered farmsteads across the rural part of the region to move to designated *ujamaa* villages starting in 1973. In Kunduchi and the surrounding area, farmers were corralled into the *ujamaa* villages of Mtongani and Tegeta.[24] Various other relocation exercises were aimed at repatriating unemployed urbanites considered to be dangerous, idle, or both. Operation *Kila Mtu Afanye Kazi* ("every able-bodied person must work") in the mid-1970s and the Human Resources Deployment Act of 1983 (known as *Nguvu Kazi*, or "hard work") both expelled urban dwellers to periurban areas to farm, usually with little success.[25] People were also directed to the city's periurban and rural edges to farm during the *Kilimo cha Kufa na Kupona* ("Farming for survival") campaign launched in response to the city's food crisis following the 1973–74 drought. Conducting research in Bunju at Dar es Salaam's northern edge in the 1970s, Marja-Liisa Swantz noted that the allocation of land as part of these directives was completely ad hoc, with no records of who owned what land or what parcels were being allocated to urbanites.[26] Some of the land being parceled out was on nationalized estates and plantations, but some of it was farmland that had belonged to the Zaramo before they had been forced to move to *ujamaa* villages.

These government relocation exercises stimulated demand for land in the periurban and rural hinterland, and with it the long, slow dispossession of the Zaramo of their former farmland. Transacting land between individuals was not unheard of before the 1970s. As noted in chapter 1, during the German period some Africans claimed Arab identity in order to claim ownership of land which they then sold;[27] "nonnative" investors also began acquiring land during the British period. In the 1930s and 1940s peripheral land within the township boundary was being subdivided and sold without freehold or leasehold tenure. It was also being accumulated beyond the township boundary, as in the case of the *liwali* (local leader) in the periurban village of Rangi Tatu who was buying land from the surrounding Zaramo who were unable to pay their poll tax.[28] Later in the 1970s land acquisition was also facilitated by payments in kind, as was the case in rural Goba, where newcomers were allocated land in exchange for harvested crops, cloth or local drinks, or token cash payments.[29]

Nevertheless, cash transactions for land before the 1970s were not widespread. Land surrounding Dar es Salaam was relatively abundant and the main population, the Zaramo, lived in scattered farms and practiced shifting cultivation.[30] This changed with *ujamaa* and the government campaigns of the 1970s and 1980s, which divorced the Zaramo living on the city's periurban fringe from their land and ushered in urbanites who were allocated or were willing to pay token amounts of money to access land on which to cultivate. At this time land itself still could not be sold; transactions referred instead to the "improvements" (buildings and trees such as mango, cashew, and coconut) on a piece of land. Yet over time such practices can morph into a common understanding that the land itself is part of the transaction.[31] Such was the rapidity of the commodification of land in Dar es Salaam that by the late 1980s land in the city's periurban and rural areas was in demand as urbanites sought small pieces of land on the city outskirts on which to produce food.[32] In her study of livelihoods in the inner-city neighborhoods of Manzese and Buguruni, Aili Mari Tripp found that by the late 1980s the majority of residents had acquired farm plots averaging 1.2 hectares in the periurban and rural edges of the city.[33] Among Manzese residents she found that farms had been gifted by relatives or friends (36 percent), purchased (23 percent), inherited (15 percent), or simply claimed in one's original village within the city boundaries (23 percent). By the late 1990s it was quite common to see locally made roadside signs advertising farms for sale in Dar es Salaam's outskirts, even though the selling of land did not become legal until the new land laws came into effect in 2001.

Many Zaramo were dispossessed by the market. It has been suggested that Zaramo sold their land for a number of reasons: to raise money for socially significant rituals and rites of passage; to take advantage of the attractive lump sums that buyers were offering; and as a result of frustration at the profound disturbance to customary tenure that resulted from *ujamaa*, various other resettlement operations, and the government designation of the land as a planning area in the early 1990s.[34] By the 1990s distress sales had become more common, with Zaramo selling their land "because of poverty, *njaa*" ("hunger").[35] The long-term impact has been the dispossession of the majority of the Zaramo from their land over three or four decades. Many stayed in the former *ujamaa* villages such as Mtongani and Tegeta as they grew into substantial satellite towns, where they formed "a landless working class," or they shifted away from Dar es Salaam altogether.[36]

This was the period when the suburban frontier began to push north into the city's formerly rural and periurban fringes. The commodification of land was further stimulated as economic liberalization policies were rolled out from the early 1990s, including the National Land Policy of 1995, which set the framework for land acquisition and occupation; the revocation of the Leadership Code, which permitted civil servants and politicians to engage in "capitalist activities"; and the promotion of private sector investment. The volume of land transactions increased and prices began to rise. Demand was driven not just by government imperatives to farm the city's edges, but also by government urban planning schemes such as the Sites and Services projects of the 1970s and 1980s that pushed the suburban frontier into the neighborhoods of Mbezi Beach and Kijitonyama in Kinondoni and drove demand for adjacent land around Kunduchi, Mwenge, and Mbezi Luis. The price of land varied substantially, with higher prices commanded by land that was proximate to formal planning areas, arterial roads, and the coast. Land prices were subsequently higher in the north and west of the city compared to the south and southwest, which saw very little infrastructure investment until the 2010s. In the early 1990s the price of an acre-sized plot ranged from TSh15,000 (US$50) inland in the then poorly connected village of Goba to TSh500,000 (US$1,679) in places closer to the sea and good roads such as at Salasala junction, Ununio, and Tegeta. In Mtongani and Kunduchi, smaller plots of land would transact for TSh1–2.5 million (US$3,359–US$8,397) because of proximity to the ocean and to the Mbezi Beach planned area where the market value of high-density plots was over TSh3 million (US$10,077).[37] By the early 2000s Wilbard Kombe found that the price of periurban land under rapid transformation was not only rising across the city, but that the average size of parcels being sold was shrinking as people subdivided their land and sold pieces off.[38] A quarter of an acre was more expensive thirty kilometers to the north in Bunju or twenty-five kilometers to the west in Mbezi Luis (TSh600,000–TSh1.5 million [US$621–US$1,552], depending on proximity to an arterial road), while land was cheaper in Rangi Tatu and Nyantira, fifteen kilometers to the southwest of the city center (TSh300,000–500,000 [US$310–US$517]). In Goba, near to Salasala, demand was so high that people reported that the average price for the average plot of land had increased from two to three dollars per acre in the 1980s to around US$1,000 for a third of an acre in 2010.[39]

Demand for land was coming from both rural and urban migrants. The latter group had moved from a rural area to stay with kin or acquaintances in the inner city, or who had lived in the inner city for some time before seeking their own parcel of land further out that would be large enough on which to build a house and conduct small-scale income-generating activities such as growing vegetables, animal husbandry, or running a small business such as hairdressing, tailoring, a small bar, or a retail shop. Being able to grow at least part of the food required for household consumption was particularly important in the late 1970s and through-out the 1980s. In the 1980s and 1990s periurban land was still relatively abundant and could be cheaply acquired, depending on where in the city it was located. Some areas filled up with people who had previously been neighbors in the inner city as word of mouth spread about opportunities further out. This happened in Mbezi Luis, which lay fifteen kilometers further west along the Morogoro Road from the inner-city settlement of Tandale from which many of its residents moved. These preexisting social networks facilitated land access for the poor; people who knew each other were less likely to charge exorbitant prices for land, and vendors were more likely to accept favorable terms of payment for buyers over longer time frames.[40] Similarly, Daniel Msangi found that relatively poor newcomers had been able to access land in the periurban area of Goba, but that over the 1990s market transactions became the dominant mode of accessing land rather than through inheritance or grants from friends and relatives, and land prices increased substantially.[41]

By the 1990s the suburban frontier was taking shape as the periurban and rural zones of Dar es Salaam were undergoing significant change. Former Zaramo farm-land, which could be thirty to forty acres in size,[42] was increasingly carved up and sold to individuals who treated the land as private property. Plot sizes were smaller—on average 4.1 acres—and land was being used for a greater variety of activities. Periurban economic activities included farming, casual labor, land sales, rental housing, trading and services in small towns, land mining, and fodder production.[43] Farming was still the dominant land use in the 1990s, but instead of supporting shifting cultivation land was now treated as private property and used more intensively. Land had become a commodity necessary for supporting income generation activities and small businesses. Land was sought for small-scale agriculture or market gardening, residential and rental houses, small business activities such as warehousing, grain milling, car workshops, tailoring, ironworking or timber, or small retail spaces for basic groceries, fruit and vegetables, or bars. These activities were often combined so that a plot could contain a residential house, a rental room, a small garden, and a bar or retail shop facing the path.[44] Land was also being hoarded by speculators, limiting the supply of land to the market and further pushing up prices.[45]

The formerly rural hinterland became a zone of enclosure and investment once again, as it had been during the Zanzibari-Omani and colonial periods. By the 1990s a large proportion of newcomers seeking land on the suburban frontier were relatively well-off people in business, politics, and the civil service.[46] Civil servants, in particular, had stable incomes (TSh50,000 average monthly salaries) and monthly transport and housing allowances (both worth TSh100,000 each); they constituted about two-thirds of new house-builders on the suburban frontier in the late 1990s.[47] It became common to see walls or barbed-wire fences constructed around plots.[48] But the advance of the suburban frontier into the periurban fringe is not a smooth story of incremental property ownership and prosperity, and there was much inequality. Davis Mwamfupe distinguished between a small number of capitalist farmers with large private farms (twenty to fifty acres) growing food for the markets in Dar es Salaam and for export; "hobby farmers" employed in the city in the public and private sectors who had bought between five and ten acres of periurban land, which they farmed as an investment; "city-based food producers" employed in the city in less well-paid jobs, who produced food for household consumption on their plots of one to three acres; "periurban food producers," who were usually indigenous full-time farmers with one to five acres; and the "land poor," who were indigenous or migrant farmers who had sold off parcels of their land to recent newcomers, who produced food on less than an acre for household consumption.[49] The inequalities between these groups continued to grow. A decade later in Mbezi Luis, twenty-five kilometers west along the Morogoro Road, Aldo Lupala found that average incomes of new arrivals were four times the minimum urban salaries in the public and private sectors.[50] He also found that 80 percent of the residents of Mbezi Luis lived on less than a dollar a day, as the commercial and self-employment opportunities of the growing neighborhood attracted people to work as petty traders and vendors, in bars and restaurants, and shops and services such as car repair. The area rapidly became a residential and commercial neighborhood in which livelihoods depended on urban employment, more localized off-farm jobs, casual labor, and self-employment. Those who had sold their land to in-coming farmers would have been among those flocking to these growing suburban centers in search of work.

Land purchased by newcomers was held under "quasi-customary" tenure, which refers to rights to customarily held land that has been transacted for cash to someone who is not indigenous to an area. The market transaction expunges the land from customary tenure, so that the land can subsequently be used, subdivided, sold, or gifted by the new owner without recourse to the wider social group.[51] "Quasi-customary" tenure as practiced around Dar es Salaam has emerged to fill the gray space created by the colonial and postcolonial bifurcation of land tenure. It is widely recognized and accepted on the ground, including at the lowest level of dispute resolution in the legal system (the ward tribunal, discussed in chapter 3). But it is not a legally recognized form of land tenure with attendant rights enshrined in law.

The administration of land in the periurban zones of Dar es Salaam is in practice devolved to the lowest level of urban administration, made up of the subward chairperson and the *wajumbe*.[52] Yet these local leaders have no statutory role or power in relation to land administration, and there is little communication between them and municipal land administrators. They were not given town planning

drawings that were drafted for their neighborhoods after they were declared planning areas in the early 1990s. Instead, subward chairpersons and *wajumbe* permit
and witness land transactions in their areas, often for a small personal fee and a
10 percent fee paid to the subward office. This self-organized process of land management at the community level has a long history, and largely worked until the
2000s.[53] From the 1960s branch and ten-cell leaders of the ruling party, who were
usually also community leaders in their neighborhoods, oversaw land transactions
despite such activity being contrary to party policy and both statutory and customary law. As demand for land and the volume of transactions increased in the
1980s, some leaders in periurban areas developed their own paperwork to record
the details of transacting parties though they were not required to do so by law
and the information was never collated centrally. By the 1990s it was increasingly
common for land transactions to be witnessed by local leaders and for the transacting parties to exchange sale agreements recording party and witness names and
the location, size, boundaries, and price of the plot. Transactions relied on local
technology such as pacing or using a rope to measure parcels and marking boundaries with physical features or poles fashioned from trees or bushes. Security
of tenure derived from being recognized by one's neighbors as having used a piece of
land for some time. The governance of land more widely in the community relied
on what Wilbard Kombe and Volker Kreibich call "social regulation," in which
neighbors recognize each other's claims and negotiate basic urban planning principles such as leaving sufficient space between plots for pathways and accepting
the legitimacy of subward leaders, who act as arbitrators in case of disputes. By the
late 1990s Kombe and Kreibich noted that public and communal land uses were
coming under increasing strain, as local leaders condoned sales of land and building projects that blocked paths or were located on slopes or hazard lands. They
also noted that social regulation was breaking down in more densely settled places
closer to the city center and coming under greater strain as prices and demand for
land on the suburban frontier continued to rise.[54]

OPENING UP THE SUBURBAN FRONTIER: SALASALA

The longest established residents of Salasala today trace their arrival to the 1970s
and 1980s. Before that time, the farmers who had practiced shifting cultivation, living and farming the land in scattered farmsteads, were mostly indigenous Zaramo,
though in-migration during the British period brought Matumbi, Ndengereko, and
Rufiji to the area. These farmers were moved to the *ujamaa* villages of Tegeta
and Mtongani during the *ujamaa* campaign of 1973 and 1974. The 1978 census
recorded the population of Kunduchi Pwani, an area that included Salasala, at
just 1,419, while the population figures for nearby Tegeta (5,323) and Mtongani
(3,270) reflected the relative size of the *ujamaa* villages by that time.[55] *Ujamaa*
precipitated the long and slow dispossession of the Zaramo, who were separated

from their former farmland in and around Salasala. When the food crisis struck after the 1973–74 drought, village administrations in Dar es Salaam's periurban and rural areas allocated land to newcomers to farm, often with no recourse to establishing who already owned, claimed, used, or had been removed from what land.[56] The same happened during the campaigns of the 1980s to encourage urbanites to farm in the city's periurban and rural hinterlands. Thereafter, as demand for periurban and rural land increased throughout the 1990s, those Zaramo who still owned land began to parcel it and sell it themselves. In addition to Zaramo farms, the former sisal estates in and around Salasala were also allocated to newcomers from the city. Many of the long-term present-day landowners in Salasala thus obtained land relatively cheaply through cash transactions with the previous farmers, or they were allocated former farmland or sisal estate land by the village administration in Mtongani several kilometers away. One Salasala resident said of the allocations, "they [government] even gave you a hoe and a bush knife for free." There was no systematic record-keeping of land allocations or transactions. Tenure was customary for those Zaramo who remained, based on customary law. For the new farmers tenure was quasi-customary. One *balozi* in Kilimahewa subward who had obtained land in Salasala in 1977 described the process of acquiring and enclosing land:[57]

> At that time we lived in Kinondoni . . . they were calling people working in town and giving them land to farm out here. It was the *Kufa na Kupona* campaign . . . this place was a Greek sisal farm. It was huge. But with nationalization people were given large areas. You just went to the Mtongani village government,[58] you went with a policeman to this place, and you chose your land. You decided how much. My father took four acres. One woman here took a large area. You put your markers down and you said "This is my land." Others were going to Kinyerezi, to Wazo.[59]

Those who acquired land in and around Salasala in the 1970s and 1980s described their experience as one of opening up a frontier. At the time the area was considered a wild landscape that needed to be tamed and made productive by the newcomers. The land was mostly described as *pori* (wilderness or scrub) inhabited by wild animals, though some of it had previously been cleared and cultivated by the Zaramo, who had tended coconut and cashew trees. The newcomers grew food crops such as paddy rice, maize, sorghum, cassava, and fruits such as oranges, pineapples, and bananas, they tended coconut and cashew trees, and they reared livestock such as chickens, goats, and cattle. Few of these farmers envisaged Salasala as a place in which to live. It was far from the city, with poor transport links and no services. Houses were few and far between and constructed with local materials of mud, poles, and thatch. Whether relatively wealthy or not, those who acquired land in Salasala in the 1970s and early 1980s considered it their farmland, to which they commuted on an intermittent basis while they continued to live and work elsewhere in the city. The better-off among them hired laborers to work on their land, including the former Zaramo farmers if they had stayed nearby on a small plot of land, or local laborers, some of whom would have been dispossessed local farmers or former sisal estate workers.

Yet it was not only commuter-farmers who were drawn to Salasala, and the population of the area doubled between the 1978 and 1988 censuses.[60] Parts of the area were densely settled in the interstices of other long-standing land uses in this part of northern Kinondoni: plantations and quarries. The original village of Salasala accommodated workers at the former Kunduchi Sisal Estate, a remnant of a German-era plantation that was sold to Arab, Greek, and Indian investors during the British colonial period and then nationalized in the 1970s. The section in Salasala was owned by Greek investors from 1936 to 1971. A small whitewashed Greek church, built in 1945, still stands next to the Bagamoyo Road at the Salasala turnoff on a small section of land that the investors were permitted to keep after nationalization.[61] The original village is now a small area known as Salasala RTD, so-called for its proximity to the Radio Tanzania Dar es Salaam site, a large open area the size of several football pitches carved out of the former sisal estate that was set aside for a broadcasting station and masts after nationalization. At the site's southeastern corner lies RTD, a densely built area of small houses that constituted the original village next to the sisal estate, at the heart of which is an old mosque. People who had arrived in the 1980s recalled that at that time the area surrounding Salasala RTD was sparsely populated by small-scale farmers, but that the settlement began to grow from the late 1980s as more people arrived looking for somewhere to build a house and maybe to produce some food. Another high-density settlement in Salasala grew at the Kunduchi quarry site, a small section of which falls in Salasala and the rest in Mtongani, now a large informal settlement nestled between the Bagamoyo Road and Kunduchi village. Only a small section, the JKT Quarry in Salasala,[62] remains active: the rest of the Salasala part of the quarry has been claimed for residential use. As large mining companies wound up their activities in the quarries in the 1990s, small-scale miners entered the quarries to mine and to build homes. Kinondoni Municipal Council subsequently drew up plans to redevelop the former quarry site on the Mtongani side for landfill and administrative purposes, and in 1999 the council tried to evict the *wavamizi* (invaders)—so-called because they were occupying hazardous public land belonging to government. This was resisted by residents who took their case to the primary courts and won a temporary injunction against their eviction, which was later overturned by the High Court. Their case was bolstered in 2006 when the then prime minister Edward Lowassa ordered the closure of the remaining mining operations at Kunduchi and a review of the decision to evict the invaders.[63] As one Salasala resident noted of Lowassa's support for the invaders, "You know you can't get rid of these people—they will say 'we won't vote for you.'" Most of the former Kunduchi Quarry site is now filled with small houses. On the Salasala side, the former quarry wall drops down precipitously behind the row of small shops referred to as *Mabanda Mengi* ("many shacks") that line the tarmac road that serves as the entrance to Salasala. The small houses packed closely together in the former quarry are invisible from the road. The area has become more densely populated since the mid-2000s, as people looking for somewhere to build and make a livelihood invaded the site and made a living crushing stones to sell as building materials by the roadside. Land inside the quarry and at RTD transacted for cash, often witnessed by a representative from the *serikali ya mtaa*, despite the ambiguity of the residents' tenure rights.

Until the mid-1990s Salasala was characterized by low-density farming, a strip of industry along the Bagamoyo Road that had been zoned in the 1978 Master Plan, and a few low-income informal settlements. Farm sizes were still relatively large, ranging from over ten hectares to less than one; the majority of farms were between one and two hectares in size.[64] This began to change in the late 1990s as more people acquired land and built houses in Salasala. Most of them had been living elsewhere in the city where land was more expensive or simply unavailable for house-building and small-scale income generation activities. The homes they built in Salasala were small and the plots open to the pathways through the settlement, though some used trees, hedges, and shrubs to mark their plot boundary. People constructed single-storey square or rectangular houses, using concrete blocks, plain iron roofing sheets, and mesh windows, configured with sitting rooms and one or two bedrooms, outside kitchens, and bathrooms.[65] They used what outside space they had for vegetable patches, poultry, goats, pigs, and zero-grazed cattle. At this time, the only all-weather road and bus service was to be found on the Bagamoyo Road, the nearest primary school and dispensary was some distance away in Mtongani, Tegeta, or Kunduchi, and the nearest secondary school was seven kilometers away in Makongo.[66] Electricity, water, and sanitation, where they existed, were privately installed or accessed (for a fee) from better-off neighbors who dug wells or paid for an electricity connection;[67] young people earned a living transporting jerry cans of water to residents by bicycle. The transformation of Salasala into a desirable residential location on the suburban frontier picked up pace in the early 2000s with two significant developments: a resettlement scheme that planted a small planned neighborhood in the middle of the Salasala farmland, and the construction of two tarmac roads connecting parts of Salasala directly to the Bagamoyo Road and the rest of the city.

Any visitor to Salasala today will note that some parts of the settlement are easily reachable by tarmac road. Salasala is flanked to the east by the six-lane tarmac road that runs north from the city center to Bagamoyo, making the adjacent neighborhoods prime commuter areas relatively accessible from the rest of the city. There are two small tarmac roads that wind through the area, neither of which was the outcome of a municipal urban planning layout; rather, they were by-products of industrial infrastructure development in the city. Both roads stop abruptly after a few kilometers in the middle of the settlement: one of

Kilimahewa's neighborhoods is known locally as *Mwisho la Rami* ("end of the tarmac"). The first road was constructed in 2003–4 and connects the main Bagamoyo Road to the Independent Power Tanzania Ltd (IPTL) plant,[68] now nestled among housing plots in Kilimahewa. The second was built in the mid-2000s as part of a resettlement project to relocate urban residents displaced by the construction of a gas pipeline by Songas, a public utility power company with funding from the World Bank for infrastructure and power development. The new pipeline connected the Songo Songo Island gas fields located two hundred kilometers offshore south of Dar es Salaam to the Ubungo Power Plant in the city, the IPTL power plant in Kilimahewa and the Wazo Hill Cement Factory in Tegeta. To mitigate the displacement of urban residents the World Bank project planned two resettlement sites at Salasala and Kinyerezi to accommodate 183 households. At the time both sites were peripheral to the city and lacking amenities such as roads, water, and electricity. The resettlement project in Salasala consisted of a small island of several hundred planned plots arranged around a road layout in the middle of the existing farmland several kilometers from the Bagamoyo Road. The plots were surveyed and laid out according to formal planning regulations and made available with granted rights of occupancy. A water storage tank connected to the city's main water supply was also provided, though it was not operational until local residents established a community organization to run it in 2009. Some existing landowners who owned large plots of farmland under quasi-customary tenure at the resettlement site were required to subdivide their land to provide residential plots for the resettlement scheme. They were compensated for the land they surrendered to the project and were offered their own residential plots in the process. Nevertheless few—if any—of the families displaced by the Songas pipeline were resident on their reallocated plots in Salasala a decade later. As one resident who had built a large house in the resettlement area commented by way of explanation, "The original resettlers were small farmers with small huts . . . and the resettlement plots had requirements to develop the plot within three years." Given that planning regulations were rarely followed up by municipal planning officials, it was more likely that the displaced families did not want to move to the resettlement site, preferring to sell the land in Salasala and stay in their neighborhood close to their existing networks, livelihoods, and transport links.

The relative remoteness of Salasala did not remain the case for long. In planting a sliver of a planned urban neighborhood with security of tenure and a tarmac road in an area where demand for land on which to build residential housing was growing, the unintended consequence of the resettlement scheme was to push the suburban frontier out to Salasala, creating a small area of high-value property that stoked demand and land prices in the surrounding area. The population of Salasala grew from 9,707 people in 2002 to 33,448 by the 2012 census, by which time Salasala had become sufficiently densely populated to justify dividing it into two *mitaa* (Salasala and Kilimahewa).[69] Keen to overcome their distance from government services, residents contributed to building offices for the *mtaa* government at Salasala and Kilimahewa. In the resettlement area a community water association was set up by residents to manage the water facilities that had been provided by the World Bank as part of the resettlement scheme. The original thirty-four members took on the burden of the cost of pumping the water from the city's main water supply to the community tank by collecting connection and user fees. By 2016 the water scheme employed fifteen staff and had expanded beyond its intended capacity to serve 283 households, supplying water (intermittently) to 485 customers.[70] The few schools in the area were joined by new government and private providers, and private dispensaries opened up. New churches and mosques were built.

As Salasala became more desirable as a residential neighborhood, existing landowners turned to building their own houses on their former farmland and subdividing their plots to sell pieces off to newcomers. Simple brokers' signs, often displaying just a name, telephone number, and the word *dalali* (broker) or *viwanja* (plots), were nailed to trees or stuck in the ground at junctions to advertise available land. As we will see in chapter 4, many of those who came after the mid-2000s built an entirely new landscape characterized by distinctive, good-quality houses largely hidden behind tall concrete block perimeter walls. But they were not the only ones attracted to Salasala: many poorer urbanites were also drawn to the possibilities that a growing peripheral residential area offered for relatively low rents and livelihood opportunities. As well as the opportunities for small-scale mining and aggregates business offered by what was left of the quarries, incremental house-building provided opportunities for day laborers, as well as a market for services such as food vending and motorcycle taxis. Some of them were able to build small concrete block houses on tiny patches of land that did not afford space to cultivate anything, but most of those who provided this labor and these services did not join the local building class; instead they rented from them.

. . .

Over a century of colonialism, state socialism, urban crisis, and economic liberalization, Dar es Salaam's suburban frontier has shifted slowly northwards from the first European suburb at Oysterbay. The original suburb was a material and imaginative frontier that symbolized the coloniality of space during the British colonial period: an exclusive, carefully planned, and relatively well-resourced oasis of good-quality housing, urban services, and secure tenure, built to suit imported European suburban aesthetics and separated from the rest of the township where very little housing or public services was provided for the majority African population. By the end of the colonial period a small African elite had benefited from the handful of housing schemes belatedly developed by the colonial state to the north of the city center near to Oysterbay; after independence the bureaucratic bourgeoisie extended their control over these and the new government housing schemes developed close by.[71] A nascent suburban frontier coalesced in and around these government housing schemes that created highly sought-after urban neighborhoods—most of which became home to those in the higher echelons of government—that offered security of tenure and the promise of public services in a city with woeful access to both. Dar es Salaam was not an isolated case. As if to prove Frantz Fanon right in his warning about the national bourgeoisie, the relationship between state-created property and class formation has been noted in other colonial and postcolonial contexts—across capitalist, socialist, and Marxist-Leninist regimes.[72] In colonial Bulawayo, West argues that demands for housing fit for educated Africans was key to middle-class formation there, while Mabogunje and Sumich describe a similar process to that in Dar es Salaam in which senior civil servants were overrepresented in the possession of public land and housing resources in the immediate postindependence period in Nigeria and in the post–civil war period in Mozambique. More recently there has been renewed interest in a new generation of state- and private-funded housing developments in Addis Ababa, Luanda, Maputo, and Nairobi, which provide opportunities for the accumulation of economic, political, and cultural capital for urban middle classes, contractors, and government officials alike.[73] To date, there have been fewer such developments in Dar es Salaam, leaving the middle class to fend for themselves in the urban peripheries.[74]

The shift northwards to the present suburban frontier, on which Salasala is located, was a slow process set in motion by the government campaigns of the 1970s to collectivize farming and to encourage urbanites to farm at the city's edge, which divorced Zaramo and other cultivators from their farmland and ushered in city dwellers to produce food. The unintended consequences of those campaigns became clear as the suburban frontier took shape in the following decades. The sweeping changes that followed *mageuzi* and the micro effects of the Salasala resettlement scheme ignited the land market in Dar es Salaam's former rural hinterland. The liberalization of land was key to middle-class formation. Transactions in land in and around Salasala increased as Zaramo farmers and settlers who had arrived in the 1970s and 1980s parceled out and sold off pieces of their farmland to newcomers in search of a plot on which to build a house. The suburban frontier was transformed from *pori* to a zone of possibility where land could be occupied, bought, hoarded, or invested in. It was also a zone of ambiguity where land rights were unclear, government urban planning was nonexistent, and public services were absent. How did this suburban frontier become a space of middle-class formation? The rest of the book turns to answer this question.

3

Land

"You know, people want to buy this land. But I tell my children they must value this land. When I am gone, they must not sell it . . . There's no better money than land," explained Rajabu as we sat in the shade of a tree in the large enclosed landscaped garden in front of his recently completed, peach-colored two-storey house. He and his wife were among those urbanites who enclosed land in Salasala that was reallocated to farmers when the Kunduchi Sisal Estate was nationalized. He explained, "My wife came to buy land from the natives here—well, they weren't natives, they had been given it for free by the government." His wife Saada later told me, "A friend of mine told me that there was farmland to buy out in Salasala. At that time it was just bush, no one wanted to live here." They purchased two large adjacent plots in Salasala in the mid-1970s, about one kilometer from the Bagamoyo Road, for TSh30,000. At the time, Rajabu and Saada lived in government accommodation in town. They were both employed, he as a civil servant and she as a secretary. They kept cattle on the land they bought in Salasala and sold milk in the city. The cattle had since been replaced by poultry, which was less labor-intensive as he and his wife got older. The current house was not the only construction on the land: the first, more modest house had been their home when Rajabu had retired from government service in the 1990s. It was now the residence of one of their children. Since his retirement from government Rajabu had worked in the private sector in town. He and Saada had constructed the current house while living in the first one. They had now been living in it for a couple of years. During that time, Rajabu had also built a string of "frames"—concrete block shops for rent—alongside the tarmac road that had been built by the World Bank as part of the Salasala resettlement scheme. The road now bifurcated his land. A daughter ran a bar out of one shop; others were rented to businesses including a hair and nail salon, a bakery, and an animal feed shop. A few stood empty. In addition to these investments, Saada had recently been buying farmland in neighboring Bagamoyo Region, and Rajabu owned inherited land in his natal village in Kilimanjaro Region.

Rajabu and Saada's story illustrates a common characteristic of middle-class practice: over several decades they had acquired land at every opportunity. Land enabled them to invest earnings, secure future income streams, project social status, and ensure social reproduction. These strategies overlapped. Buying land with cash acted as a form of saving as well as providing a basis for house-building, social status, and inheritance. Incremental house-building, the main use of land purchased by the newcomers to Salasala after the late 1990s, was widely seen as the most prudent use of money that was not required for immediate house-hold consumption in a context where mortgage financing was not widely used. House-building was itself understood as a form of saving, as owner-occupiers no longer paid rent to landlords, even though the cost of house-building was itself a huge burden over many years. Relative to other parts of the city where land and rental prices were more expensive, Salasala and its environs offered the possibility of building a modest and respectable lifestyle around one's own home.

In addition to owning land on which to build a residential house, over the years Rajabu and Saada had invested what they could in acquiring land and mak-ing it productive. In Salasala they had invested in agricultural projects, rental shops, and a bar; others built small rental rooms on their property. Those with the necessary connections complemented their land in Salasala, most of which was owned under quasi-customary tenure,[1] by purchasing a formally planned plot with granted right of occupancy in one of Kinondoni's planned residen-tial areas (for example at Boko, Mbweni, Mivumoni, or Kigamboni) where they intended to build another property for either residential or rental purposes at some point in the future. Such land was considered the most secure and valu-able land it was possible to acquire in the city. In addition, many suburban resi-dents had bought farmland in neighboring Bagamoyo Region or around Kibaha (a town located thirty kilometers to the west of Dar es Salaam, in Coast Region). One of Rajabu and Saada's neighbors, Renata, had a small farm in neighboring Bagamoyo District on which she cultivated vegetables and fruits. She was seek-ing buyers in town willing to place irregular orders. In addition to her city-based full-time job with a multinational company, during the cultivating season she would drive to her farmland on weekends to supervise the work. Maintaining a claim to inherited family land in a rural home region was also common. Others acquired land in other towns and cities outside of Dar es Salaam where they had worked or gone to school. Such land could become the basis for investment proj-ects such as building a house or other rental property. Land was also acquired in and outside of Dar es Salaam for children's inheritance.

Land was the most valuable material asset for middle-class suburban residents, and a considerable amount of effort went into scoping, acquiring, enclosing, securing, and exclusively using it. Land was also the most valuable asset of land-poor residents, many of whom suffered the consequences of the layered enclosures that took place from the mid-1970s. As noted in chapter 2, many Zaramo farmers who cultivated in Dar es Salaam's rural hinterland were removed from their land during the villagization campaigns. They were subsequently dispossessed when their former farmland was then enclosed by city dwellers and other settlers who claimed or were reallocated the land by government, or who bought land from the Zaramo themselves. As demand for land rose in the 1990s and 2000s, remaining Zaramo parceled their land and sold it to newcomers who built houses enclosed within perimeter walls (maps 7 and 8). Those who sold all of their land moved away to find farmland elsewhere or for waged labor in the inner city or the satellite towns around Dar es Salaam.[2] Others remained on much smaller parcels of their own land or entered into caretaking agreements with the new settlers. Over time the hinterland's former farmers' most valuable asset shrank, becoming too small to support established livelihood activities or to invest in new ones.[3]

By the mid-2010s there were almost no farmers left in Salasala who had inhabited the land since before the 1970s. Some had managed to hang on to a small amount of a larger piece of land they had acquired at that time. These early settlers were recognized by subsequent arrivals as local leaders, partly because later arrivals purchased land from them, but also because they often took on local leadership roles in the party-state bureaucracy, such as *mjumbe* or CCM branch secretary. One early settler who gradually sold most of his land but managed nevertheless to stay in Salasala was Ahmed, an elderly man who had migrated in his youth from Lindi in southern Tanzania, residing first in Chanika, an outer settlement in Ilala, then in Kawe in Kinondoni. He explained that he came to Salasala in 1973 and bought a large piece of land from Zaramo farmers, "who sold to get money and then left the area. The land was just farmland and it did not have much value."[4] As if to underscore the point, Ahmed, who lived in a small house built with local materials on what was left of the land he had bought, added, "When we came Hassan was living there," as he gestured towards a distant hill. "There were no other residents. . . . You could meet lions," he recalled. As he gradually sold off small pieces of the Zaramo farmland he had purchased, Ahmed precipitated a further round of enclosure. As an early settler he became the *mjumbe* for the area, consolidating his position as landowner, land seller, and local leader connected to the ruling party structure. Ahmed's small unwalled plot and mud-brick house suggested that he was not a member of the middle class, but he nevertheless held a position of authority in relation to his neighbors. One neighbor—whose plot was even smaller and less well-positioned than Ahmed's—explained that he had bought his plot from Ahmed in the 1980s and

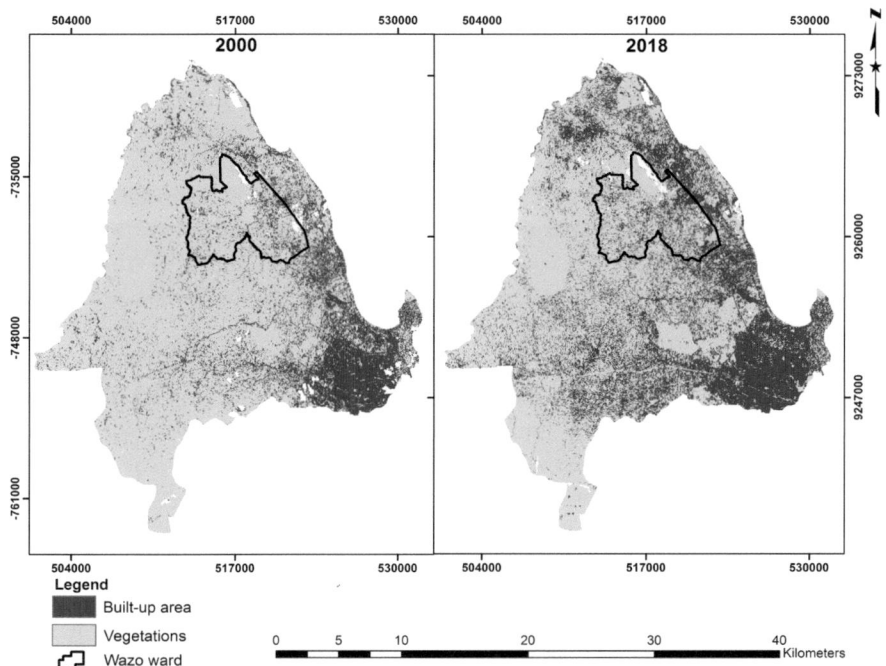

MAP 7. Kindondoni District and Wazo Ward land use change, 2000–18. Drawn by Kelvin Kamnde, Department of Geography, University of Dar es Salaam, 2018.

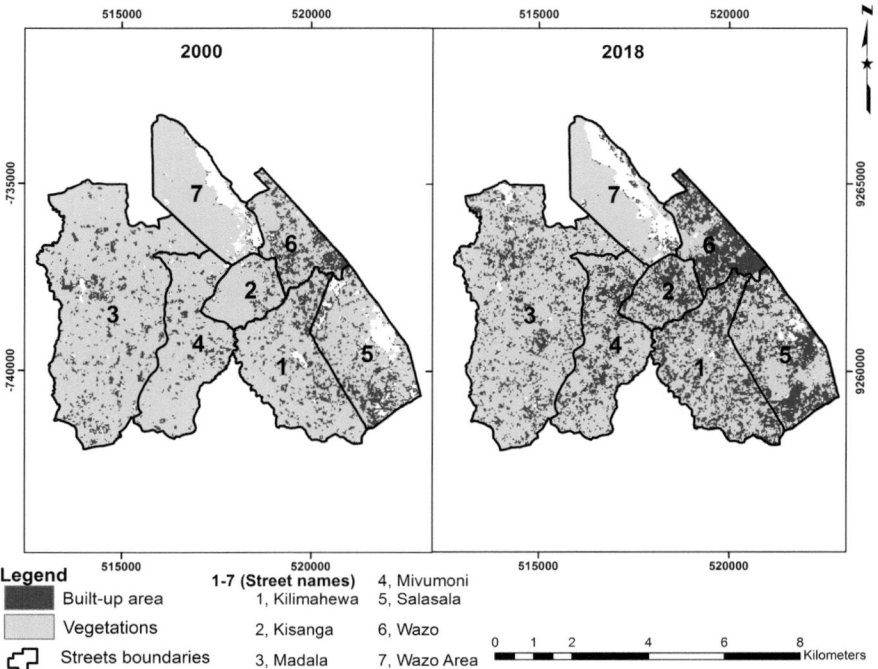

MAP 8. Land use change in subwards of Wazo Ward, 2000–18. Drawn by Kelvin Kamnde, Department of Geography, University of Dar es Salaam, 2018.

that the surrounding area had attracted more residents from 2001, such that "by 2006 it was getting full." He explained that Ahmed often adjudicated in land boundary disputes between neighbors since he was the one who had parceled the land and sold the plots to newcomers. Another *mzee* (elder), George, who had also enclosed Zaramo farmland in the 1970s, participated in the further enclosure of land where he had settled in Kilimahewa. When George retired from the army in 1979 he was living in Manzese, a large informal settlement close to the center of town. The land he had acquired in Kilimahewa was formerly part of the Greek-owned Kunduchi Sisal Estate, which was nationalized in 1971. Makonde farmers had been resettled on the former estate but, George noted, "they were selling this land . . . they didn't want to stay . . . they moved to Karege in Bagamoyo."[5] He bought thirty acres of farmland from the Makonde but found it difficult to maintain such a large farm while still living in town. As more people seeking land came to the area in the 1980s, he was drawn into a further round of enclosure through subdivision. He explained, "I was alone, and they could invade easily, so I had to give them land." By the time I met him in 2017, he was living in a house in need of repair on a small plot, surrounded by neighbors to whom he had sold small parcels of the farmland he had earlier acquired from Makonde farmers.

In these frontier stories we see contrasting dispositions in relation to land: better-off residents think of land as an asset that is always better kept than sold, while poorer residents see land as an asset that can also be a drain. If one lacked the money or inputs necessary to make land productive, it could be sold or subdivided to free up cash for other more pressing matters, such as when a family calamity required cash, or when a deceased relative bequeathed land that the family could not afford to keep up. One Kilimahewa resident recounted a WhatsApp discussion with her neighbors about a piece of land being offered for sale to neighbors by grandchildren following the death of their grandmother. The group members advised the grandchildren that they should keep the land, perhaps to cultivate vegetables or to raise poultry; but the grandchildren felt they had to sell the plot because they couldn't afford to fence, build, or pay taxes on the land, and they needed the cash that the sale would generate.

The control and use of land was therefore central to class reproduction in Salasala. Four decades after the Zaramo were forced to leave their land during the villagization campaigns of the mid-1970s, this was no longer a rural hinterland that supported shifting cultivation and scattered farming. Rather, through the incremental and interlinked processes of dispossession, commodification, and enclosure, Salasala's landscape had been transformed into a plotted residential neighborhood in which the small, modest homes of the land-poor nestled in between the walled, aspirational houses of the middle classes. Yet the apparent achievement of enclosure in so many concrete block homes and walls belied the ongoing work necessary to secure them.

FIGURE 3. An empty plot secured with a wall and a caretaker building, Salasala. Photo by author, July 2015.

RISKY TRANSACTIONS

Acquiring and holding on to land on Dar es Salaam's suburban frontier was a risky undertaking. Buyers were routinely duped by brokers, neighbors encroached on boundaries, strangers invaded unenclosed land, family members feuded over plots, and government agencies could demolish unauthorized constructions to accommodate public services or changes in land use. Risk was literally written on the landscape: spray-painted signs on doors and walls vividly proclaimed the intentions of plot owners, brokers, and neighbors (*"nyumba hii haiuzwi,"* this house is not for sale; *"ogopa matapeli,"* beware conmen), or the edicts of underresourced municipal land enforcement officers condemning structures that violated planning regulations (*"simama,"* stop; *"bomoa,"* demolish; *"ondoa,"* remove; or simply a large red X). In such an unpredictable environment the middle classes were better placed than others to secure their land by drawing on connections to strategically useful individuals and their experience of and confidence in dealing with government bureaucracy, not least because many members of the middle classes were part of the bureaucracy. As Wilbard Kombe notes, when it came to controlling land in Dar es Salaam, "one has to know who and how."[6]

FIGURE 4. A warning to prospective brokers and buyers painted onto a wall around an empty plot in Salasala: *Hapa hapauzwi, ogopa matapeli* (this place is not for sale, beware conmen). Photo by author, April 2018.

Land transactions could be hazardous. It was rare to hear someone describe their own experience of this because to do so would reveal their lack of skill in relation to land acquisition. But most people could recount stories of people they knew who had fallen afoul of unscrupulous brokers, vendors, surveyors, or local government officials. In Kilimahewa Juu one *balozi* told of a pastor who bought land adjacent to him for TSh5 million, started to build a house on it, but was then removed from the plot by the real owner when it was revealed that he had been scammed by *matapeli* (conmen) who had posed as the seller and a neighbor. In a rare admission of his own vulnerability when navigating the land market, the *balozi* went on to recount his own experience of getting his plot surveyed. In exchange for his TSh400,000 the surveyors placed beacons on his plot and gave him a document, but when he discovered these to be fake, "they had disappeared. They were conmen surveyors."[7]

Transacting unplanned land on the suburban frontier provided ample opportunity for such *matapeli*. A transaction usually involved the seller and buyer, perhaps mediated by a broker, and witnessed by the local *mjumbe* who verified, in consultation with neighbors, that the seller owned the land in question and that the boundaries were correct. The plot should not contravene planning regulations such as being located on hazardous land (river valleys, floodplains, gulleys) or within sixty meters of a trunk road, nor prevent any anticipated developments in relevant town planning drawings that showed the location of land zoned for residential use and public goods such as markets, police posts, schools, and health centers. A written record was then endorsed by the *mjumbe* and marked with the *serikali ya mtaa* (subward government) official stamp, and copies kept by the seller, buyer, and the *serikali ya mtaa* office. A fee was usually paid to the *mjumbe* and any other witnesses, and an additional fee of 10–15 percent of the value of the transaction was sometimes paid to the *serikali ya mtaa*. These procedures were developed across the city from the 1980s as local leaders in unplanned areas attempted to keep up with the land market. In fact, lower local government had no legally mandated role in land delivery and management, and in practice oversight of such transactions was often improvised. This was partly a function of necessity, since subward offices and *wajumbe* did not have copies of the town planning layouts that were drawn up for their neighborhoods following the declaration of Dar es Salaam's outer wards as planning areas in the early 1990s. The only map I encountered in a subward office was in Kilimahewa, where a copy of a map of the Salasala resettlement scheme was taped to the wall. This covered perhaps a third of the subward. In one corner of the map, the words "forged document" had been painted over with correction fluid. None of the subward offices in Salasala (Salasala, Kilimahewa, or Kilimahewa Juu) were able or willing to provide records of land transactions in their areas. The Subward Executive Officer in Kilimahewa reported that the majority of land transactions in the area were not registered at the *serikali ya mtaa*.[8] No local land cadastre existed. In practice transactions could be witnessed for a personal fee or a plot sale could be endorsed on land not meant for residential use. *Madalali* could fraudulently sell an empty plot by working together with real or fake *wajumbe* or neighbors. Vendors might themselves be fake: One young man recounted his experience of going to inspect a plot for potential purchase in the periurban area of Mabwepande, where two men purported to be selling a twenty-five meter by twenty-five meter plot for TSh500,000. The young man's suspicions were aroused when the sellers insisted the transaction be completed in cash on the spot without going to the *serikali ya mtaa*, since they had all the paperwork and an official stamp with them. My interlocutor did not buy the plot.

In this frontier environment the artifacts of plots and buildings were not to be trusted: survey beacons,[9] maps, and even the measurement unit of plots were all subject to physical shifts as well as to shifting meanings and interpretations. One neighbor might move another's beacon to increase the size of their plot, or they may place fake beacons on their boundaries to materialize their claim to land. A plot might not really be for sale, nor belong to the person apparently selling it. The absence of maps and a land cadastre meant that any claim to land relied on the testimony of neighbors who might be real or fake. Documents, signatures, and certificates were routinely fabricated. In Kilimahewa a copy of the official stamp of the *serikali ya mtaa* was available for use at the photocopy shop opposite the office. One surveyor described the widespread practice of *kupika data* ("cooking data"), in which "you have a title and the survey but when you check the beacons and the GPS you find that the plot should be somewhere else." Land in Salasala was difficult to pin down.

NAVIGATING THE WARD TRIBUNAL

The challenges of buying and securing land on the frontier were nowhere more evident than in the local court system. Across the country, the number of land cases filed with District Land and Housing Tribunals (DLHTs) has been rising steadily.[10] A significant proportion of all land cases in the country were filed in Kinondoni District,[11] where the relative density of people with both the will and the financial means to dispute land through the legal system reflected the specific nature of frontier suburbanism in Dar es Salaam's northern suburbs. Below the DLHT, a lower tier of land conflict resolution was provided by the ward tribunals that provide a cheaper, nonprofessionalized system for dealing with land disputes in urban areas. Ward tribunals were established in 1985 as part of a broader reorganization of local government and were officially purposed with maintaining peace and stability in neighborhoods by hearing and mediating local conflicts related to land, marriage, and debt. They were designed to deal with land or property to the value of TSh3 million. In practice in Salasala the ward tribunal heard cases regarding higher-value property because very few parcels of land in the area were worth less than that sum. Ward tribunals were closely supervised by Ward Executive Officers and made up of *wazee* (elders), many of whom had previously held party or lower local government positions. Professional lawyers were not involved in ward tribunal cases.[12] There was a fee (TSh10,000; US$4.6 in 2016) to lodge a case at the ward tribunal, and land cases attracted an additional fee (TSh100,000) if a site visit was required.

In recent years, land cases have taken up an increasing amount of ward tribunals' time. This was the case at the Wazo Ward tribunal located in Salasala. Many of the cases concerned minor infringements on small pieces of land.[13] For example, in one case a transaction was being disputed in which a vendor and buyer were arguing about the size and price of a plot postsale. The buyer claimed that when the sale was agreed the vendor had stated the size of the plot in meters, and that she only discovered afterwards that the plot measurements were in *miguu* (steps),[14] meaning the plot was smaller than she had been led to believe. Conversely the vendor was accusing the woman of attempting to increase the plot size by changing the unit of measurement on the sale agreement from "m" for *miguu* to "meters." In addition, she had been causing trouble with her new neighbor over the location of their latrine, which she claimed was located on her (enlarged) plot. The tribunal had looked at the informal sale agreement and agreed with the vendor that the woman had changed the unit of the plot size on the sale agreement from *miguu* to meters. They directed her to change the unit of measurement back to *miguu*. The woman announced that she did not accept the judgment and that she would take the case to the DLHT.

In other cases more valuable assets were at stake, such as in the case brought by a young man who had sold his plot for TShs10 million (approximately US$4,593 in 2016). He and the buyer agreed that the payment would be made in installments, with a first payment of TSh7 million to be followed by the remaining TSh3 million at a later date. They also agreed that on completion of the payment the buyer could demolish the existing building on the plot and reuse the materials. The buyer did not complete the payment, yet proceeded to remove the doors from the existing structure. Despite his summons to attend the tribunal, the buyer was absent when the case was heard. Instead, a letter was read out from the Kinondoni DLHT stating that the defendant wanted the case heard at the district tribunal and not at the ward tribunal. Circumventing the ward tribunal was a common tactic in disputes over higher-value property. Another case had been brought by a man (Buyer Two) who had bought a plot through a bank auction. The plot in question had previously belonged to Buyer One, who had taken out a bank mortgage to finance the purchase, but who had subsequently defaulted on the loan. The bank had repossessed the plot and put it up for auction, whereupon it was bought by Buyer Two. However, thereafter Buyer One proceeded to start building a house on the plot. Buyer One also did not attend the ward tribunal, instead sending a letter stating that he did not trust the ward tribunal and that he wanted the case referred to the Kinondoni DLHT.

Land risks on the suburban frontier were not confined to land transactions alone, but could become long-standing disputes over boundaries. This was the case in a conflict over the boundary between two adjacent plots belonging to Dora and Leila, two middle-class women who both lived in the planned area of Mbezi Beach. They had invested in adjacent plots in an unplanned part of Salasala, where an *mzee* had been slowly selling off parcels of the land he had enclosed in the 1970s. Leila had bought her plot (115 × 90 *miguu*) from the *mzee* in 1998 and had gifted it to her sister on her wedding day. When the sister later died, her husband returned the plot to Leila, who gave the plot to another relative. An *mlinzi* who had previously cultivated the *mzee*'s land continued to guard Leila's plot, which remained undeveloped with just a small temporary structure in one corner—a common strategy to mark ownership of a piece of land before building on it. In 2010 the *mzee* sold an adjacent smaller plot (27 × 27 *miguu*) to Dora. Leila's complaint was that Dora had encroached on her plot by demolishing the concrete boundary pillars that separated the two plots and replacing them with a line of ashoka trees inside her plot. Leila also alleged that Dora had further encroached on Leila's plot by building a wall close to Leila's temporary structure. Leila had brought the case to the ward tribunal, having failed to resolve the matter with Dora directly. At a ward tribunal hearing in April 2016 (one of a series of hearings for this case) Leila called four witnesses to support her case: the *mjumbe*, who corroborated Leila's story; a smartly dressed neighbor in Salasala who verified the plots and the structures on them, but didn't know much about the boundaries; a third man, who also had an investment plot in the vicinity and confirmed that the pillars had demarcated the boundary between the two plots, but who couldn't enlighten the tribunal as to who had put up the pillars, trees, or concrete block wall; and finally a relative of Leila's who described how, on visiting the site in 2014, she had been surprised at how close Dora's concrete block wall was to the small building on Leila's plot. Thereafter Dora called her first witness, a woman who had witnessed the transaction when Dora bought the plot, who was asked questions about the proximity of Dora's wall to Leila's existing building. When Dora's second witness was called and it transpired that she was absent from the tribunal because she had been unable to leave work, the hearing was adjourned. Dora asked for a summons to be sent to the witness so that she could get time off work, and Leila asked if it was possible to talk to the witness by telephone, both of which were denied by the tribunal.[15] This particular hearing, which was neither the first nor the last in the case, had lasted almost three hours and had required the synchronous presence of the two disputants and six witnesses, the absence of one of which brought the proceedings to a halt. The episode made evident that the work of securing land in the absence of a granted right of occupancy required the maintenance of good social networks, and a substantial amount of time and energy.

This small sample of cases from the Wazo Ward tribunal in April 2016 demonstrates the range of conflicts and challenges that frequently arose during the course of acquiring and securing land on the suburban frontier. While the cases reveal the audacity and skill required to navigate the various characters and institutions involved in the sale of unplanned land, they also underscore the risk that one might not be successful. Achieving some semblance of land security was an arduous and lengthy process. The bundle of competencies, social networks, and experience that enabled land to be acquired in the market and secured via bureaucratic means, as well as the possibility of failure, was a defining feature of middle-classness. It distinguished the middle classes from the elite, who could rely on greater economic and political power to secure their assets and who were therefore far less likely to experience the challenges faced by the middle classes in acquiring and securing land; it also distinguished them from the poor, whose relative lack of economic and social resources limited them to smaller, less valuable parcels of land that they struggled to secure. Some middle-class residents were well-placed civil servants who were able to use connections to acquire a formal plot in one of the few planned residential development schemes in the city.[16] Some used their networks and paid cash to push the paperwork for a planned plot through the Ministry of Lands more quickly, or to lean on officials to grant a residential title for a plot located in an area designated for public services. The elite did this too, but on a grander scale.[17]

Middle-classness also entailed competence in acquiring relatively high-value unplanned land. Knowing how to navigate the bureaucracy around land was less daunting for those with more formal education and experience with valuable assets. This meant knowing that when buying a plot via a broker the site should be revisited without the broker in order to verify ownership and boundaries from unmediated neighbors; that town planning layouts at the municipal planning offices should be consulted to check that a plot was not on the site of an anticipated public service or road; and that land in a valley or floodplain or within a road reserve should be avoided. One broker in Kilimahewa noted a hierarchy of class-based practices among his clients based on the extent to which they exercised caution when buying land. "People who buy cheap land don't go to the *serikali ya mtaa*, just to the *balozi*. The middle classes go to the *serikali ya mtaa* to check who really owns the place before buying it. . . . Some come with their lawyers."[18] Others considered the *serikali ya mtaa* to be below them, engaging very little with what they considered to be unprofessional and unreliable local officials. Zacharia, who worked for a mobile telecommunications company, had bought a plot of land in an unplanned part of Salasala and was in the process of obtaining formal title to his land. Discussing the process, he claimed, "I don't even know where the *serikali ya mtaa* office is. I never go there, I have nothing to do with them. I just go straight to the ministry." A similar tactic emerged in the above accounts in which the ward tribunal was dismissed in preference for the DLHT, where the dispute would be handled by legal professionals with reference to statutory land law rather than customary or just principles. This was an expensive option. While disputing a land case even in the ward tribunal required time and money, fighting over plots of land in the DLHT was a strategy available only to the upper-middle classes and the elite. Even if such a strategy was employed simply to hold on to land by calling an opponent's bluff, it revealed a certain level of knowledge and experience with land transactions and an unwillingness to subject one's property to the judgments of nonprofessionalized, local institutions.

SECURING PROPERTY

The accumulation of land was a precarious enterprise, and not always a successful one. As well as the risks associated with transactions and securing boundaries described above, unplanned land was also at risk of reclamation by the state. Dar es Salaam's residents were periodically reminded of this when the demolition of houses was beamed into living rooms and bars courtesy of local television news crews. Demolitions were usually small-scale, targeting clusters of buildings in contravention of planning regulations, though they seemed arbitrary given the scale of planning violations in the city. They could be highly controversial, as in the case of the demolition of over one thousand homes built in the road reserve along the Morogoro Road in Kimara in August 2017.[19] It was clear from discussions about these events with residents in Salasala that many people thought that those whose properties were demolished should have known better than to build within the road reserve.[20] This was in spite of the fact that what made this episode controversial was not just the scale of the demolition of the housing of a range of social classes—including the Bongo Flava star–turned Chadema MP Professor Jay—but that the usual road reserve width (60 meters) did not apply to the Morogoro Road, where it was 121.5 meters.[21] Nevertheless, Salasala residents felt that it was not bad luck or arbitrary state power: it was poor judgment on the part of those who had built close to a major road. Similar sentiments were expressed about the removal and resettlement of former residents from the flood-prone Msimbazi Valley near the city center to Mabwepande on the city's northern periphery:[22] those who were resettled by the state should not complain, because they should not have built in the flood plain in the first place.

Less dramatic, but no less devastating for those affected, was the smaller-scale demolition of properties constructed in unplanned settlements in order to make improvements to public goods. One such demolition of high-quality houses and other structures took place along a roadside in Salasala in November 2015. Salasala sits above the main water pipe that supplies the city from the Ruvu River to the north. Although the placement of water beacons along the road above the pipeline made residents aware of the pipe's location, when the pipe was to be replaced and expanded in 2015 they nevertheless fell afoul of seemingly arbitrary government planning rules. As one woman complained, "One day DAWASCO came and put an X on the side of our building.[23] I wasn't given any information, they just came, they didn't tell me anything, there was no explanation. When we arrived here we could see a beacon on the other side of the path, but not on this side [where her property was located]. Then they just came one day with the Field Force Unit and destroyed the buildings.[24] We saw the caterpillar coming, so at least we were able to dismantle some of the materials before it got to us."[25]

The fact that land was vested in the president on behalf of the people generated a background hum of insecurity in unplanned areas throughout the city. Even though building in informal areas was the norm, the potential demolition of one's house by a government agency could never be ruled out. Land and property constituted the bulk of most families' assets. For this reason, people were keen to have their plot surveyed in order to obtain a leasehold title (granted right of occupancy) from the Ministry of Lands, Housing and Human Settlements Development. This was a relatively new development, driven by the scarcity of urban land and the possibility that one's plot, boundaries, or house might be subject to dispute or even destruction. One never knew when documents might be needed, and they held out the promise of defending a plot from endless negotiation. It marked a shift away from previous modalities in which those who had built on periurban unplanned land were not exercised by their lack of title and derived their sense of security from their neighbors.[26] Customary or quasi-customary arrangements were no longer deemed sufficient. As a resident of Salasala explained, the impetus to have one's claim to land formally secured with a title arose because, "if you get a formal title deed it is signed by the representative of the president. If you get a customary title deed it is signed by local officials . . . so it is the same government but different levels. It is better to have the formal title because that is the highest level of legitimacy you can have."[27] According to planning law, since the outer suburbs of Dar es Salaam had been declared "planning areas" in the early 1990s, landowners were permitted to survey their plot and submit their planning application to the municipal planning department.[28] Obtaining a title would not stop a potential demolition, but it would guarantee the leaseholder the right to government compensation in the event of their removal by a government agency. The fact that people were entitled to compensation by law if they were displaced from permissible land after twelve years of occupation did not seem to allay fears, not least because compensation was never paid at market rates, if it was actually paid at all.[29]

The problem was that getting a title was expensive, tedious, and slow, involving multiple stages, payments, and authorizations at the municipal and ministerial levels. It began with the survey. Private surveyors routinely charged between TSh700,000 and TSh1 million (US$309–US$442 in 2018) for an average-sized plot survey at the time of research, and the few surveyors at the municipality were unlikely to entertain individual requests for plot surveys unless incentivized. The survey proceeded with a site visit to take the details of the plot, for which most surveyors used GPS technology. Boundaries with neighbors and paths were noted and agreed at this point, a base map prepared and then compared with the town planning drawings held at the municipality (for Salasala these dated from 2004, before most of the development of the area took place). The municipal land registry was also consulted, where hard copies of existing formal title deeds were kept. If all was in order and requisite fees had been paid, the beacons were installed on the ground to demarcate the plot boundary. The file was then submitted to the Commissioner for Lands in the Ministry of Lands, Housing and Human Settlements Development, where further checks were completed and an "offer" of a granted right of occupancy was issued detailing the fees to be paid in order to obtain the final title deed. These included: a premium calculated relative to the size and location of the plot, one year's land rent, certificate fees, stamp duty on the certificate and duplicate, and fees for registration, survey, and deed plan. On payment of these fees the Commissioner for Lands signed the title, which was then passed to the Registrar of Titles, who also performed a series of checks before entering the details into the Land Registry.

This is a fairly schematic outline of the process, but the point to note is that files could be held up by all manner of irregularities or missing bits of information at any stage, and they had to be moved through the system by the applicants themselves, necessitating numerous visits to the ministry building and waiting in corridors for civil servants who might or might not be at their desks. This is why those who could, paid others to shepherd their files through the system for them. Until 2022, I had not encountered a single Salasala resident who had successfully navigated this process to obtain a granted right of occupancy on unplanned land.[30] Some had gotten as far as receiving an "offer" from the Commissioner for Lands that they deemed sufficient for their immediate purposes, delaying the outlay of more money until the conversion of an offer to title was either financially possible or bureaucratically necessary. Others who wanted to convert their offer to a title had gotten stuck at some point in the process, either for lack of cash, a technical problem with their application that created a bureaucratic hurdle, or simply due to bureaucratic inertia. People complained of the multiple visits to surveyors and to municipal or ministry offices that were necessary to see a formal title application through to fruition. One such resident was Rajabu, who by 2018 had not managed to secure formal title deeds for the land that he and his wife had acquired in Salasala in the 1970s. After the land had been surveyed and approved by the municipality, the application had stalled at the Ministry of Lands when it emerged that, according to the ministry's maps, Rajabu had constructed his second, larger house directly over the World Bank–built tarmac road that ran through Salasala to the resettlement scheme. He lamented, "The maps at the council and the Ministry of Lands show that my property is on the road, which as you can see is not the case . . . but they can't give me a title for a place that is where the road is. So the maps are wrong. They need to redraw them."

The attempt to legally secure land was one of a set of practices that sought to secure property and life at the home and *mtaa* scales. Those who had lived in Salasala since the early 2010s routinely told of the insecurity that had plagued the suburban frontier, especially at night. Security problems for these residents ranged from opportunistic break-ins to armed robberies of properties and vehicles.[31] While the relative wealth of Kinondoni's residents inevitably drew attention, Salasala residents also pointed out that the area was vulnerable because it was a growing community populated by a constant stream of unknown newcomers attracted by the availability of land. The amount of ostensibly open space—mostly plots on which people had not yet constructed walls or buildings—though diminishing, was seen as a problem because it provided thieves with potential hiding places. Residents felt further discomfited by the fact that the nearest police station, six kilometers away at Tegeta, was underresourced. Getting a police post for Salasala was often mentioned by the middle classes as a priority local issue.

Those who could took security matters into their own hands. Houses were built with security in mind using heavy doors, window and door grilles, concrete block walls, and metal gates. Night watchmen were a regular feature. Zacharia, for example, had hired a watchman after his house was burglarized and his computer equipment stolen while he and his wife were out at work and the domestic worker had gone out briefly to the local shops. Neighbors also cooperated with each other on security. It was common for the residents of a cluster of houses to erect a wooden barrier across a path leading to their homes and to contribute money to pay night watchmen who would stop anyone attempting to pass after dark and ask whom they were going to see. Others put pressure on errant neighbors to build on their undeveloped plots, to minimize cover for potential criminals.

These strategies required financial and social resources, as well as property to protect. Undertaking them was a marker of middle-classness. The upper-middle classes who had colonized the planned plots in the Salasala resettlement scheme had gone a step further by providing their own security at night. In 2012 they founded a group to deal with the insecurity they were experiencing. The chairman of the group noted that at that time in Salasala "the problem was armed bandits. They came to steal . . . they even killed three or four people."[32] As another member explained, these neighbors decided to set up a rota to patrol the streets around their houses using their own cars: "These *bodaboda* were bringing men with guns . . . so after six in the evening we stopped anyone on the street and asked them what they were doing, where they were going . . . we were using our cars. If we found someone and they couldn't explain what they were doing, we would call each other and be there. And then you are faced with ten cars . . . now we are sleeping very well."[33]

This group of men felt they had contributed to a fall in property crimes in their area, pointing out that they no longer needed to patrol at night, and that some residents who had fled their homes had been encouraged to come back. The chairman noted, "We made this a calm area . . . we are close to the police. We repaired their land rover." The security initiative undertaken by these residents echoes a wider nationwide campaign to encourage *ulinzi shirikishi* (participatory policing) following a police reform program in 2006. *Ulinzi shirikishi* builds on a longer history of community policing in Tanzania known as *sungusungu* that goes back to the 1980s.[34] The Salasala group used the same term to refer to their own efforts. The aim of *ulinzi shirikishi* was to enroll citizens in the organization and remuneration of their own community security patrols, and to work with police when criminals were apprehended by handing them over and assisting with any subsequent investigation. These community patrols made up of youths were organized by the *serikali ya mtaa*, although in practice their reliance on community contributions strained their sustainability.[35] What distinguished the Salasala residents' efforts was that their security group operated independently of the *mtaa* government. They patrolled their own streets at night and invested directly in their relationship with the police based at Tegeta station. The subward chairman explained that Kilimahewa also had an *mtaa* security group similar to *ulinzi shirikishi*, made up of twenty youths who patrolled the streets at night and were paid via a TSh5,000 (US$2.3) levy on the bills issued by the water users' association.[36] It was unclear whether the *mtaa* security group was operational by 2016. The *sungusungu* group established by the upper-middle-class residents of the Salasala resettlement scheme may have been "close to the police," but the extent to which their poorer neighbors benefited from this proximity was perhaps reflected in the often-repeated anxiety about security among poorer residents, many of whom did not think that matters had improved.

REGULARIZING LAND

When I next visited Rajabu in 2017, he was supervising laborers on the unwalled, empty plot adjacent to his home. They were cutting down and burning the trees that stood on the plot to make charcoal. Rajabu explained that his main goal was to clear the land so that his daughter could begin to construct a house on it. He did not want the plot to remain vacant. Since the then Minister of Lands, Housing and Human Settlements Development William Lukuvi had announced the previous year that the government would audit, claim, and reallocate "idle land," owners of empty plots had become jittery. According to the minister, the move would reduce land conflicts, enable a more equitable distribution of land, and help investors.[37] Although the minister's comments were mostly addressed to rural landholders, the large number of enclosed yet undeveloped plots in Salasala gave people cause for concern. There seemed to be a shift underway in how government intended to treat land and those suspected of hoarding it. The seizure of former prime minister Frederick Sumaye's farmland near to Salasala, at Mabwepande, raised concern for many.[38]

The election of John Magufuli to the presidency in October 2015 reinvigorated the central government's interest in land, and urban land in particular.[39] A new Master Plan for Dar es Salaam was finally published in 2016, seventeen years after the previous Master Plan for the city had expired.[40] A domestic tax drive was rolled out. Tax collection, including land and property taxes, was digitized and recentralized in the Tanzania Revenue Authority.[41] Deadlines were set for the payment of existing and outstanding taxes, with the threat of repossession used as a stick. There was also a renewed commitment to urban land formalization and regularization programs.[42] Land titling had been an active policy objective in rural areas, particularly agriculturally valuable ones, since the passing of the New Land Policy in 1995 and the subsequent Land Acts of 1999.[43] Urban land titling programs had been somewhat slower, despite former president Benjamin Mkapa's commitment to surveying and titling land across the country.[44] Three government programs had focused on regularization of urban informal settlements: the Unplanned Settlements Regularization Program, the Property and Business Formalization Program (widely known by its Swahili acronym MKURABITA), and the National Program for Regularization and Prevention of Unplanned Settlements, which by 2018 had delivered a total of 103,065 surveyed and regularized plots across urban areas nationwide.[45] Urban land titling remains a key objective of the Ministry of Lands, Housing and Human Settlements Development.[46] In 2021 a fresh World Bank loan of USD150 million was agreed to register two million plots across forty districts, including in Dar es Salaam.[47]

The pursuit of formal land rights on the suburban frontier—obtaining a granted right of occupancy—had exercised many residents, as we have seen, but it had generally been an individual endeavor in which few had succeeded. Soon after President Magufuli came to power, however, the government began to make a series of announcements encouraging citizens to obtain land titles. Widespread land titling, argued Magufuli and Minister of Lands William Lukuvi, would solve land conflicts, give people security, and enable access to credit. The Ministry of Lands opened offices in all twenty-six regions of the country to serve land title applicants, and encouraged communities to work with an approved list of private companies to survey whole neighborhoods. In fact Magufuli and Lukuvi undermined lower levels of land administration at the municipal and district levels, claiming that their staff were not to be trusted. Land officers, they charged, were routinely duping title applicants and engaging in unscrupulous land practices.[48] Councils were banned from surveying and planning land in April 2016,[49] and in November 2018 the Lands Department of the Dar es Salaam City Council was closed down for the irregular issuing of land titles.[50]

The move against local government officers dealing with land and urban planning was part of a wider strategy of Magufuli's presidency to shift the charge of corruption that had been leveled at the government of his predecessor, Jakaya Kikwete, from government in general to the bureaucracy in particular—in other words, from politicians to bureaucrats and administrators. The slogan for the 2015 election campaign that brought him to power, *hapa kazi tu* ("only work here"), valorized the public display of hard work over laziness, negligence, corruption, and extravagance. Once in power Magufuli positioned himself as *kiongozi wa wanyonge* ("leader of the downtrodden") in his attempt to apportion blame on the corrupt and exploitative bureaucratic classes rather than on those at the very top of government.[51] While his anticorruption drive targeted prominent businessmen and politicians connected to Kikwete and top-level bureaucrats (such as at the Tanzania Revenue Authority, Tanzania Ports Authority, and the Prevention and Combating of Corruption Bureau),[52] he also launched an attack on the bureaucratic "middle stratum," which he claimed was operating against the interests of the poor and by extension the nation.[53] He boasted of "bursting the boils" in the public service (*kutumbua majipu*), and he carried out drives to root out ghost workers and those with fake qualifications.[54] Public servants' allowances, perquisites, and travel were also cut, leading to frequent complaints about the lack of money in circulation among the middle classes, who had benefited the most from these practices under presidents Mkapa and Kikwete.[55] The legitimacy of wealth was now routinely questioned: had you acquired your assets gradually through hard work, or had you made a quick profit from a scam? Public servants faced the additional burden of having to follow their jobs from Dar es Salaam to Dodoma after Magufuli pledged to complete the move to the new capital that had begun in 1974. They had to scramble for scarce rental accommodation and plots of land on which to build new houses far from the lives they had built in Dar es Salaam.

Within a few years of Magufuli's first term a general uneasiness had set in among the middle classes. They might be accused of shoddy work, lateness, or of not having proper documents; they might be sidelined or sacked; or they might be reported by an acquaintance for something critical uttered in public or posted on social media. The secret police (Tanzania Intelligence and Security Service) were said to be everywhere. Across the country, four newspapers were banned for criticizing the president; journalists, activists, and opposition leaders were harassed;[56] opposition parties' rallies were banned; and bloggers were required to register with the government for a hefty fee, failure to comply with which carried a fine or a jail term. Salasala residents complained in hushed tones that *hakuna demokrasia* ("there is no democracy"). By the 2020 election that delivered Magufuli's second term, the gains that the opposition had made in the 2015 election were more or less wiped out. Having won 45 percent of the legislative vote and the control of local governments in most urban areas in the 2015 election,[57] the 2020 parliamentary election reduced the number of directly elected opposition MPs in parliament from 68 (out of 263 seats) to just 8. CCM also won all of the urban *mitaa* positions in the 2019 local government elections after the main opposition party, Chadema, boycotted the election citing arbitrary deregistration of its candidates.[58]

For all the government's zeal for land titling, the implementation of the land regularization program did not proceed smoothly on the ground in Dar es Salaam. In the three adjacent neighborhoods of Salasala, Kilimahewa, and Kilimahewa Juu, private surveying companies had approached the subward governments and undertaken to conduct collective neighborhood surveys. Each subward agreed on an overall price with the surveying company, the cost to each resident varying among the three subwards from TSh200,000 (US$92) to TSh350,000 (US$161). The company would survey the subward and produce a town planning drawing containing the necessary cadastral details of all plots. The town planning drawing would then be agreed with the municipality before being sent to the Ministry of Lands, where the title deeds would be prepared (for which applicants would have to pay extra). These costs were high in relation to many residents' ability to pay, but far lower than the cost of an average survey for an average plot. Yet given the government's long-term ambivalence towards land rights in urban unplanned settlements in general and towards rapidly urbanizing former periurban and rural areas in particular, the regularization process was potentially radical. It offered the very real prospect of access to secure land rights for the urban majority. Whether or not this materializes has yet to be seen.

By August 2018, two years after the regularization drive was announced, the plot survey in Salasala had not yet begun. A large area of land that had been zoned for industrial use in the 1979 master plan had since been invaded and turned into residential plots. The subward chairperson had been liaising with officials at the Ministry of Lands who refused to regularize the plots for residential use because they considered the house-builders to be invaders who were squatting on government land zoned for industry. In Kilimahewa Juu a surveying company had been appointed and a local committee tasked with aiding the surveyors in their work, which they had begun in April 2018. But in 2019 the surveying ground to a halt as a result of a land dispute in which several well-built, walled-in houses had been built in a disused quarry that had been earmarked by the municipal government for a secondary school and a health center. There had been more progress in Kilimahewa, where the surveying had been completed and residents were being invited to community meetings to verify their plots on the town planning drawing; but the cost recovery was slow, with only around 400 of the 950 eligible households in the *mtaa* having paid the survey fee. In April 2019 the Minister for Lands announced a cap on the survey fee of TSh150,000 (US$66) in an effort to speed up the regularization process; a further cut in the fee to TSh130,000 (US$57) and access to "plot loans" was announced in August 2021.[59]

· · ·

It is too early to know the full impact of the government's regularization drive on the suburban frontier.[60] But in early 2022, while some residents of Salasala were complaining about the cost and bureaucracy of the regularization project, Rajabu had finally managed to collect his title deed. The surveying project had produced an accurate map of the neighborhood, and his house no longer appeared on the road. The new map removed the final obstacle to obtaining his title. The deed for his three-quarter-acre plot cost Tsh1.2 million (US$522). While the promise of secure land titles may appear to take the side of the urban poor, land titling and registration rarely protects the poor against dispossession by the market.[61] In addition, it strengthens state control over land, raises domestic tax revenue, and provides opportunities for land officials to collect additional fees.[62] It also shores up the enclosure of land by the middle classes that has slowly unfolded on the city's edges since the 1970s. The acquisition of land, which sped up after the value of bare land was recognized in the new National Land Policy of 1995 and the Land Acts of 1999, has been central to middle-class formation on the suburban frontier. The regularization drive offers a new strategy for the middle classes, who have been investing in land and attempting to secure their claims by navigating transactions, the local and district land courts, and the bureaucracy. Middle-classness is formed through acquiring land as an asset, and protecting that land through a suite of learned practices. Those who could afford the title fees now had the option of securing their land with a granted right of occupancy. Despite the different approaches to questions of land, accumulation, and inequality taken by presidents Mkapa, Kikwete, and Magufuli over twenty-five years, the colonization of the sub-urban frontier by the middle classes nevertheless continued. During the *kipindi cha Magufuli* (Magufuli era), building may have slowed down, hampered by the lack of cash circulating in the economy, but land transactions and house-building did not stop.

4

Landscape

The scramble for land and the ensuing house-building activity that has taken place in Salasala since the turn of the twenty-first century have transformed the formerly periurban zone into a desirable suburban landscape. One- and two-storey residential houses built of cement blocks and topped with the latest roofing sheets, flanked by carports and gardens and enclosed within cement walls, now dot Salasala's rolling hills. These suburban landscapes have become central to the boundary work through which middle-class distinction is achieved.[1] The spatial and topographical features of the suburban landscape, the state of repair of roads and other infrastructure, the style and density of houses and the materials used to build them, and the embodied experience of traversing and living in these neighborhoods are all experienced and evaluated by residents according to a relational hierarchy of urban space in which people higher up the social hierarchy deserve to live in better places. In the previous chapters the coloniality of space was examined in relation to land law, land administration and housing policies, and the ways in which an emergent middle class maneuvered these to access land and housing in the colonial and postcolonial city. In this chapter I turn to examine the ways in which the coloniality of space shapes urban residents' aesthetic engagement with the built environment of the suburban frontier to show how the aesthetic politics of landscape has become integral to middle-class formation.

Landscapes are constructed, lived, and imagined spaces that are historically, geographically, and socially shaped.[2] Despite the association of the global middle classes with particular landscapes of urban consumption such as the home, the suburb, and the shopping mall,[3] the role of landscape in middle-class formation and reproduction has received little sustained attention. In Africa, landscape research to date has been mostly concerned with rural communities.[4] Urban research has only recently begun to pay attention to the qualities and aesthetics of urban space, the conditions of its production, and urbanites' lived experience of urban built environments.[5] The continued salience of colonial representations of urban landscapes has emerged as particularly significant in cities such as Luanda and Maputo, where the cement city of the colonizers and the temporary materials of the city of the colonized are read locally as both reflecting and producing social differentiation.[6] As Claudia Gastrow notes in Luanda, it is widely held that the *cidade* (the formal core of the city) is the place of "good urbanism," good people, and good development.[7] In Dar es Salaam as in Luanda and Maputo, landscape aesthetics are not only a matter of taste and social judgment, but are also deeply informed by the coloniality of space.

As we saw in chapter 1, colonial Dar es Salaam was divided into three racially distinct zones that came to represent distinctive types of urban landscape. These became known as *uzunguni* (the place of the European), *uhindini* (the place of the Indian), and *uswahilini* (the place of the Swahili or African). In this chapter I argue that this colonial frame still has resonance for many of Dar es Salaam's residents. At first glance it might seem that the development of the suburbs as a distinctive landscape modeled on *uzunguni* has allowed the middle classes to find space for themselves in the city at a distance from *uswahilini*. But in the same way that the middle classes are not the elite, the suburban landscapes they have built are also not quite *uzunguni*. On closer inspection, these suburbs seem unfinished: many homes are arranged irregularly, most roads are untarmacked, and responsibility for the provision of services such as water, electricity, and sewage falls to the individual homeowner. They are also heterogenous: smaller, older houses, constructed by poorer residents with cheap materials, intersperse the better-appointed homes and cluster together on smaller plots unmarked or secluded by cement block walls. In contrast to other postcolonial cities where the wealthy and upper-middle classes have retreated into exclusive private enclaves and walled compounds,[8] the landscape of Dar es Salaam's suburban frontier is shaped by both the middle classes and the urban poor. The polycentric governance of urban land and planning that is a hallmark of the coloniality of space in Dar es Salaam makes it very difficult for the middle classes to protect the landscape they have built by retreating into exclusive suburban enclaves. The machinations of the land market and the widespread lack of formal land titles make insurgent house-building in the suburbs almost impossible to police. A far more fragmented landscape emerges as relatively low-density, good-quality residences stand next to smaller houses on more densely arranged plots. This in-between position, of having built suburban landscapes of distinction yet being unable to protect them from infiltration by poorer urban residents, captures a defining characteristic and central tension at the heart of contemporary middle-classness in Dar es Salaam.

THE COLONIALITY OF SPACE: ENFRAMING THE CITY

The seeds of the coloniality of space were contained in colonial urban planning practices that sought to impose order on what were considered chaotic, dirty, and dangerous urban landscapes. Early twentieth-century concerns with order in the colonial city betrayed racist environmentally determinist assumptions about the influence of the environment on human behavior, particularly in relation to air, light, and sanitation. The ills of urban space were diagnosed in terms of congestion and unsanitary conditions that prevailed in native quarters, where narrow alleyways that wound through areas of native huts were considered unhygienic and threatening. The disorder that the British perceived in African urban space "was seen as a sign of a lack of proper regulation, betraying . . . incapacity or irrationality."[9] The prescribed solutions included the demolition of native huts, the creation of straight, wide, regular streets, and racial segregation on sanitary grounds.[10] Such measures would not only improve sanitary conditions, they would also allow air, light, and the colonial gaze to travel more easily through urban space. Colonial urban planning aspired to create space where there was congestion, and discipline where there was chaos.

The British colonial disposition towards African urban landscapes can be understood as an instance of what Timothy Mitchell has called "enframing." In his analysis of nineteenth-century British colonial power in Egypt, Mitchell shows enframing to be a colonial strategy of authority that operated by dividing and containing space, separating insides from outsides, and providing a vantage point from which space could be apprehended and surveilled by the colonizer.[11] Garth Myers's analysis of British colonial urban planning in eastern and southern Africa also finds enframing at work in colonial urban planners' attempts to impose a racially segmented order where they found disorder, the demarcation and separation of the private inside from the public outside, and the construction of highly visible public buildings that provided elevated points from which the city could be surveilled.[12] Buildings such as Government House in Nairobi, Ng'ambo Civic Center in Zanzibar, and Munali Secondary School and the Governor's Village in Lusaka served to impress upon the colonized the colonizers' representation of what they considered to be the modernizing benefits of British colonialism. British colonial notions of order and discipline were diffused throughout the city and the countryside through the microphysical effects of urban planning on the body and the metaphysical effects of education on the mind.

The concept of enframing captures both the material and the psychological effects of colonial authority. Building on Edward Said's *Orientalism*,[13] Mitchell shows that the effect of colonial enframing served both to separate and mutually constitute colonized and colonizer.[14] The representation of the European as rational, modern, and civilized relied on the representation of the African as irrational, backward, and uncivilized. So it was with the landscapes of the colonial city, where colonial rule grappled with a paradox: the representation of the colonial city as ordered, spacious, and clean relied on the representation of native urban landscapes as chaotic, congested, and unsanitary, even though this very representation provoked colonial anxieties about native urban space. Native landscapes were to be divided and separated from European landscapes, but they were also absolutely necessary to the European representation of the modern colonial city.

The effects of the enframing of colonial urban space on the colonized have been powerfully conveyed in the writing of Frantz Fanon and Ngũgĩ wa Thiong'o.[15] From the perspective of the colonized the colonial city was experienced as a space of physical and psychological violence. For Fanon, the colonizer's space was seen from the outside as a space of order, modernity, and comfort as evidenced by the quality of buildings, the provision of street lights and permanent roads, and the abundance of food. Fanon observes that "the streets of his town are clean and even, with no holes or stones."[16] He describes the native town as the negative opposite of the colonizer's space, characterized by congestion and "starved of bread, of meat, of shoes, of coal, of light."[17] In Fanon's rendering of colonial urban space, the landscapes of the colonizer and the colonized were built, imagined, and experienced as separate compartments of the colonial city. Writing about postcolonial Kenya over two decades later, Ngũgĩ w Thiong'o insisted that the traces of colonialism remained scattered across contemporary African cultures and landscapes, and "the mental universe of the colonised."[18] In the work of Ngũgĩ and Fanon, colonial alienation entailed not only the reordering of material space, but also a psychological struggle in and for the spaces of cultural production in the postcolony such as the community center, the theatre, the university, the hospital, and the street.[19] The coloniality of space emerges from the insistence that colonial and postcolonial worlds have been shaped not just by the exertion of colonial power over the material landscape, but also by the less visible but no less devastating spatial and psychological effects of that power. Those effects continue to shape how people think about and experience the landscapes that have been produced.

In this chapter I describe the colonial enframing of Dar es Salaam as constituted of the separate, contained landscapes of *uzunguni, uhindini*, and *uswahilini*. I then turn to the ways in which these colonial landscapes resurface in middle-class suburban residents' representations of contemporary urban space. It is perhaps surprising that the colonial enframing of Dar es Salaam has so much currency in the city today, not least as Dar es Salaam has been reframed multiple times through the postcolonial state ideologies of nationalism, socialism, and neoliberalism.[20] All have left traces on the city's material landscapes and the geographical imaginations of its inhabitants. Most notably, the entire city was enframed by the socialist government as a space of exploitation and consumption, shaped by and for colonial and imperial interests, that was not to be further privileged in a social-ist postcolonial state pursuing a rural agricultural development strategy.[21] Yet the colonial enframing of the city has lingered on into the postcolonial period. To argue that traces of colonial enframing continue to have currency both in the built environment and in the ways that urban residents experience and make urban space in contemporary cities is not meant to imply a lack of agency among urban dwellers who simply reproduce colonial modes of doing and being.[22] Paying attention to the aesthetics of landscape reveals the endurance of the coloniality of space in the legal, material, and imaginative legacies that shape land tenure, the quantity and quality of urban housing, ideas about what good urban space looks like, why some people live in better places than others, and why residents make frequent references to *uswahilini, uhindini,* and *uzunguni* as both actual neigh-borhoods and distinctive kinds of landscape. In other words, showing how the coloniality of space works in contemporary Dar es Salaam is central to an under-standing of the spatial politics of class. Middle-class suburban residents repeatedly draw attention to the aesthetic qualities of order and low density that distinguish the suburban landscape—and them—from *uswahilini* and the urban poor. In the same way that the British enframing of the colonial city needed the native town to define itself against, so too does middle-class suburban self-representation rely on the presence of *uswahilini*. Middle-class suburban residents in Salasala continue to enframe *uswahilini* as a chaotic, disorderly landscape and to distance themselves from it. And yet this enframing strategy, this projection of power, is only partial, as the suburban landscape falls between *uswahilini* (unplanned, lacking services) and *uzunguni* (low-density, serviced homes). While the suburban middle classes can build walls around their houses, they cannot protect the suburban landscape from insurgent house-building by the less well-off. It is difficult to assert authority over the landscape in the unplanned city.

ENFRAMING DAR ES SALAAM

The foundations for the enframing of Dar es Salaam as a city divided between dis-tinctive landscapes characterized by race, architecture, and urban planning were laid during the German colonial period. The first building ordinance, published in 1891, demarcated three zones of different building construction: a zone stretching from the east of the town along the harbor, in which "European-style" buildings could be constructed with permanent materials; a zone set back from the har-bor around India street, in which buildings of "solid materials" were permitted; and the rest of the town, in which local building materials were permitted. The ordinance reflected the Germans' concern with control over space, property, and health. It regulated the construction of permanent buildings by Arabs, Indians, Africans, and Europeans; African constructions with local materials could always be removed at a later date. The Germans allocated to themselves the healthier eastern part of the town, away from the western end of the harbor where the Sultan had established the first buildings, which now became the location of noisy and polluting activities such as the floating dock, coal warehouse, quarantine area, and leper colony. Other health measures taken to protect Europeans included various efforts to improve air flow and sanitation, such as the construction of a small network of open drains, the leveling out of land to remove pools of stagnant water, and the destruction of Africans' huts that were thought to be a source of humidity, disease, and general displeasure for Europeans.[23]

Thus divided, urban space was to be contained in a new road layout. The European administrative and residential area was expansively laid out around a network of straight, wide streets connecting government houses with the harbor, projecting "grace and permanence" and facilitating European security.[24] The district chief and former representative of the chartered company Deutsch-Ostafricanische Gesellschaft, August Leue, was anxious to replace the formerly narrow streets that had provided cover for local fighters during the Bushiri Uprising against the Germans (1888–89) with wider thoroughfares that could be more easily surveilled and controlled.[25] The Indian business quarter was to be contained within a series of semicircular roads behind the European administrative area that stretched along the harbor-front. There were initially no roads laid out specifically for Africans. As discussed in chapter 1, over time Africans were removed from the European and Indian zones.

This blueprint for the town was consolidated with the publication in 1914 of the second building ordinance. These regulations were explicitly framed in terms of racial segregation, reserving Zone One for Europeans, Zone Two for Indians, and Zone Three for natives.[26] The "native quarter" developed at the western end of the town on a coconut plantation that was sold in 1901 by the Sultan of Zanzibar to a German investor, and on which Africans were able to settle from around 1905. By 1913 it had become the largest African settlement in Dar es Salaam, housing around two-thirds of the town's nineteen thousand Africans in sixteen hundred houses.[27] The administration laid out a road network for this native quarter on a densely arranged grid pattern, again with the aim of surveillance and control.[28]

The enframing of Dar es Salaam as divided between and contained within these zones lived on in British urban planning from the 1920s, despite the fact that racial segregation was not permitted within the terms of the League of Nations mandate under which Britain administered Tanganyika. In practice, people and buildings often transgressed the zone boundaries.[29] Nevertheless, the enframing of the city as comprised of three racially distinct and internally organized landscapes entered local parlance. The zones became known as *uzunguni* (place of the European), *uhindini* (place of the Indian), and *uswahilini* (place of the Swahili; map 3). As well as being racially inscribed, each zone was also understood as a distinctive, contained landscape within a hierarchy of landscapes. *Uzunguni* was the government area in the city center housing grand official buildings and European residences, which extended northwards along the coast and incorporated the suburban development of Oysterbay from the 1930s. It was characterized by low-density, high-quality single- and two-storey buildings, arranged regularly along wide, paved, and lit streets. Houses built to European standards contained interior kitchens and bathrooms and many large glass-paned windows.[30] During the German era a botanical garden extended across a large area of the European zone in the city center, and well-tended tropical trees and verdant greenery remained a feature of *uzunguni* during the British period. The location of this zone along the coast also enabled Europeans to benefit from the sea breeze. *Uzunguni* not only contained the administrative and residential buildings of the colonial power; it also cared for them when sick (the Ocean Road Hospital) and catered for their leisure needs (the Gymkhana sports club and golf course, the shops on Acacia Avenue). Africans such as domestic workers were tolerated in *uzunguni*, but were otherwise excluded.[31]

The commercial and residential area dominated by Dar es Salaam's Indian community, *uhindini*, contained a mixture of two- and three-storey stone buildings and more temporary local constructions that doubled as home and *duka* (shop). It was considered overcrowded and unsanitary by the British.[32] The area underwent a process of gentrification from the late 1920s, when the British replaced the prevailing German tenure system with right-of-occupancy tenancies that came with attendant building standards and plot-alignment requirements.[33] The resulting rebuilt environment began to reflect the relative wealth of the Indian community. A large number of three- or four-storey buildings with businesses (usually shops) on the ground floor and residential apartments on the upper floors were constructed in architectural styles ranging from classical to Indian and interspersed with the religious buildings of different Indian communities.[34]

Uswahilini began life as the "native quarter" and developed into the neighborhood known as Kariakoo, extending to Ilala in the 1920s. A building-free "neutral zone" (later "open space") separating the native quarter from Zone Two was planned by the Germans and executed by the British on commercial and sanitary grounds.[35] From the 1920s Kariakoo developed into a densely populated African neighborhood, characterized by rows of Swahili houses arranged in a grid pattern around the town's main fresh food market. Living conditions were poor and basic infrastructure lacking, despite the fact that the colonial government collected revenues from urban Africans. In 1930, Africans in Dar es Salaam paid land rent (£1,740), municipal house tax (£1,051), hut and poll taxes (£3,650), traders fees at Kariakoo, and the municipal eating house (£2,210) and *pombe* (locally brewed alcohol) market fees (£720), yet the African areas were neglected.[36] In theory the density of housing in *uswahilini* made the provision of public services there easier, but they never materialized on the scale required. Instead, investment was mostly directed at *uzunguni*.[37] Europeans paid no house rents or service charges, yet had their "hedges cut and drives gravelled for nothing."[38]

The dividing and containing of Dar es Salaam into three racialized zones characterized by different standards of urban planning and architecture emerged over time in an ad hoc and reactive way, born of the colonial impulse to racially segregate and control urban space, and was subsequently shaped by a lack of commitment to comprehensive urban planning and the willful neglect of African neighborhoods.[39] Despite its ad hoc development, the colonial enframing of the city provided a simple and powerful geographical imagination of the city's landscapes in which an "urban entitlement" to space, housing, and infrastructure was widely understood in terms of a racial hierarchy.[40] The effect on Africans was to impose "a psychological atmosphere of African inferiority" that lingered on into the postcolonial period.[41] The *Nationalist* newspaper captured this coloniality of space when it noted, in 1968, "We have failed to dismantle the myth of '*uhindini*', '*uzunguni*' and '*uswahilini*'. As a result, negative attitudes of judging people according to the 'racial zones' they live in still persist."[42]

The tripartite enframing of the city survived into the postcolonial period as the landscapes of *uzunguni, uhindini*, and *uswahilini* became recognizable in many urban areas across the country. These landscapes still carried their colonial racial connotations but now also reflected distinctions of social class.[43] Beyond Oysterbay, formally planned *uzunguni* landscapes where the elite and upper-middle classes resided could be found in Gangilonga (Iringa), Mlimani and Area D (Dodoma), Isamilo and Capri Point (Mwanza), Forest Hill (Morogoro), Loleza (Mbeya), Kijengi (Arusha), Shangani (Mtwara), and Shanty Town (Moshi).[44] In these neighborhoods—which were often small relative to the rest of the town—the orderly wide streets, large plots, and basic public services laid down during the colonial period were matched by spacious houses, well-tended gardens, and carports secured behind gates and walls.

In contrast, by the 1990s *uswahilini* areas housed the majority of the urban poor in unplanned settlements that had developed on marginal and sometimes hazardous land close to urban centers. In Dar es Salaam *uswahilini* was synonymous with cramped conditions and state neglect. Water, sanitation, and electricity services, if they existed, were provided by individuals, as was housing, which was mostly accessed in six-room Swahili houses. Families rented rooms and shared cooking and cleaning facilities in courtyards. Houses were densely arranged according to the preferences of their builders rather than in alignment with one another. Cars could go no further than the fringe of the neighborhood: *uswahilini* was navigable only on foot by those who knew the place well, and the impenetrable nature of *uswahilini* to outsiders lent it an air of refuge. Daily life took place in public view on verandas, in courtyards, and in-between spaces.[45] Homes provided business premises, particularly for women who conducted their tailoring, food preparation, and brewing businesses from a room, courtyard, or veranda; rooms and kiosks became small retail shops or vegetable stalls. Streets became impromptu performance spaces at night for local musicians, or spaces of celebration for weddings and Eid.[46] *Uswahilini* invited commentary in popular music by *Bongo Flava* artists such as Professor Jay and Diamond Platnumz, who claimed it as the experience of the city for the majority and criticized the lack of jobs and opportunities, poor housing and roads, uncollected rubbish, and the random violence meted out to its residents by the city authorities and society at large.[47] *Uswahilini* and its residents gained a reputation for mastery of the scam and the deal, but the fact that residents of *uzunguni* could be equally creative, for example when it came to improvising an electricity connection, reminds us that the tripartite enframing of urban space is not all-encompassing.[48]

BETWEEN USWAHILINI AND UZUNGUNI

In a discussion with the councilor for Wazo Ward, in which the *mitaa* of Salasala, Kilimahewa, and Kilimahewa Juu were located, I asked him to describe the area he represented. His response immediately mobilized the tripartite enframing of the city's colonial landscapes to interpret urban space more broadly: "It's a middle-class area. If you compare it to Manzese—we can say people of the lower level live there; if you go to Masaki, Oysterbay, then high-level people live there. Here . . . it's in the middle. But there is *uswahilini* inside."[49] His response captured the way in which many Salasala residents reflected on their community with a mixture of aspiration and trepidation. Salasala, like many of its residents, was in the middle. Not fully one thing or another, it was not *uswahilini* but neither was it *uzunguni*. Pockets of both could be found in Salasala. The planned area that stretched across the hilly terrain of Kilimahewa that had begun life as the World Bank–funded resettlement scheme approximated *uzunguni* with its sea views, well-ordered street layout, low-density plots, community water scheme, and impressive houses standing behind tall gates. But it was unclear whether this meant that Salasala and other suburban areas like it could therefore be understood as *uzunguni*. Residents who had built impressive houses in the planned area of Kilimahewa were unequivocal that it could. When I discussed the benefits of living in Salasala with Richard and Peter, who both worked in banking and finance, Richard claimed, "We call it Salasala City! Here it is planned, World Bank–financed. This is *uzunguni*—well organized, no local beer stalls . . . a well-planned area." Peter added, "Not like Manzese . . . there it is highly populated and unplanned."[50] In a separate conversation with Rehema, who had moved from the inner-city informal settlement of Mwananyamala to Kilimahewa in 2008, she compared the two areas directly: "Here there is a breeze! But there it is too congested. There's no noise and disturbance here, it's like being in the village. There it is noisy, people are going to bars and nightclubs. But not here. Houses there are packed tightly together. Here there is no congestion. It's like *uzunguni*."[51]

Despite the claims of Richard, Peter, and Rehema, pockets of *uswahilini* could be found in Salasala in the marginal spaces of the old quarry and the original Salasala RTD settlement, where narrow paths wound between small, densely arranged houses. Even in the resettlement area of Kilimahewa, not all of the streets were tarmacked, water did not run all of the time, and the provision of sanitation and electricity was down to the individual homeowner. Such conditions typified the rest of the Salasala landscape, populated by a mix of houses in terms of size, quality, and architectural distinction, built on irregularly organized plots, and traversed by earth roads and paths save for the two short tarmac roads that connected the planned area and the IPTL power plants to the main Bagamoyo Road. Zacharia, who worked for an international mobile telecommunications company and who had built a large house close to Kilimahewa, reflected, "There's no word to describe this place. There is *uswahilini* for the packed places downtown, and there is *uzunguni* for the planned places like Masaki and Mikocheni. But we don't have a word for places like Salasala. It's not *uswahilini* because it's not packed; but it's not *uzunguni* either because it's more mixed."[52] Located somewhere between *uzunguni* and *uswahilini*, there was unease among Salasala's middle-class residents about the landscape they had built, what it said about them, and how they might be able to protect it from slipping further from the ideal of *uzunguni* in the future.

One particular source of anxiety for middle-class residents was the state of the roads in Salasala. The earth roads were an inconvenience during the rainy season when they became hazardous or impassable. While residents complained about the damage this did to their cars, there was also an underlying concern about what the slippage between residents' aesthetic aspirations and the material reality of their neighborhood revealed about their place in the hierarchy of landscapes. Although the two short tarmac roads that formed the central arteries through Salasala made the area better served than most other neighborhoods that had grown up in the formerly periurban zone, the majority of roads in the settlement were made of earth. In addition to the general degradation of earth roads over time, the seasonal rains made many of the roads impassable for weeks, causing great damage that required regular repair. The municipal council possessed a grader, but communities had to raise funds to pay for the fuel, labor, and equipment hire. Many residents were unwilling to contribute money to the *serikali ya mtaa* (subward government) for this purpose. In April 2015 the *serikali ya mtaa* in Kinzudi, neighboring Kilimahewa, wrote to all residents to request contributions to a road fund that would be used to regrade the main roads through the neighborhood. They were looking to raise TSh4.5 million (US$2,260). Showing me the letter, local resident Zacharia was unsure whether he would contribute anything. Later he admitted that he had not. Why should he pay, he argued, when he could not be sure that the *serikali ya mtaa* would use the money to hire the graders? Things got particularly bad after 2017, when Kinondoni Municipality's graders were "loaned" to the newly created neighboring municipality of Ubungo. Neighbors were left to their own devices to

FIGURE 5. A path damaged by rain in Salasala. Photo by author, June 2018.

do what they could with the roads that affected them. People found inventive solutions, filling holes and gulleys with palm fronds, bits of broken-up masonry, and sandbags. Some even entered into agreements with private rubbish collectors to fill particularly large gulleys that opened up in paths during the rainy season with truckloads of collected rubbish that would otherwise go to the municipal dump. A more expensive solution was to hire the municipal grader privately. This was the preferred solution for a group of neighbors who lived in and around the planned area of the Kilimahewa resettlement scheme (discussed in more detail in chapter 6). Some among this group had connections with the municipal council; all of them owned good-quality cars. While the private hire of the public grader temporarily resolved the issue of private mobility and damage to cars in their immediate neighborhood, it did little to address the state of the roads in the wider area.

FEAR OF USWAHILINI

The *uzunguni/uswahilini* enframing of urban space was a common refrain among middle-class residents and *mtaa* administrators in Salasala. Despite the fact that the newly constructed landscape did not quite fit this frame, the *uzunguni/uswahilini* framework still had currency as a way of dividing and containing urban space that served middle-class residents' geographical imagination of the city. This is the coloniality of space at work: in everyday parlance the landscapes of *uzunguni* were referred to, often in passing, as elevated, breezy, low-density, planned, ordered, and sedate; the landscapes of *uswahilini*, in contrast, were described as congested, chaotic, disordered, threatening, and unpredictable. In fact the representation of the orderly nature of the Salasala landscape relied on the simultaneous representation of the disorderly and dangerous landscapes typical of *uswahilini*. Fear of *uswahilini*—the densification of buildings, the subdivision of plots into smaller and smaller parcels, the invasion of open land by squatters—threatened to thwart the aspirations that middle-class residents had for the future of Salasala. The recognition that *uswahilini* might not be containable in the future was a source of considerable anxiety.

In a discussion at the Kilimahewa Juu *mtaa* office, the *mtaa* executive officer observed in a matter-of-fact manner: "Here there are two zones, Kwa Babu and Msiige. Kwa Babu—that place is like Manzese. But Msiige is planned."[53] Manzese featured regularly in middle-class residents' geographical imaginations of the city. As one of the oldest and largest informal settlements in Dar es Salaam, it was often conjured up to signify a generic "*uswahilini*." Afterwards, as I walked through Kwa Babu with two of the *wajumbe*, I asked them what the executive officer had meant. "When people come here," one *mjumbe* explained, "they know their status. They look at the other buildings . . . they are squatters." His companion chimed in, "It is an area of poor housing, it is *uswahilini* . . . *Uswahilini* is down at the bottom of the valley, *uzunguni* is at the top of the hill."

Middle-class residents were dismissive of *uswahilini* areas in Salasala. Residents of *uswahilini* were routinely referred to as "squatters" and considered as impediments to the development of the area. Yet the definition of "squatter"—always used in English even among Swahili speakers—is open to different interpretations. Originating in English land law and imported to Tanganyika during the colonial period, the legal definition of squatting refers to the occupation of land without tenurial rights.[54] However, as we have already seen in chapter 3, the tenurial rights of the majority of residents of Dar es Salaam's former rural hinterland are ambiguous, since the rights of nonindigenous landholders occupying urban planning areas where customary rights have yet to be extinguished or compensated have not been settled in law or bureaucratic practice.[55] Despite this ambiguity, middle-class residents routinely referred to low-income residents of Salasala as "squatters," even though their low-income neighbors' tenurial rights were most likely equal to their own. Rather, it was the landscape aesthetic of *uswahilini* that marked low-income residents as "squatters." The middle classes prided themselves on the quality and orderliness of the landscape they had built. Their spacious houses built with modern materials on good-sized plots legitimized their occupation of land, regardless of their legal status. In contrast, residents of *uswahilini* were considered illegitimate users of urban space, occupying land in a haphazard manner that contravened basic official urban planning requirements such as leaving sufficient space for paths between buildings. Words such as *ovyo* (disorderly, reckless; valueless, worthless) and *mazagazaga* (a slang word for haphazard) were often used by middle-class residents to describe how people built in these areas.[56] Squatters were considered to be an eyesore and a nuisance. Two recently squatted areas in Salasala, one in a disused industrial site that was subsequently earmarked for a public health facility and a school by the municipality, the other in the old Kunduchi quarry, demonstrate the point. The first site was squatted and then parceled into large plots on which modern houses were built, while the second was developed by poorer residents into an area of lower-quality housing. Despite the fact that the middle-class squatters were depriving the area of planned public services, it was only those who had built in the former Kunduchi quarry area who were referred to as squatters.

The arrangement and density of housing was of particular concern to Salasala's middle-class residents, who were keen to maintain the area's suburban residential character. *Uswahilini* areas offended middle-class residents' aesthetic judgment about order in the landscape. People in *uswahilini* "settled randomly," as one resident complained, and they needed "to be educated about how to build their houses," as an *mjumbe* observed. David, who worked for the Catholic Church, explained, "*Uswahilini* . . . means that a place is constructed irregularly, it is a place that is difficult to govern because people just do what they want, it is a place where people live anyhow. The construction of houses—there is no planning. The fire truck cannot pass! There is no organization. The government just leaves you there [i.e., does nothing]."[57]

The smaller, irregularly arranged plots and more congested living conditions characteristic of *uswahilini* areas were a threat that had to be guarded against. I discussed this point with Elizabeth, a middle-aged nurse who had constructed a modest, well-built and carefully decorated house on a large plot that she had inherited from her mother in Msiige, the zone in Kilimahewa described by the executive officer as "planned." In fact Msiige was not formally planned by the municipal council. Rather, the relative order and arrangement of the larger plots in that part of the *mtaa* was a conscious attempt to approximate the landscapes of *uzunguni* rather than *uswahilini*.[58] Picking up the executive officer's distinction between areas in Kilimahewa, she explained:

> Most of the people in Kwa Abarikiwe [an area in Kilimahewa] and Kwa Babu, they didn't buy their plots. They were given their plots [by the government during the campaigns of the 1970s and 1980s]. But here, people came from town to buy. There [Kwa Abarikiwe and Kwa Babu] is *uswahilini*, where people live like they do in Man- zese. But those small small plots you won't get here. 10×10—you can't get them. People come here for big plots, 30×30, 40×40, 70×70. People who want small plots go there. Here, people want to keep it like this, so they don't sell small plots.[59]

David's and Elizabeth's descriptions of the different types of urban landscape demonstrate the apparently benign and banal ways in which the coloniality of space shapes everyday representations of urban space. Urban space is separated and contained—now by the market—into areas of small plots and big plots between which people make an aesthetic choice. In this rendition of urban space, unequal access to land is simply a natural outcome of who chooses to build where according to aesthetic preference. The disorderly and chaotic landscapes of *uswahilini* reflect the failures of its inhabitants who did not purchase their land or who chose small parcels, who built their environment haphazardly, and who failed to plan properly. Yet despite Elizabeth's assertion that the exclusive landscape of Msiige could be maintained through residents' vigilance over land sales, the multivalent nature of land transactions and construction activities meant that controlling plot sizes—and the aesthetic appearance of the landscape—was very difficult to achieve in practice.

MIDDLE-CLASS PLANNING

Middle-class residents who had obtained land from the 1970s onwards thought of themselves as pioneers who had brought order, improvement, and value to a landscape that they considered to have been previously empty.[60] These residents often described the landscape as having been *pori* (wilderness or scrubland) before they cleared the land to farm or to construct a house, or to pay TANESCO to put up the first electricity pole.[61] Zacharia, who had been a relatively early settler when he bought land and started building a house near to Kilimahewa in 2008, was

FIGURE 6. Middle-class planning, Salasala. Photo by author, July 2018.

proud of the way his area had changed from undeveloped land to a built environment. It suggested that he had made a shrewd move in buying the land in the first place, despite the initial reservations of his wife who had considered Salasala too far from the city center. Having first visited him in 2012, on my return in 2015 I was astonished at the speed with which new, impressive buildings had gone up in his neighborhood, where there had previously been grass, shrubs, and trees. "Do you recognize the place now? Can you see how it has grown?" Zacharia exclaimed proudly as he gave me a quick tour.

The congregation of the middle classes on the suburban frontier has brought with it various attempts to impress a new vision of urban order on the landscape by naming places and streets in a context where few individual streets are signposted.[62] Scattered across northern Kinondoni were a small number of street signs that signified global consumer culture (Old Trafford Street, Beverly Hills), African political leaders (Mwinyi Street, Madiba Street), Swahili words that conjured up histories of cooperation and neighborliness (*Amani* [peace] Street, *Upendo* [love] Street), and personal names where recent housebuilders had given their name to a path on their land. These new street signs declaring new place names contrasted with the preexisting practice of referring to places by the name of a significant individual or group who had lived in an area, or that referred to a distinctive physical feature.[63] Such localized place names and histories were being overwritten by more recent settlers who wanted to represent the landscape in a more modern idiom, such as in Msiige, where the area formerly known as *Kijiji cha Wagogo* (village of the Gogo people) was now commonly referred to as "Best One" after the name emblazoned across the smart and modern two-storey office building that had been constructed on a central plot in the vicinity by two recent arrivals. In contrast, Kwa Babu was so called after a well-known medicine man set up in the area in the early 2000s; Kwa Abarikiwe was named after the settler who enclosed the land in the 1970s and gradually parceled it out to newcomers; and Mbuyuni was so named because of the very large baobab tree that stood near the Salasala junction on the Bagamoyo Road and was said by long-term residents to be a place of spirits that had caused many road traffic accidents. These places and their localized names coincided in middle-class residents' geographical imaginations with spaces of *uswahilini*. Near Zacharia's house was *Usukumani*, a group of small houses and kiosks where a group of people from the Sukuma ethnic group had long lived. Looking at *Usukumani* from his walled and spacious house across the valley, Richard, who had retired from working in a bank, commented, "My neighborhood is good, it's not like those small shacks over there [pointing towards *Usukumani*]—over there it's like Manzese. That's *uswahilini*." When I asked Zacharia who lived in *Usukumani*, he shrugged and said, "They are just tenants."

In contrast, those who had acquired land from the original inhabitants from the 1970s onwards and who had built large storey houses saw themselves as pioneers who had made the former scrub land more productive. They had had a vision for the area, and that vision did not include *uswahilini* or squatters. One of those pioneers was Rajabu, whom we met in chapter 3. He and his wife had bought their land in 1975, and had become prominent members of the early Salasala community. Rajabu had been the secretary of the Salasala Community Development Association (SACODEA) in the early 1990s. SACODEA had brought together approximately fifteen early settlers, including the CCM branch secretary and the *mtaa* chairperson, to discuss issues pertaining to the development of their neighborhood. At that time, Rajabu explained, "we were really setting up on our own, there was no government here—the administration was coming from Mtongani. Back then this place was a village."[64] SACODEA had wanted to preserve the area as a farming green belt, which would have protected the members' large farm plots. They lobbied the prime minister's office, the Ministry of Agriculture, and the Dar es Salaam Municipal Council to no avail. "We couldn't get it," Rajabu lamented, "and then those stone quarries were squatted." He was referring to the incremental settlement of the former Kunduchi quarry in Salasala. The implication was that the squatters had effectively thwarted the SACODEA members' attempts to protect their land, as well as SACODEA's authority over the area's development. SACODEA ceased to function, because, Rajabu said, "people with different interests moved into the area." Describing the landscape that subsequently developed, Rajabu swept his arm from his plot towards the quarries: "When the quarries were finished, they were settled randomly. The area that is planned in Salasala starts here and goes inward [he gestured towards Goba]. The rest [gesturing the other way, towards the quarries] is squatters."

As Rajabu experienced, middle-class residents had limited power to protect the landscape they felt they had constructed. Some residents recognized this fact, as Richard and Peter demonstrated:

> Richard: This place will become congested. This area was all farms ten years ago. Now it is a town. We are predicting this place will be congested, and we will be *wazee* [elders] . . . but we don't want to be disturbed with noise and traffic.
> Claire: Why will this place become congested?
> Peter: If the government was strong . . . .
> Richard: Look at Masaki [next to Oysterbay]. It was very nice, it was executive, but now there are bars, it's noisy. So from this experience we think this area will go the same way. Here one hundred houses are planned [those built in the Kilimahewa resettlement scheme], around us the rest is not planned. People can settle, they can do whatever they want. It will be horrible. We are working with the *serikali ya mtaa* to make sure there are no unplanned houses. We don't have control.

· · ·

This lack of power sat uneasily alongside the sense of natural authority over suburban space that many middle-class residents felt. The enframing of urban space was an everyday practice of distinction mobilized by middle-class residents to define themselves and the space they had built against the less desirable landscapes of the city. Drawing on colonial and socialist tropes that measured the right to be in the city in relation to building materials and urban productivity,[65] middle-class residents framed their self-built neighborhoods as evidence of their legitimate presence on the suburban frontier. In liberalized Tanzania, socialist ideas about the self-reliant, hard-working rural citizen were recast in terms of suburban respectability, now measured by the individual's hard work in building a good house in an ordered neighborhood. In defining the landscape they had constructed in opposition to *uswahilini*, many suburban residents considered their use of space to be of higher quality, and therefore more legitimate, than poorer residents' buildings and use of space. Their attention to maintaining neighborhood roads and paths, plot sizes, architectural design and finishing; their acquisition of land through the market rather than by invasion or government grant from the 1970s; and their appropriate use of space for residential rather than noisy business purposes distinguished the suburban landscape from the noise, congestion, and haphazardness of *uswahilini*.

Yet *uswahilini* was not easily contained. *Uswahilini* was necessary to the enframing of middle-class suburban landscapes, but it also provoked anxiety. In examining this enframing and its contemporary manifestations, this chapter has shown that paying attention to landscape can help us to grasp the in-between, unsettled nature of middle-class subjectivities in Dar es Salaam. Richard and Peter identify the central tensions at the heart of middle-class life on the suburban frontier: How to protect one's stake in the landscape? How to make the landscape fit the frame? How could *uswahilini* be kept at bay? This is the coloniality of space at work in the postcolonial city. Middle-classness emerges as an unstable condition of being in between multiple binaries; between *uzunguni* and *uswahilini*, rich and poor, property owner and squatter. The material reproduction of the suburban landscape and the social reproduction of the middle classes is far from inevitable.

5

Domestic Architecture

CHARLES AND SALMA

Charles and Salma's house in Kilimahewa was not yet finished, but it was already impressive. It stood in one corner of a large plot enclosed by a two-meter-high concrete block wall. When they moved into the house in 2012 it was one of the few inhabited houses in their neighborhood. At that time, the surrounding area was occupied by grass, trees, one or two modest houses, and a few improvised fencing poles marking out nearby plot boundaries, some of which enclosed ambitious two-storey concrete block skeletons. They had started building the house six years previously. Charles and Salma's house occupied a single floor in a unique bungalow layout. Occupying only one floor rather than two meant that the house was not too ostentatious. Yet the architecture made a clear statement about the status and taste of its builders, confidently mixing global and local influences to produce a unique design that met the family's needs while reflecting a sense of their place in Tanzania and the world.

As Charles said, when he designed the house, he knew that what he wanted was a house with four bedrooms—a clear aspiration to distinction in a context where three bedrooms was considered to be the standard marker of success. Encountering the actual building, however, the complex roof seemed to most clearly articulate Charles's sense of social status—an origami puzzle of gabled and hipped shapes in modern imported red roofing sheets that rose and fell over the building like a small mountain range. The external concrete block walls had been smoothly finished with plaster and were awaiting paint, their corners picked out with decorative plastered quoins painted in an accent color. A tiled veranda and staircase (the house was built on a slight slope) flanked by concrete doric columns atop concrete balustrades leading to a heavy carved wooden Swahili-style front door jutted out of the house towards the thick metal gate that slid aside to allow entry and exit to the walled compound that enclosed the house. On another side an imposing bay feature containing three double windows extended the bungalow into the expansive plot. Towards the back of the bungalow a second tiled veranda, also flanked by concrete doric columns and balustrades, served as the everyday entrance to the house. This smaller veranda led from where Charles and Salma parked their cars, through a small cloakroom, into the large kitchen at the back of the house. It was easier to use this entrance than to use the actual front door for everyday coming and going, as the front door was secured from the inside with heavy metal bars. An electricity meter and a series of small security lights were fixed to the external walls, as well as a satellite dish and two air conditioning units, one for the living room and one for Charles and Salma's bedroom. Behind the cars, a water storage tank sat on top of a three-meter-high concrete block tower. The rest of the plot had been cleared except for a mature cashew tree in one corner, the only remnant from the land's previous life. An electricity cable hung across the plot connecting the house to the TANESCO pole in the street that Charles and Salma had paid to have installed. In the other corner, sections of large concrete pipes and piles of aggregate were scattered around the spot where an eighty-meter-deep well was to be dug. Since the house was designed with internal water facilities, water was delivered regularly by truck to fill the external storage tank. After three months of living in the house, however, Charles and Salma had decided that the water deliveries were too expensive, and they had begun to plan a well instead.

Once inside, a visitor would pass through the large kitchen, the walls of which were lined with bespoke dark wood cupboards and worktops, a free-standing electric oven, a microwave, a sink, and a large fridge-freezer. Shiny pale tiles on the walls and floor and highlights of pastel-colored paint lightened the room. If the domestic worker was cooking, the visitor might notice the oppressive heat in the kitchen even in Dar es Salaam's cool season, as the only ventilation came through the mosquito netting at the windows that looked out onto the concrete block walls enclosing the plot. From the door of the kitchen they would enter the dining and living rooms at the heart of the house, which were partly open-plan: large curved arches and pale shiny floor tiles connected the two rooms; but they were also partly separated by a section of structural wall and a series of transitional steps between them and the corridor that led to the sleeping quarters, necessitated by the slight slope on which the house was built. Beyond these public rooms at the heart of the house, the bedrooms were accessed via a large empty space—effectively the entrance since it was behind the large heavy front door—that led from the living room. The children's wing contained four rooms: two bedrooms for three children, a playroom containing a sofa and a television, and a bathroom containing a bath and flush toilet. The master wing was located back along the open-plan corridor and up some steps, and contained a large master bedroom and dressing room furnished in matching dark wood furniture, and an en suite bathroom.

In the dining and living rooms the overall effect was of space, light, and carefully curated décor. Large double windows constructed from high-quality local wood and secured with bespoke decorative iron grilles let light into these rooms. Charles, a university graduate in his forties who worked for a consulting firm, preferred these wooden frames to the popular, cheaper aluminum windows. His wife Salma, also a university graduate and a middle-ranking civil servant in her forties, had chosen all of the furnishings. A modest glass and black aluminum dining table with six matching chairs stood alone in the center of the large dining room, which was painted the same pastel peach as the kitchen; a cream and gold ceiling fan hung above the table; and a plumbed basin for hand-washing at mealtimes had been installed in the corner by the window. The living room was furnished with low-backed sofas in dark fabric and accent cushions, bought from one of the new shops selling imported furniture located along the industrial strip on the Nyerere Road. They were arranged in an L-shape facing the large flat-screen television with surround-sound speakers in the corner of the room; between them a small glass-topped coffee table stood on a gray rug with an abstract design. A four-foot-high traditionally carved wooden soldier figure stood in one corner of the bay window between two sofas. Above the coffee table a modern aluminum candelabra containing three bulbs in frosted upturned pendants was suspended from a ceiling rose; additional lighting was provided by uplighters on the walls and small lights embedded in the ceiling. The walls were topped with white coving carved with a flower design to match the ceiling rose, and finished at the bottom with a skirting trim of dark shiny tiles. The windows were all dressed with matching pale coffee-colored curtains hung from wooden curtain poles and secured with gold hold-backs. Salma intended to complement them with silver patterned net curtains, which would give a shine effect. On the freshly painted cream walls were hung a few items including a small framed professional family photograph positioned high up above the sofas, a small local painting of a vase of flowers hung above the television, a large plain clock, and an air conditioning unit up in one corner. Salma intended to hang a larger picture of herself and her husband on the wall by the arch to the dining room so that it would be easily seen by visitors as they passed from one room to the other.

THOMAS AND ROSEMARY

Thomas and Rosemary worked in routine administration in central government offices in Dar es Salaam. They lived in a modest house in Salasala. It was in quite a good location, not far from the tarmac road, but the area had become more popular in recent years and their neighborhood was changing fast. When Thomas bought the land, about ten years before he and Rosemary were married in 2014, there were fewer buildings in the vicinity. By 2015 they could no longer park their pickup and their small four-by-four-wheel-drive vehicle in front of the house, as newcomers had bought small plots and built their houses encroaching onto the path that led to Thomas and Rosemary's house. Beyond their house, the path narrowed further as it dropped down a steep hill and meandered through the houses built on the hillside. It was passable only on foot, and neighbors had to secure it with sandbags during the rainy season. Thomas and Rosemary had to park their cars on a yet-to-be-developed plot of land nearby.

Thomas and Rosemary's house was perfectly comfortable for them and their three children, containing a living room, three bedrooms, a kitchen, and a bathroom, with a higher-quality finish than many of their neighbors' houses had. But they aspired to something better, and to that end they had bought land further out on the suburban frontier, where they planned to build a larger house in the future. At the front of the existing house, they had built a distinctive small veranda with curved arches and finished with a bright pastel paint and white trim. Thomas often sat there, especially if he was drinking bottled beer with a friend in the evening, but it faced the concrete block wall of a neighbor; and since they hadn't yet completed their own wall enclosing their plot, it was open to passers-by on the other side and therefore lacked privacy. As Rosemary opined, there was little space inside or outside their house. Sitting in the living room, one could watch pedestrians through the windows as they navigated the sandbags on the path outside. The neighbors' walls abutted the space outside their kitchen door where Thomas kept a small chicken coop. The rest of the house, a square shape with a half-veranda at the front, was painted a sage green color. A simple hipped and gabled roof constructed with regular roofing sheets sported a satellite dish. Inside, the wooden window frames and mosquito netting were secured with plain metal grilles. They had managed to connect to electricity via a branch initially installed by a neighbor who was the first in the neighborhood to connect to the grid, but there were no water or sanitation services to connect to in this part of the city.[1] At the back of the house stood a four-thousand-liter water tank that was refilled by a delivery truck with a long hose every three weeks. Thomas used jerry cans to bring the water inside the house. One was placed in the kitchen, and the other was used to top up a larger water tub in the corner of the bathroom.

In the living room, terracotta-colored matte floor tiles contrasted with pale painted walls and cream and brown patterned curtains tied in the middle to let the light in; net curtains provided extra privacy. Ongoing improvements were in evidence from the freshly painted walls and freshly splashed unpainted wooden doors. A neutral-colored low-backed L-shaped sofa was pushed up against two walls facing the small flat-screen television attached to the opposite wall. On the floor in the center of the room was a large brown rug on which stood a low coffee table with a glass top and dark wooden legs. It sheltered four nesting tables covered in imitation leather, which could be moved around to serve drinks to guests. On the other side of the living room a wooden dining table covered with a brightly colored plastic tablecloth and four matching chairs was pushed up against the wall. On either side of the doorway to the kitchen stood a water cooler and a chest fridge. The small kitchen contained a gas-canister-powered freestanding oven and storage for food, cooking utensils, and crockery; there was also a small charcoal stove that was placed on the external steps outside the kitchen when used for cooking. A corridor to bedrooms and a bathroom containing a latrine led away from the living room, concealed by a hanging curtain, the fabric of which matched the window curtains. Another matching curtain was hung across the inside of the front door. On the walls were placed a picture of Thomas and Rosemary's wedding reception, two photographs of Thomas, and a wall calendar with a photograph of Lake Victoria.

NYUMBA NZURI (A GOOD HOUSE)

Charles, Salma, Thomas, and Rosemary were all members of Dar es Salaam's middle classes. Charles and Salma came from upper-middle-class families. They had masters' degrees from Tanzanian universities and they both aspired to pursue PhD's; they had stable jobs with good salaries in the private and public sectors; their three children were studying in good private boarding schools; they had both traveled internationally for work to Europe and China; they each owned farms in their home regions, and they owned two houses (one in Dar and one in Dodoma, where Salma's office had relocated after President Magufuli's drive to complete the government's move to the capital city). Both sets of their parents also owned property in Dar es Salaam. Thomas and Rosemary came from lower-middle-class families and were the first generation in their immediate families to own property in Dar es Salaam. They both worked in rank-and-file positions in central government offices. Thomas had a diploma from a college in Dar es Salaam, while Rosemary had a bachelor's degree from a Tanzanian university and was seeking sponsorship to pursue a master's degree in business studies. Their three children were enrolled in local English medium primary schools. In addition to the house they owned in Salasala, they both owned plots of land in their home regions, as well as the plot they had bought on the very edge of Dar es Salaam's suburban frontier, where they planned to build a larger three-bedroom house. The plan was to eventually live there, and to rent out the house in Salasala.

Despite the differences between them, Charles, Salma, Thomas, and Rosemary all had the capacity to build *nyumba nzuri*—a comfortable house constructed with permanent materials, some modern conveniences and aesthetic flourishes. The focus on houses in this chapter builds on the earlier analysis of middle-class property-making through acquiring land (chapter 3) and shaping landscape (chapter 4). Here I shift the focus to the new styles of domestic architecture favored by the middle classes building on the suburban frontier and the ways in which house-building is intimately related to the making of middle-class property and the properties of middle-classness. The good house and the practice of building it are key to being middle class in Dar es Salaam.

Scholars of social class have been less interested in housing compared to other attributes such as occupation and education. Yet there is recognition—most of it from European and North American contexts—that housing is related to social class in a number of ways, from political economy approaches that analyze housing as property or an asset that is owned or rented,[2] to historical cultural analyses of the relationship between class, gender, and domestic interiors,[3] to architectural analyses of middle-class suburban architecture,[4] to sociological and geographical analyses of housing types, aspiration, and gentrification.[5] More recent work on the anthropology of architecture and material culture has turned attention to how individual buildings "make people."[6] The housing of the new global middle classes has attracted considerable anthropological attention since the turn of the twenty-first century. This work has pushed class analysis in new directions by examining the ways in which middle-class distinction is achieved through the domestic arrangements and aesthetics of consumption in places such as China, Hungary, India, and Vietnam.[7] In these accounts domestic architecture and interiors are treated as significant sites through which middle-class subjectivity is expressed,[8] as well as signaling new tastes and patterns of consumption associated with new configurations of ideology, identity, and belonging.[9] As I show in this chapter, this is particularly salient in the autoconstructed city where self-built houses are about building the self as much as they are about constructing a place to live.

In Tanzania, as in much of Africa, self-built domestic architecture is political.[10] It is not only a question of who is able to build what kind of house and where, but also one of aesthetic politics. Building materials, architectural styles, and the speed with which a building is constructed are all significant. Where do materials and styles come from, and what do they signify? What is the rhythm of building, and what does that reveal about the wealth and moral worth of the builder? In colonial Dar es Salaam, as we have seen, legitimate urban residence was associated with productive employment and housing constructed with permanent materials.[11] Given the paucity of land, and later housing, provided for urban Africans, most lived beyond any urban entitlement in self-built structures of temporary materials. During the socialist period, after a brief spell in the early 1960s during which the National Housing Corporation constructed some urban housing, the socialist state reframed housing as part of self-reliance, opting instead to provide land on which people could build their own houses—though as we have seen in chapter 1, the supply of land was never able to keep up with demand. The materials with which people built their houses, and their interior furnishing and arrangements, either confirmed allegiance to the state's socialist ideology or suggested that one's affinities lay instead with bourgeois-capitalist ideals. As Anne Lewinson notes, "sparse utilitarianism, neatness, and an emphasis on accommodating people rather than things characterised the *ujamaa* interior décor."[12] Young unmarried women who enjoyed comfortable living arrangements that appeared to be far beyond their means could be suspected of being someone's mistress, and thus a threat to the gendered social order based on marriage and the nuclear family. During the Operation Economic Sabotage campaign in 1983, when people were encouraged to report suspected illegal activities among their neighbors to the authorities (such as obtaining luxury or everyday items on the black market), people resorted to burying or hiding domestic appliances, cash, building materials, or even cars and motorcycles.[13] The status of building materials was more ambiguous. Building with concrete blocks, rather than with temporary materials, was originally promoted by Nyerere in the early independence period. Concrete would build a modern socialist self-reliant nation of factories, government buildings, and homes. Tanzania's first concrete factory was opened in Wazo Hill (near to Salasala) in 1966. It was nationalized in 1974 and constantly hampered by production problems related to the lack of skilled labor and the rising costs of importing oil and spare parts. Nevertheless, Tanzanians took to building in concrete blocks with enthusiasm, when concrete could be purchased. By 1977 Nyerere was trying to reverse the preference for concrete, encouraging people to build instead with burnt bricks, which could be more easily manufactured locally. Yet concrete blocks remained popular because they signified permanence and modernity, despite Nyerere's complaint that building in concrete— or "European soil"—was a sign of a colonial mentality.[14]

UWEZO: THE CAPACITY TO BUILD

Today the self-built house is a barometer of *uwezo*,[15] or the capacity to build. The self-built house is the most durable and visible evidence of a person's capacity to meet theirs and their family's needs, as well as a public statement of aesthetic judgment and moral values. The size and style of a house, and the speed with which it is completed, are read by the builder, their family, friends, and neighbors as a statement on who they think they are, their place in Tanzania and the world. On the contemporary suburban frontier, smaller buildings in more densely built areas, often without exterior paint or concrete block perimeter walls and which might be poorly finished or in need of repair, are read as having been built by those with less financial capacity, who have prioritized other investments (such as in local businesses, trade, or a farm elsewhere) or whose capacity has been stretched by competing demands (such as children's school fees, an unexpected bill for health care, or obligations to relatives). These houses do not necessarily lack architectural flourish or attention to aesthetic detail, but the scale of such buildings and the resources required to pursue their builders' aesthetic ambitions are more limited. At the other end of the scale, the wealthy build more ostentatious two- or three-storey villas surrounded by tropical gardens and high concrete block walls. Such

FIGURE 7. A typical *nyumba nzuri* (good house), Salasala. Photo by author, September 2012.

buildings are often admired, but they can also be read as evidence that a builder has developed too high an opinion of themselves, or has enriched themselves in illegitimate ways and is therefore not of respectable character. Houses built by the middle classes occupy the interstitial ground between high- and low-quality housing: their houses are neither too big nor too small, neither too ostentatious nor too humble. They are the material manifestation of *uwezo*: the capacity to build something of good enough quality. These houses are distinguishable by the attention paid to relatively modest details of architectural design and interior space. Building something more elaborate than the template of the Swahili house and choosing the most up-to-date paint colors, roofing materials, and sofa designs take on significance as elements of an emerging middle-class domestic style. The capacity to build also captures the sense of achievement when a house is ready to be lived in—not necessarily finished, but livable.

Houses are big, unpredictable projects that consume money, time, imagination, and emotion. To build a house is a huge effort, often taking many years. A house may not be completed, as the many half-built, empty ruins that litter the new suburbs testify. People start too big, run out of cash, are distracted by other claims on their resources, or even die. Yet building too fast can also be problematic. Neighbors note who is building what in their vicinity and at what speed; new constructions of unknown provenance still invite speculation about the builder and the legitimacy of their apparent wealth. To build slowly and incrementally is more respectable. Neighbors recognize the familiar rhythms of cash flow, materials acquisition and the faster and slower phases of the development of the building, and are reassured that their new neighbor is of good moral character.

The capacity to build draws attention to the *process* of building as much as to the house itself. Charles, Salma, Thomas, and Rosemary were all architects of the houses they had built: they had imagined, designed, planned, project-managed, and decorated their houses with skill and care. They had also been frustrated by and had persevered with their building projects. The experience of building a house over many years oscillated between the capacity to aspire and the possibility of disappointment, and is central to middle-classness.

DOMESTIC ARCHITECTURE
AS MIDDLE-CLASS PRACTICE

House-building has long been recognized as a skilled activity,[16] yet the buildings that are constructed by ordinary self-builders are rarely considered as architecture. Despite the fact that a large proportion of the built environment in African cities is constructed in this way for residential purposes, most surveys of architecture in Africa focus on vernacular or colonial buildings or contemporary projects built by professional architects. They have little to say about the way that the majority of urban residents either experience or make architecture in their daily lives. The kinds of houses that have been built by Charles, Salma, Thomas, Rosemary, and others are invisibilized: neither sufficiently traditional in style, materials, or method to count as "vernacular architecture" nor sufficiently authored by trained architects to count as architecture. The analysis of domestic architecture developed here takes its lead instead from David Adjaye's continental photographic survey of architecture, which challenges ideas about what counts as architecture in Africa.[17] The residential architecture included in this collection covers the whole range of urban domestic buildings from shacks to modest concrete block bungalows to apartment buildings to villas.[18] Significantly, many of Adjaye's residential buildings are ordinary houses made out of cement blocks, much like Thomas and Rosemary's, and Charles and Salma's houses in Salasala.

If the houses built by Dar es Salaam's middle classes can be considered as examples of African domestic architecture, what then are their architectural characteristics? This is a distinctively hybrid form of domestic architecture in terms of its styles, influences, and materials. It is not "vernacular architecture" in the sense of using traditional architectural forms, materials, or methods. It is also not the Swahili house—the single-storey square or rectangular design with gable roof and an extendable series of rooms opening onto a central corridor with shared space at the back. Domestic architecture among the middle classes is now more open to experimentation with spaces and shapes such as complex roofs, imposing columns, curved walls, open-plan spaces, and double-height rooms. This architecture is global in the sense that ideas can be plucked from any place and any

FIGURE 8. An elaborate floor plan with circular living room takes shape on a building site among more modest houses. Photo by author, April 2016.

time. Classical columns, Chinese gateways, and modernist concrete sunshades in improvised shapes adorn bungalows and villas. House-builders get inspiration from social media, television, neighbors, and their own experiences of traveling—whether within the city or further afield. For example, there were several houses in Charles and Salma's vicinity that had external wall corners decorated with the same concrete quoins picked out in accent paint colors, yet this design is less common across the city. Floor plans experiment with new shapes and layouts such as hexagon-shaped living rooms and internal balconies. External walls are finished from the palette of newly available paints in rainbow colors, or are even mixed for the customer to create a bespoke hue. Outside space is also carefully curated, with attention paid to the design of perimeter walls, decorative paving stones, and garden features such as lawns, flowers, and trees, sometimes with a separate space for poultry, gardens, or other small business activity. Heavy metal gates provide another opportunity for ornamentation, the more imposing the gate suggesting the wealthier the occupant.

Building materials are also a hybrid of the locally made and the imported. Cement blocks are the most popular building material in Dar es Salaam and are made from mixing cement, local sand, and water. Cement production in Tanzania has expanded since the early 2010s (from three plants to twelve by 2022) but it is also imported from Kenya, the Middle East, Turkey, and Pakistan to try to keep up with demand. Cement blocks can be bought from one of the small factories that have sprung up across the suburbs in which young men feed block-making vibrator machines with different ratios of cement, sand, and water to make different-quality blocks that are then cured and stacked along the roadside for sale. Alternatively, the cost-conscious house-builder can rent a manual block-making machine, hire a few casual laborers, and oversee the block-making process themselves on their building site. Iron grilles for windows and doors, and decorative concrete blocks, are made by small local businesses and distinguished by their design; bespoke designs are more expensive. Complex roofs sport the latest roofing sheets made to look like tiles using a combination of aluminum, zinc, and galvanized iron and coated with granulated PVC in red, green, or blue. Interiors are organized with specialized uses in mind (sitting room, dining room, bedroom), and most domestic activities can in principle take place inside the house (as for example with internal kitchens and bathrooms). Small details differentiate these interiors from those with less space, time, and resources to curate their domestic space as they might wish.

The private spaces of the house, such as bathrooms and bedrooms, are demarcated from the open-plan family living spaces by solid wood internal doors (rather than a curtain hung across a corridor or doorway), large windows facilitate time spent inside (rather than outside in the compound), and there is attention to interior design details such as cornicing, ceiling roses, and painted skirting trims (rather than fading paint or undecorated internal walls). Rooms are less cluttered with previously popular mass-produced consumer goods such as soft toys, antimacassars, plastic flowers, religious images, and scripture quotations, or large wall calendars produced by Tanzanian parastatals. Furniture is either imported or made locally to appeal to a globalized IKEA aesthetic. There is a preference for low-backed, large-cushioned neutral fabric sofas rather than the cheaper and previously ubiquitous locally made wooden sofas with thin cushions; shiny surfaces on tables, floors, and TV cabinets predominate over the previously popular dark, natural materials such as local wood and textiles; walls are adorned with framed photographs of nuclear family members, certificates, and graduations rather than mass-produced religious or parastatal wall-hangings.

What makes the domestic architecture of the middle classes significant, however, is not only the particular configurations of design, materials, and décor. For builders like Charles, Salma, Thomas, and Rosemary, architecture is also an everyday practice. Building a house is a huge undertaking. People are always thinking about their building project, real or imagined: how to save money to buy bags of cement; what kind of decorative blocks to buy; how to fit the shape of the house they want into the parameters of the plot they have; what not to do the next time they build. Domestic architecture is achieved through an ongoing process of experimentation. The middle classes have the capacity to build, and the production of domestic architecture is central to middle-class practice and experience.

AGNES AND ARNOLD

Agnes was a lecturer at a higher education college in Dar es Salaam. She and her husband, a legal professional, rented a house in an inner suburb near to his job and their daughter's school, but they had been building a house in Salasala for several years. In fact her husband had bought the land in Salasala in the late 1990s when it was cheap and relatively easy to obtain. They started to build in the mid-2000s. The house had been designed by Agnes's husband and a friend of his who was an engineer. It was a curious shape. In order to secure their claim to the plot, they had initially built a small two-bedroom building with a simple gabled roof. Later her husband and his friend had designed a more ambitious three-bedroom bunga-low with a large circular living room and veranda, which they positioned behind, but not adjoining, the original building. They subsequently decided to join the two buildings together by constructing a large concrete block linking room that could become either a storage room or a garage. Both buildings had been finished in high-quality materials with matching dark wood window frames and a smart paint scheme (pale green walls, black skirting trim and fascia boards, white win-dowsills, external cornicing and internal veranda walls). They were roofed with locally manufactured concrete tiles. Agnes explained that they were more cost-effective than roofing sheets, which have a lower life span in the tropical environ-ment, although when building the roof they had also discovered that, since the tiles were much heavier than roofing sheets, they required a lot more wood in the roof to hold them up. Constructing the roof had therefore been more expen-sive and taken longer than they had anticipated. Inside the larger building, the stump of a decorative column hung down from the ceiling of the living room like a concrete stalactite, awaiting a decision on what form its design would take.

As Agnes walked me around, she explained that building the house had been a learning process and that she now knew what she would do differently next time. She would insist on smaller rooms ("What do you need all that space for? It's just status"), and she would avoid wasting space, as she felt they had done with the cor-ridor that ran from the living room past the bedrooms to a dead end. They were considering putting a door at the end of the corridor so that one could pass from one building to the other via the garage. She would not buy materials imported from China again; she was disappointed with the sinks they had installed in the original building that were already corroding. Durability was key, she said: the quality of materials was very important, because if something was not dura-ble then it would have to be replaced and end up being much more expensive. She was pleased with the decision to only have one en suite bathroom (attached to the master bedroom) and one additional bathroom. So many people don't think about maintenance when they build, she said, they just want to have a big house.

Why would you need three en suite bathrooms, she asked me: who is going to clean and maintain them? Outside in the compound, she showed me her main current problem: what to do about the huge volume of rain that ran off her neighbor's roof over the boundary wall and straight into her plot.

FLEXIBLE HOUSES

A new concrete skeleton frame had been attached to the front of Clara and Cosmas's house since I had visited the previous year. When I asked Clara what they were doing, she replied, "Oh it's just Cosmas's latest thing, he's always doing something . . . the house is never finished." When I visited again, over three years later, the red roofing sheets of the house had been extended out over the concrete frame to provide an area of very welcome shade over the front entrance. Since it was a hot February, we spent much of the time sitting under the new canopy to enjoy the breeze and the view of the Indian Ocean, from where we could admire the new trees that Clara had planted in the garden, the ornamental bird feeder she had bought on impulse from a roadside trader, and the small solar panel that stood next to it. We speculated about what species the new trees Clara had planted might be (one had produced an unidentified fruit, which later turned out to be a grapefruit); what could be put in the bird feeder to attract birds; and the benefits of the new mobile solar panel (and the problems caused when the supply switched between it and the TANESCO system). At the back of the house, they had also extended the two back bedrooms since my last visit, adding two small en suite bathrooms.

Domestic architecture in Dar es Salaam is endlessly reconfigurable. Regardless of the scale of available resources—whether the builder is poor, middle-class, or elite—all building projects require the ability to design, problem-solve, and adjust. What differs is the scale of the project and the materials used. Over the long time period during which a house is being constructed, ideas germinate, are tried out, revised, and amended, each new layer of the building produces new questions about how the whole fits together, and solutions are arrived at through trial and error. The experimental nature of domestic architecture is partly enforced by the incremental manner in which most people finance their house according to available cashflow. Since it takes several years to get a house up to at least a basic living standard, there is plenty of time to think about alternative ways of doing things. Domestic architecture is also malleable because most house-builders do not use the services of professional architects. Instead they effectively project-manage the building of their own house, designing floor plans, entrances, and window grilles, sourcing their own materials, and contracting labor when necessary. House-builders conjure the house they want in their imagination, and then seek a local builder who can translate that image into the phases of a building: the foundation, the walls to the lintel, the top of the walls, and the roof. Since the different phases are dependent upon having large amounts of cash to buy materials and pay labor, there is often a long time lag between them, and different parts of the building might be completed by different builders and laborers, who might themselves have different ideas and ways of doing things.

The slow tempo of building means that many of the more aesthetic finishing touches are attended to after moving into a house. Charles and Salma's interior was mostly finished when I first visited them, but three years later the finishing touches had been completed, with the exterior walls of the house and the plot perimeter painted in matching cream tones, the balustrades and columns picked out in white, and a decorative plant border installed at the base of the bay window. There was still more work to be done replacing the earthen floor of the plot with patterned paving stones and trees. They had also started work on the next house in Dodoma, where Salma's office had relocated. The new house was now taking up most of their time, resources, and energy.

The flexibility and open-endedness of self-built houses means that they can be reconfigured to meet a family's changing needs. As children arrive and grow, or elderly parents need home-based care, new bedrooms can be added or refashioned out of spare rooms or storerooms. Houses and plots can also accommodate economic activity. Home-based enterprises range from the more capital-intensive and ambitious to the smaller and more popular. Robert, an accountant for a Tanzanian safari company, had built a modest house in Salasala with his wife over a decade. The house itself was a simple bungalow topped with plain roofing sheets. Robert and his wife had had to balance building the house with educating their three children, who had all attended good secondary schools and were now pursuing diplomas and certificates. To help pay fees, Robert and his wife used the space in the compound behind the house to invest in a large chicken house for a thousand modern-breed chickens; the chickens and eggs were sold to local catering businesses and provided an income stream with which to pay the fees for the children's education. Others kept one or two zero-grazed cattle on their plots and sold milk to neighbors, or grew fruit, vegetables, or plants either for home consumption or to sell to neighbors. Women with good kitchen facilities made use of these to generate additional income, such as preparing spice mixes for sale or offering cookery classes to neighbors' children. Baking cakes was becoming a popular home-based enterprise among women with ovens at home, selling cakes to neighbors and relatives for family occasions and celebrations.

ZACHARIA AND ZAINAB

Zacharia and Zainab's house had gone through a number of transformations. Zacharia bought the land in 2004 for a good price, at a time when Salasala was still considered by many to be far from the city center. He bought his plot, wedged between two others on a piece of sloping ground, from the landowner, who had acquired the land as a much larger farm years previously. He was now selling off small parcels. Using local laborers, Zacharia started to build a two-storey house into the slope of the plot, and managed to complete a split-level ground floor before going abroad to study for a master's degree. When he returned he discovered that cracks had appeared in the walls. The laborers who had made the bricks on site had mixed too little cement with sand to make the blocks, so that they could sell the unused bags of cement themselves to make extra money. This had weakened the construction and caused the walls to crack. Zacharia realized that building a house on a slope required more technical expertise than he had appreciated; he also realized that he needed to choose and supervise his builders and laborers more carefully. The whole lower ground floor of the house had to be demolished and rebuilt with a proper foundation. He paid an architect US$760 to produce a plan for a three-storey house on the site, which clearly indicated structural details such as the number of steel rods required for the outer supporting concrete pillars. Zacharia proceeded to personally oversee the building work on weekends. By 2012 he had a middle management job with an international telecommunications company and several building projects (the house, a local shop, and another small shop near the Kariakoo market in the city center), which he attended to in sequence. Once the two shops were up and running, he focused on the house, putting his monthly salary into the purchase of materials for the next phase of building.

When I first visited Zacharia's house in 2012, the original upper ground floor of the house at the top of the slope still stood, housing the caretaker's room, a room for Zacharia's sister, and lots of bags of cement. The lower ground floor was in the process of being completely rebuilt. This time Zacharia had employed a builder recommended by a relative, and he was personally overseeing the work every weekend. The materials for the foundation alone had cost US$12,700. Although Zacharia had paid an architect to draw up the plans for the redesigned building, in practice he didn't completely follow the architect's vision for the house. The lower ground floor, according to the architect's drawings, comprised a double garage and back entrance to the house. A decade later the lower ground floor was still the main living space in the house, containing the living/dining room, two bedrooms and a bathroom, as well as the main front door. Up to three cars could be parked—if one knew how to angle them—between the back of the house and the perimeter wall.

By 2015 Zacharia had married Zainab, who worked in the city as a medical professional. Although wedding preparations had somewhat stalled the building process, they had nevertheless been able to finish the interior of the lower ground floor to a comfortable standard and were living in that part of the house. In addition to the living space that they occupied on the rebuilt lower ground floor, a domestic worker had a room and used a small kitchen area in the old upper ground floor building as well as an outside cooking area. Both were only accessible from the lower ground floor by a small path cut between the house and the perimeter wall, via the main front door. They had laid the slab for the first floor, where they intended to put an internal kitchen. The first floor was a building site, in the middle of which was a large plastic tub. A hosepipe snaked through a window, its bunged head hanging into the tub. The hose was connected to the neighbor on the other side of the street, whose large three-storey house had already existed, behind its high walls, when Zacharia had started building his own house. The owner—a man who owned several businesses in the city center, whom Zacharia and Zainab hardly ever saw—had dug a well on his plot and was supplying several neighbors for a fee. Zacharia's long-term plan was to build a well with his immediate neighbor on the other side: he said it was cheaper if you did it together. They had also had to pay attention to security after thieves had tricked the domestic worker into leaving the place unattended during the day; Zacharia's computer and some other small electrical goods were stolen. The mirrored PVC windows were now covered with bespoke iron grilles, the heavy wooden door was fortified with three locks on the inside and an iron grille on the outside, and the perimeter of the plot had been secured with a high concrete block wall and heavy sliding metal gates. They also employed a night watchman.

Things changed again in 2017: their first child had arrived and Zacharia's mother, who was unwell, was staying with them in the original upper ground floor building. The first floor was still under construction, and they had laid the slab for the second floor, where Zacharia intended to put the master bedroom and a study. Zacharia was toying with the idea—a suggestion from one of his friends—of building an external curving staircase that would lead from the car parking area to the first floor of the house. Building had stalled again anyway as Zacharia had been laid off from the telecommunications company. Many middle managers in international companies had had similar experiences as the business environment had become more difficult, he said: Coca-Cola and Tanzania Breweries had just gotten rid of a whole layer of management. Rather than try his chances in an increasingly competitive labor market, Zacharia had decided to invest his retrenchment package in starting his own business making bespoke logo cloth carrier bags. He had taken several trips to China in recent years to investigate machinery and other business opportunities. By 2018 he had bought his first machine and was waiting for it to clear customs. A few years later he had finished building a small factory in one corner of the plot and had started production with four employees. In the house, the open-plan living room and kitchen was now in use—mostly by the domestic worker and the nanny, though their bedrooms were still in the old upper ground floor building. Zacharia was anticipating turning the second floor—now a building site—into a master bedroom and bedrooms for their two children.

· · ·

Dar es Salaam's middle classes are a diverse social group that includes office workers, civil servants, employees in the private sector, and the self-employed, with varying levels of education, income, and assets. What they have in common is the capacity to build and the experience of building *nyumba nzuri*. Building a good house demonstrates *uwezo* or the capacity to build. The design and décor of these buildings stake a claim to middle-classness through their architectural influences and incorporation of new consumer goods from paint colors to roofing sheets, to water coolers and IKEA-style sofas. In addition to the style of these houses, the experience of building is also central to middle-classness. Located between the capacity to aspire and the possibility of disappointment or failure, house-building is both a material and an emotional undertaking—almost a test of one's middle-classness. Those without the *uwezo*—material, social, practical, emotional, aesthetic—are less likely to complete a house to their satisfaction. These self-built houses are flexible, but in their dwelt state they are also often a compromise between the builders' vision and the realities of what could be afforded, what architectural desires could be achieved in practice, and whether the resulting built form itself coheres and endures.[19] In their not-quite-as-imagined state, with unfinished upper floors, decaying fixtures, yet-to-arrive infrastructure, and encroaching neighbors, these houses capture both the desires and the frustrated aspirations that characterize middle-classness in Dar es Salaam. Yet read against the context of the city in which they have been built, the increasing number of *nyumba nzuri* in places like Salasala indexes the growing inequality that has characterized the postliberalization era in Tanzania. Hidden in plain sight, these houses say what cannot be said about inequality and social class in Dar es Salaam.

6

Lifestyle

In 2016 a large modern private-hire hall opened in Salasala. Three storeys high and painted dark pink, it could accommodate up to three hundred guests for events such as confirmations, weddings, and send-off and kitchen parties. A year later Salasala got its first juice bar and a gym, both of which opened on the main tarmac road through the *mtaa*; and by 2018 a smart new Catholic Church had been built by the local congregation. This was the frontier of domestic investment in the city, not only for those looking for land on which to build a house and a life, but also for those looking to capitalize on the opportunities that the suburban frontier presented. The inner suburbs of Sinza, Mikocheni, and Mbezi Beach, where land was far more expensive, were already densely built and had already been colonized with malls, bars, supermarkets, private schools, and private-hire halls: Salasala and other parts of northern Kinondoni were the future.

In her ethnography of professionals living in Dar es Salaam's inner suburbs in the mid-1990s, Anne Lewinson noted that much celebratory activity, such as weddings, baptisms, and confirmations, was home-based but publicly accessible.[1] Send-off parties for brides-to-be in *uswahilini* would be organized and celebrated in homes that were not walled off from the public path; attendees would spill into the street, and music and celebrations would be heard in the surrounding neighborhood. The event was as much about community building and the sharing of prosperity and life events with kin and neighbors as it was about celebrating one family's success at marrying a daughter. For those who could, such events were also an opportunity to demonstrate wealth and status in a newly liberalizing polity—the size of the celebration, the nature of the facilities (additional chairs, awnings, music), and the quality and quantity of guests, food, and drink all indexed the status of the celebrating family. Weddings were the most common events held in and around homes, but Lewinson noticed that confirmations and first birthdays were also conspicuously celebrated among those who could afford to do so: a particularly lavish first birthday party conducted within the gardens of the walled compound of a wealthy family in the city's then periurban fringe was exceptional in the mid-1990s. Fast-forward to the present, and two things are notable about contemporary suburban lifecycle and other events: a wider range of events now warrant conspicuous celebration, and those celebrations have become increasingly privatized, withdrawing into the walled plot or an invite-only event in a private space.

This chapter examines the lifestyles that are taking shape in the new homes and businesses populating the suburban frontier that are aimed at middle-class leisure and lifecycle events. The chapter begins with a discussion of homes as places of class reproduction through forms of labor, self-improvement, leisure, and new ways of celebrating lifecycle events. I then turn to three new significant sites dotted across the suburban frontier where the middle classes congregate—the private-hire hall, the private English-medium primary school, and the bar. Middle-class boundary work—the lifestyles, values, and aspirations through which social boundaries are maintained—starts in the home but goes beyond it, embedding itself in the city's wider fabric.[2] Starting with everyday activities in and around the home, the chapter follows the middle classes out of their houses and into the private-hire halls, private schools, and modern bars that are so central to middle-class distinction. These are spaces of consumption, leisure, learning, and bodily transformation where the services and consumer goods on offer are aimed at meeting new middle-class tastes and desires. Middle-class life in Dar es Salaam radiates out from the home to include the private nursery, the private school, the boarding school, the office, the mall, the supermarket, the outdoor bar, the private-hire wedding hall, the gym, and the hair and beauty salon, all of which are scattered across the city's northern suburbs yet nevertheless function as a kind of middle-class ecosystem held together by the private cars used to navigate between them. This is not so much an enclave of middle-class exclusivity as an archipelago of middle-class sites and services stretched across the suburban frontier.

DOMESTIC LIFESTYLES: LABOR, LEISURE, AND SELF-IMPROVEMENT

Middle-class homes are sites of both productive and socially reproductive labor. During my time in Dar es Salaam, parents cared for elderly relatives who had come to stay with them to access better health care in the city; they managed their domestic workers and helped their children with homework; they dealt with the rat problem or the electricity meter, prepared evening meals, and caught up with their obligations to multiple WhatsApp groups. They also managed their multiple income streams from the home, sometimes in lieu of waged work but often to compensate for low salaries: they ran livestock projects such as chickens or stall-fed cattle, sold milk or other produce to neighbors, took orders for cakes to be made for special events, ran small shops or managed rental rooms on the plot, or even managed small factories producing vibrated bricks or small consumer goods. Investments away from the home also needed to be attended to via mobile phone calls to in situ workers or caretakers. Agricultural investments in rural home regions or the neighboring districts to Dar es Salaam such as Kibaha and Baga-moyo were common. Vegetable gardening and livestock keeping supplemented the household food stores or could be distributed to neighbors and kin, but for some families home-based businesses constituted an important part of the house-hold income. Smaller plots could accommodate one or two zero-grazed cattle that provided milk for consumption and for sale; larger plots had space to allow more cattle to graze. Producing chickens, which were in high demand among local bars and hotels, was also a popular activity, with specialist huts housing up to fifteen hundred *kuku wa kisasa* (modern chickens) squeezed into plots.[3]

Josephine and Michael's lifestyle was a good example of this domestic multi-tasking. They lived in an attractive, modest bungalow enclosed within high con-crete block walls in Salasala. Josephine rued the fact that they had no garden space to speak of, since the house took up most of the plot, and what space was left between the house and the sliding gate was occupied by their two cars. They both had good jobs in the formal sector, Josephine with an international mining com-pany and Michael with the Open University of Tanzania, but they also maintained several businesses to provide them with the additional income that they needed in order to pay their children's private boarding school fees. Josephine had been running a small hardware shop in Kariakoo in the city center, but she closed it down in 2016 as she found it a strain to work full-time in a demanding job while running a business that she could only physically attend to on Saturdays. Thereaf-ter she turned her attention to agricultural production on the ten acres of land she had bought in Kibaha, where she hired a few seasonal laborers to produce vegeta-bles. During the planting, growing, and harvesting seasons, she would drive there every Saturday to supervise the laborers. To irrigate the land she had had a one-hundred-meter well dug that used a pump powered by a generator, but she had found it expensive to run and was subsequently considering installing TANESCO power to the land instead. She also needed to do more market research, as the local hotels and supermarkets she had first sold to in Dar es Salaam wanted a more pre-dictable supply than she could offer. Her husband, Michael, was more interested in property. He was currently supervising from afar the construction of a small apartment block for rental in the northern town in which he had grown up.

Middle-class suburban lifestyles and investment strategies were reliant on the labor of others. Domestic workers were routinely employed in middle-class households as live-in workers (usually housed in small rooms constructed spe-cifically for domestic laborers outside in the compound rather than in the house) or drop-in laborers who lived nearby and came to the house on specified days. Lower-middle-class households were more likely to engage such labor sporadically. Household labor was gendered. Female domestic workers did cooking, cleaning, washing clothes, and caring for older relatives and preschool children in the family home, while men were employed for the purposes of security, maintenance, vegetable gardening, and livestock keeping. Women were commonly paid between £7 and £20 a month, depending on the employer's budget and inclination based on their assessment of the worker's skills and ease of replacement. Domestic workers could be recruited locally, especially if they were not required to "live in," but it was more common to seek someone recommended by family or friends with connections to rural areas that were considered to produce reliable domestic or agricultural workers.

Such practices often relied on stereotypes about particular ethnic groups. Salma, a mid-ranking civil servant, had recruited her domestic worker from Bukoba. She explained that "the local people [in Dar es Salaam] are not good. One of my husband's workmates was going home to Bukoba so we asked him to look out for someone suitable." On the other hand Rosemary, a routine office worker in a government office, paid one of her poorer neighbors to help her with the housework rather than bring someone from her home area of Kilimanjaro. She explained, "Chagga girls are not interested in this kind of work. To come to the city and look after children for TSh50,000 a month? They would rather stay in the village and drink *pombe* than do this work for that amount of money. Many Chagga are educated, they have a plan . . . this is not the kind of work they want to do."[4] Zacharia lamented that his domestic worker, whom he had also brought to Dar es Salaam from a rural area, did not speak English. He and his wife were considering sending their children to an English-medium preschool, where they felt they would be more likely to start to pick up useful skills. Male domestic workers were sought from agriculturally productive rural areas. Their duties included tending the garden, preparing soil for planting, weeding, watering, harvesting, tending livestock, milking cows, maintaining water supplies, and doing low-key household maintenance. They were also responsible for security, including opening and closing the gates when people arrived or departed by car.

Middle-classness was thus reproduced in the home through control over the labor of domestic workers and the everyday practices of interacting with, while differentiating oneself from, those domestic workers. Social and cultural distinction was also achieved through other domestic lifestyle practices such as self-improvement, diet and exercise, and leisure.[5] Middle-class homes provided space for self-improvement: pupils did homework under parental duress, young adults studied for graduate courses to gain professional qualifications, and there was much talk about, and some effort to actualize, bodily improvement through diet and exercise. Helen, a graduate in her early twenties, lived with her parents in Salasala and had managed to secure a temporary job in a national bank after graduation from university with a bachelor's degree. She worked in the city center, getting a lift in the mornings from Salasala in her brother's car. They would routinely leave at six in the morning and be in town by seven thirty. Several nights a week Helen went to evening class at the end of the working day. She was studying for an accounting qualification with the aim of securing a permanent post at the bank. She would regularly come home late, around ten o'clock, after the rest of the family had eaten, and be up again at five the next morning to commute to work. She also developed a routine of getting up in the middle of the night to study as exam time approached.

Many members of middle-class households expressed desire to lose weight, eat healthily, and do more exercise. Some men preferred to exercise at the gym. For the upper-middle classes there were several in the city's international hotels and in the original *uzunguni* neighborhoods of Masaki and Oysterbay. Others preferred to use one of the new suburban gyms located in mall developments in Mikocheni or Mbezi Beach as they drove home from work. Picking up on local demand, the first gym in Salasala opened in July 2017. Other men, and some women, preferred to go for a run closer to home on weekends. As we shall see, some men were members of social groups that organized collective exercise classes on Saturday mornings, and in 2020 two new suburban running groups were established (Salasala Hills Runners and Goba Roads Runners). Many middle-class married women with families struggled to find time for exercise, often talking about it but finding it harder to put plans into action. Several women complained that, since they had moved to their new houses in Salasala from inner suburbs closer to the city center, commuting took so much of their time that it simply was not feasible to go out for a walk or anything else once they got home in the evenings, as it was too late and too dark, and therefore not safe. The fact that most married women also cooked or supervised the evening meal (if it had been cooked by a domestic worker) made exercise in the evening even more difficult.

Both men and women took an interest in eating healthy foods for health and body shape reasons. People were aware of the rise of hypertension and consumption-related health problems in Tanzania,[6] often through personal experience or the experience of a friend or family member. What this translated to in practice varied widely. Josephine, for example, liked to eat her main meal at work during the day and have "something light" at night when she returned home, as she did not want to go to bed on a full stomach. She had an impressive modern kitchen in her home, with shiny black work surfaces and kitchen cupboard doors, but as she herself admitted, she rarely used it. Most of the cooking was done by the female domestic worker who cooked in the small modern kitchen that had been installed next to her sleeping room in the out-building adjacent to the main house. Many women tried to avoid fried foods, although it was a common way of cooking meat or fish quickly for the family evening meal when they returned home at night. Women struggled with these issues and debated with each other as to what they could do. Advice circulated on WhatsApp groups, such as threads purporting to advise "30 uses of apple cider vinegar for weight loss," even though apple cider vinegar was not available in Tanzania at the time. Driving through the suburbs to a family baptism one Sunday afternoon with Clara, her sister, and her niece, they agreed that the problem was *lifestyle*: you had to change your lifestyle. This meant changing your diet and trying to do more exercise. There was a time, Clara said, when she and her sister would try to walk together in the evenings. But, she lamented, "how can we have time for that, now?" As a business owner and a mother, she was often busy with the business or family matters until late at night. Her sister added in solidarity, "It's difficult to lose weight, but easy to put it on." We all agreed. They discussed the different diets they had been trying, such as cutting out meat, starch, or sugar. One family member had lost weight rapidly on the "cabbage soup" diet (but then put it back on). Clara's sister told us about one man she knew who had cut out beer and only drank wine instead, in an effort to lose weight. Then she told us about how she had managed to lose weight over four months in the previous year by not eating any starch. But on a trip back to her village, "everyone was eating [starch] and I was not eating; they said 'why are you not eating?' And so I ate the [starchy] food, and it seemed as if my body was craving it!"

Homes were also sites for relaxation and leisure. Large flat-screen, stand-alone, or wall-mounted televisions were the centerpiece of many sitting rooms, powered by subscriptions to DStv, a South African satellite service providing access to local channels such as ITV and Channel 10, international channels such as Al Jazeera, BBC World News, channels showing Hindi films, sport, and African channels such as East African Television, music channels, Nigerian movie and Pentecostal channels. These were bundled into packages that cost upwards of US$8 a month and that could be renewed from a mobile money account on a mobile phone. Weekday late afternoons saw children, dropped at home by their private school bus or other organized transport, make the most of the fact that they had control over the television for a while. If the television package was live and the electricity was on, the most popular pastime was watching international kids' channels such as Cartoon Network and Nickelodeon or playing computer games. In the evenings, older family members switched between local news, BBC World or CNN, Nigerian Pentecostal or American Christian channels, or *Isidingo*, an English-language South African soap opera. At other times of the day when family members were not around, domestic workers might take the opportunity to watch Hindi films or locally made Swahili dramas, two genres hardly ever chosen by members of the family.

DOMESTIC CELEBRATIONS, GATES, AND CAKES

One Sunday afternoon I was invited to Rosemary and Thomas's house in a densely settled lower-middle-class suburban neighborhood on the edge of Salasala to celebrate the baptism of their second daughter. After the service at their local Catholic church, they held a celebration at their modest three-bedroom house for Thomas's relatives and some of their neighbors. When I arrived at mid-afternoon the celebration was in full swing. Guests were finishing their buffet lunch, which consisted of high-status celebratory foods such as pilau, rice, beef stew, chicken, plantain, and watermelon. Thomas's female relatives arranged themselves on the modern low-backed sofas set against the walls around a large coffee table in the living room, facing the wall-mounted television that was playing English-language cartoons on Nickelodeon. They were not watching the television, but rather were talking among themselves as they passed the baby around. Thomas and his male relatives sat outside on the floor of the veranda drinking bottled beer. Rosemary and her domestic worker Mama Anna—a neighbor who helped Rosemary out with cooking, cleaning, and childcare three days a week—moved around inside the house, Mama Anna clearing plates and bringing bottled sodas and beers while Rosemary fussed over the baby, took photos on her smartphone, and sat to talk to her guests. Thomas and his brother went off on foot to the local *duka* (shop) to buy more bottled drinks. The front door of the house was open, as was the gate to the plot, and throughout the afternoon neighbors and children drifted in and out and were fed by Mama Anna from the buffet laid out on a table pushed up against another wall. The openness of the celebration to neighbors was striking in comparison to other events I had attended in wealthier households, where only family and close friends were invited and the gates to the plot were firmly closed.

The baptism cake was brought out at the end of the afternoon. It was a modest cake, a single layer of plain sponge covered in red icing with white decorative piping, presented on a round silver cake tray. I commended Rosemary on the cake, and she explained that she made her own cakes because she had her own oven, but that she had asked a friend to decorate this one as she wasn't very good at it herself. The cake was cut by the parents and slices handed out to everyone present. I noticed that Rosemary did not eat the icing. "It's too much sugar," she said by way of explanation, "I'm trying to lose weight." In fact it was quite common for people to avoid eating cake icing, as it was widely considered to be too sweet. People would take slices of sponge, leaving a heap of stiff icing collapsed in the middle of the cake tray like a deflated balloon.

Large, elaborate cakes have increasingly become a mark of distinction for all manner of celebrations in middle-class households. I encountered them, and their cutting and consumption, as set pieces at celebrations held in homes and private-hire halls to mark baptisms, birthdays, wedding anniversaries, and school graduations. After a decade of liberalization, Anne Lewinson noted that "an elaborately decorated multi-level cake had become common at elite weddings."[7] Since then the cake trend has continued to grow, making its way into smaller home-based celebrations and not only for the elite. Home-based celebrations are usually marked by smaller cakes than those common at large events such as weddings, but the cakes are rarely made at home, since home baking and cake decorating are skills that are not widely practiced by either domestic workers or most middle-class women, partly because they require specialized equipment (ovens, mixers, tins, piping equipment) that are neither widely owned nor used, even in middle-class kitchens. Instead, cakes are new commodities that index new tastes and definitions of sophistication. Decorated cakes with personalized messages are commonly commissioned from one of the growing number of bakeries and specialist cake-making businesses in the city. In 2018 a customer could expect to pay around US$20 for a large round simply decorated sponge cake. More elaborate cakes, such as graduation cakes topped with mortar boards and scrolls made out of sugar icing, ranged from US$35 to US$75. However, in recent years the cake economy has sparked interest among women and girls more widely, with middle-class women entrepreneurs turning to cake-making as a home-based business, and school girls enrolling in cake-making classes at suburban baking businesses during school holidays.

Cakes are symbolic in several ways. They have become a marker of new patterns of consumption associated with events that might not have commanded such a ritual in the past such as birthdays, anniversaries, and retirements. The size of the cake and the splendor of its decoration reflects the social status and good taste of its commissioner. The fact that the decoration is rarely consumed further underscores the boundary work that cake performs in distinguishing the middle classes from the poor, as an expensive, very sweet and refined foodstuff that has little nutritional value, confected for aesthetic rather than eating pleasure. The sharing of cake has become a new way of affirming social relations, particularly among kin, taking the place of a whole roasted animal at events. At household events centered on the family such as birthdays and baptisms, and at larger extended family events such as weddings, cakes are prominently displayed and filmed being cut before small pieces are skewered with cocktail sticks and fed by the celebrants to their guests who are called to the cake in order of seniority.

SUBURBAN LIFESTYLES AND ARCHIPELAGIC SPACE

The suburbs came alive on weekends as people poured their energy into house-building or improvements, home-based businesses, and social activities. Weekends were the time for checking on one's building project, for supervising the delivery of timber or sand for a home extension or improvement, for driving into town to pick up a spare part or for food shopping in the markets and suburban supermarkets, or for checking on one's *duka* in the suburb or in Kariakoo, the main commercial hub in central Dar es Salaam. Suburban hair and beauty salons were full of women having their hair and nails done for the week ahead. Women attended rotating savings and credit group meetings. For Christians, Sunday mornings were for attending church and being seen there in one's best clothes. Children attended Bible study classes after the service. Weekends were also the time for middle-class married couples, or groups of men, to socialize with friends and associates in suburban bars that served bottled beer and roasted meat, and showed international football matches on large (or small) television screens. Some places were so popular that those who wanted to eat roasted meat on a Saturday or Sunday afternoon had to get there early or be prepared to wait for hours. New businesses have opened in the suburbs in order to meet the growing demand for consumer and lifestyle goods such as hair and nail products and services, freshly baked bread and cakes, and imported wine and spirits, while new bars and open-air garden restaurants, juice bars, and private-hire halls dot the landscape. One of the newest garden bar-and-restaurants in Salasala boasted a swimming pool for use by patrons. These new businesses, facilities, and activities were nodes in archipelagic space, spread across homes and sites throughout the city's suburban frontier that could only be efficiently navigated by private transport.

New supermarkets selling imported goods were popular with the middle classes. The supermarket landscape in Dar es Salaam has drastically expanded from the four small supermarkets that existed in the city before liberalization, and there are now many to choose from, located in large and small mall developments in *uzunguni* and its adjacent neighborhoods (Mikocheni, Mbezi Beach), at the large Mlimani City shopping mall near the University of Dar es Salaam, and at growing satellite centers on the city's periphery such as Tegeta. Kibo Commercial Complex was one such peripheral mall in Tegeta. Several storeys high and towering above its neighbors, it was built in a striking architectural style with an unusually shaped façade covered in shiny silver-gray cladding. Kibo offered a modern retail experience compared to the small local shops that surrounded it. Set back from the road and surrounded by ample car parking, here customers could park in a dedicated space, enter the large brightly lit mall, and browse all manner of imported consumer goods directly on the shelves, unlike the local *duka* model in which a small range of items displayed behind a counter was passed to customers, sometimes through a grille, by a worker.[8] Indeed, middle class practice at such local shops was often to be served in their car or to send a junior passenger to the window to complete the transaction for them. In the early 2010s not all of the units in the Kibo Commercial Complex were occupied, but it already contained two branches of local banks, several nail and hair accessory shops, an imported clothes shop, a mobile phone shop, and an anchor supermarket; later additions included a café and a nightclub. This was where Salma drove at weekends to get her nails done, and where she and her husband did their shopping for processed food items (fresh food was bought at the local market). Salma had considered opening a beauty supplies shop in the Complex where she could sell wigs, fake hair, make-up, and nail art products, but she thought the rent too high. Zacharia preferred to use a smaller supermarket in Mbezi Beach. It was further away from Salasala than Tegeta, but he felt it had more goods there at a better price. He regularly bought imported food items like yogurt and juice, and personal grooming products such as imported body spray.

Weekends were also the time for the celebration of established lifecycle events such as baptisms and weddings,[9] as well as new rituals such as school graduations.

FIGURE 9. Kibo shopping center, Tegeta. Photo by author, September 2012.

Although many of these events were organized around long-standing rituals that took place in recently built places of worship in the suburbs, the associated celebrations have undergone significant inflation in terms of their size and cost. Many of these celebrations are held in the new suburban gardens, bars, and hotels. In the rest of the chapter we turn to examine three key sites of middle-class practice: the wedding hall, the primary school graduation, and the bar.

WEDDING CULTURE AND THE PRIVATE-HIRE HALL

As we sat on the sofa looking through her wedding photo album in her living room in Salasala, Rosemary narrated the key events captured in the photographs. The first images were posed photographs of Rosemary before her send-off party. She was professionally made-up and wearing an elaborate white and silver dress. The photographs were taken by a professional photographer in a hair and beauty salon specializing in wedding beauty, inside which was a stage on which the bride could be photographed posing on a chaise lounge in front of a decorative mantlepiece surrounded by plastic flowers. Rosemary's send-off event was held that evening in a private-hire hall in Dar es Salaam. Two hundred guests were invited, including a large number of rural kin who had hired a bus to transport them from Kilimanjaro to Dar es Salaam for the wedding events. The proceedings were overseen by a professional master of ceremonies (MC). The photographs of the event showed Rosemary and her mother sitting in front of a decorated stage. Each image recorded a different group of guests standing with the bride and her mother with the gifts they had brought: her family, the groom's family, the wedding committee, the send-off committee. As Rosemary noted, it was common practice to tell people what you wanted to receive at your send-off, and the photographs showed Rosemary sitting behind a growing pile of pots, pans, and kanga.[10] There was also a photograph showing Rosemary being given away by her father to her father-in-law. The images of the wedding day itself showed Rosemary in an elaborate white dress with long train, flanked by six bridesmaids dressed in identical long red dresses. The church wedding was followed by a beach photo shoot at Oyster-bay in the original *uzunguni*, and then a reception at a suburban private-hire hall to which three hundred guests were invited.

Weddings are important social, cultural, and economic events and a regular feature of middle-class social life. They sit at the apex of a wedding culture in which weddings, their planning, and peripheral events seep into the everyday. People experience wedding culture in numerous ways: as members of organizing committees that require numerous meetings and WhatsApp messages; as remote participants receiving photos and videos via WhatsApp of a live wedding in another city that they can't attend; as bridesmaids, spending a whole Saturday going to another suburb to get measured for the dresses; or simply watching the popular documentary-style television series *Harusi Yetu* ("Our Wedding"), each episode of which follows a different couple through the stages of the wedding process. Middle-class wedding culture is pervasive, but it is also spatialized. Weddings and their associated parties provide rich fodder for the *ukumbi* economy, private-hire halls that are dotted across the city.

The ubiquity of middle-class wedding culture has been driven by wedding inflation, in which the number of events associated with an average middle-class wedding, as well as the size, spectacle, and cost of these events, has increased substantially.[11] The list of events that are now commonly organized as part of a typical wedding in a middle-class family includes the kitchen party, *begi* (bag) party, send-off party, wedding ceremony, wedding reception, and family/wedding organizers' postparty. For Christian weddings taking place in a church, the ceremony and reception take place on the same day (usually a Saturday). In Muslim families the ceremony often takes place at a mosque or at home on the Friday preceding the formal wedding reception, which creates an additional event to those listed above. The kitchen party and *begi* party are the most recent additions to middle-class wedding culture. They are prewedding parties exclusively for women and men respectively, although kitchen parties are far more common than their male equivalent. Karen Tranberg Hansen described attending kitchen parties organized in the home by and for women of wealthier households in Lusaka in the mid-1990s, during which the bride-to-be would be instructed on how to keep her future husband satisfied, and was presented with a series of gifts "for the kitchen."[12] In Dar es Salaam Lewinson described the kitchen party as a new ritual for the bride-to-be, her female kin, colleagues, and friends.[13] Tanzanian kitchen parties resembled those in Lusaka, being women-only parties during which marital advice and gifts were presented to the woman getting married. The Dar es Salaam events have since become more elaborate, taking place in private-hire halls rather than homes and requiring contributions from attendees. Separate from the kitchen party and more of an established tradition is the send-off party, organized by the bride's family before the wedding in order to bid her farewell before she joins her husband's family. In the mid-1990s in *uswahilini* send-off parties were held in and around the family home on the Friday night before the Saturday wedding.[14] They are now routinely held in private-hire halls for those families wishing to distinguish themselves from *uswahilini* culture. Many of these wedding events—kitchen party, *begi* party, send-off, wedding reception—as well as peripheral activities such as preparing the bride—are now private events held in private-hire halls or commissioned from specialist providers such as the wedding hair, beauty, and photography salon. These businesses were increasingly prominent on the suburban landscape, as middle-class residents not only formed the base of their clientele but also invested in such businesses themselves.

Wedding inflation is also discernible in the scale and spectacle associated with contemporary middle-class weddings. Lewinson's descriptions of the weddings of her professional interlocutors who lived in *uswahilini* in the mid-1990s highlight the distinct urbanity of these events, which brought the different rural marriage traditions of brides and grooms together with emerging city practices to carve out a distinctive Dar es Salaam wedding tradition. Viewed from the present, her descriptions offer an insight into the inflationary practices that characterize contemporary middle-class weddings. For example, the typical reception hall setup in the mid-1990s provided dressed tables for the wedding party and the families of the bride and groom. All other guests were arranged on plain chairs facing the high table, and the hall was simply decorated with kanga. In contrast, at an average middle-class wedding in the 2010s, all guests were seated at dressed tables and chairs and the entire hall was bedecked with fabric and fairy lights in the wedding colors (the color scheme for the event chosen by the wedding committee). Food and drink, the MC, entertainment, and wedding photography were now commissioned from a growing market of specialist providers. Food, for example, was no longer prepared by the female kin of the groom, but was paid for as part of the hire hall's catering service. In the mid-1990s a key marker of distinction at Christian weddings was the presentation and sharing of a whole roasted goat or a small decorated wedding cake. Whichever was presented, the wedding couple would ceremonially cut and feed mouthfuls of it to their parents-in-law, symbolizing their willingness to join with their new family.[15] Contemporary weddings may contain both meat and cake traditions and their symbolic joining of two families through marriage. However, as with other celebration cakes, wedding cakes have become bigger and more elaborate affairs, purchased from professional bakers and consisting of multiple tiers decorated in the wedding scheme colors.

The grander scale of contemporary weddings is reflected in their cost. Contributions to weddings among Dar es Salaam professionals in the mid-1990s were in the range of TSh5,000 for women and TSh10,000 for men.[16] By the mid-2010s average contributions had greatly increased. As Salma noted matter-of-factly, her cousin's kitchen party had accommodated 150 guests and invitations had required a contribution of TSh200,000 (US$90). The send-off party for the same nuptials accommodated 300 people, each of whom had contributed TSh100,000 (US$45), and the minimum contribution for the wedding itself was TSh50,000 (US$22). In fact, Salma pointed out, it was routinely possible to spend up to 15 million shillings (US$6,730) on a wedding. Her sister's reception for 200 people in one of the new suburban private-hire halls had cost TSh2.2 million (US$987) for the hall hire and decoration alone. Food per head had cost an additional TSh15,000 (US$6.7), which, she pointed out, was far better value than the up-market beach hotels that charged US$50 per person. Other costs included the MC and DJ, possibly other entertainers, the videographer and photographer, the clothes for the bride's and groom's attendants, car hire, drinks including champagne and spirits, and the cake. As the mother of a recently married young bank professional, who had invited 500 people to his wedding, argued, "It's a once-in-a-lifetime thing, so you want to hold a big party."[17]

THE ENGLISH-MEDIUM PRIMARY SCHOOL

In the mid-2010s, Wazo Ward had five government primary schools and three government secondary schools serving a population of around ninety thousand.[18] They were generally underresourced and lacking sufficient teachers. Middle-class residents did not send their children to these schools. Instead, they enrolled their children at one of the growing number of private English-medium primary schools that have become significant nodes in the archipelago of goods and services patronized by the suburban middle classes in northern Kinondoni. These new primary schools were central to parents' strategies to reproduce middle-classness in their children. Good-quality primary schools—as judged by pupils' performance in national exams—were the first step towards a selective private secondary school, tertiary education, good social networks, and lucrative employment. They have also become places where new rituals of middle-class distinction have developed. The primary school graduation ceremony is a case in point, bringing parents and students together as a community of shared interest to celebrate the school and its pupils' achievements and to ensure its future success through collective fundraising. Primary school graduations have become increasingly common, and are even held at some nurseries. School graduations were not exclusive to private schools, but I was told that the graduations held at government schools were far less lavish affairs. In the same way that middle-class wedding culture had become more commercialized and exclusive, primary school graduations had also become an occasion for marking social distinction.

One Saturday in August 2017 I was invited to attend the primary school graduation of Clara's son. As the chair of the committee for gifts, she had been busy preparing for weeks, attending after-work meetings and WhatsApp exchanges with other parents. The event was organized in the same way as a wedding, with parents forming a series of committees to take responsibility for various elements of the event (food, decorations, gifts, costumes). Each family contributed TSh250,000 (US$112) for the event, which was to be held in the school's walled grounds. The school that Clara's son, Joseph, attended was one of a cluster of private English-medium primary schools located in Mbezi Beach, an established planned middle-class suburb in Kinondoni not far from Salasala. It catered to pre- and primary-school children, some of whom boarded at the school and some of whom were brought in from the surrounding suburbs, including Salasala, by a fleet of yellow school buses. The school occupied a large plot of land, most of which was empty ground currently used for sports; but the school expected to expand in the future and was holding on to this prime spot.

On the day of the graduation, the school courtyard was set up as if for a wedding, with a raised platform and high table in one corner, and facing it, lots of plastic chairs arranged in rows under awnings to keep the sun off the seated children and parents. As we arrived mid-morning I noted that few parents were present, though by early afternoon most of the chairs were taken. The graduands—Grade Seven students who had completed their exams—entered the school courtyard in their school uniforms, dancing in formation to loud bongo flava music, and took their seats in front of the platform, where various dignitaries were seated flanking the headmistress. One of the teachers, taking the role of MC, opened the proceedings and invited the headmistress to the podium. She had a long list of special guests to welcome, including the district education secretary, the ward education secretary, and various other officers from local government and neighboring private secondary schools, including some of the country's best, although none of these invitees were yet present.

We sat through various speeches. The headmistress gave a speech documenting the history of the school, which was established in 2007, and its performance in national examinations. She noted that they had risen up in the national rankings, positioned most recently in the eighties out of over eight thousand schools nationwide, with most students achieving A or B grades. There was much cheering at this news. The headmistress then proceeded to give the results for the last three years, including where the school was ranked and the percentage of students gaining grades A, B, or C.

The Grade Six and Seven students were then invited to perform their goodbyes to each other. They performed rehearsed dances to a number of contemporary hits, both Tanzanian and international (Diamond Platnumz, R. Kelly). One performance had boys and girls wearing kanga; in another spoken word performance, Grade Seven students recited a four-verse poem in English praising the school and the teachers. There then followed a speech by the chair of the School Committee, the theme of which was the rejection of *tamaa* (desire, temptation). He entreated the pupils to follow the example of those who never gave up and eventually succeeded such as Henry Ford, who, he noted, took a long time to make his business successful, and Bill Gates, who dropped out of Harvard but became a successful businessman. He invited the students to ask their parents how they had succeeded. His message was a distillation of the values of aspiration, self-control, and hard work.

It was then time to celebrate the students. Each pupil was called to the stage and presented with a school mug (bought by the gifts committee) and a certificate. This was followed by the prize-giving, in which students were presented with prizes for the best performance in each of the academic subjects, sports, and overall performance. Gifts were then presented to the teachers. After this came the most important part of the day: the fundraising. As two of my companions murmured, this was the whole point of school graduation ceremonies. This one was led by a parent, who explained that the purpose of the fundraising was to improve the security of the school by completing the brick wall that currently ran partly around the open grounds next to the school buildings. Completing the wall would also, of course, secure that ground's enclosure and the school's claim to it. TSh18,000,000 (US$8,076) had already been raised; the goal in today's fundraising was to reach a target of Tsh30,000,000 (US$13,460). Despite the fact that there were only around one hundred parents and family members present, the parent fundraiser did indeed manage this, cajoling other parents over ninety minutes to part with their money for the good of the school. Parent after parent stood up to pledge to the roving microphone five million, one million, or 500,000 shillings. Later in the car on the way home, there was some weariness among my companions about the fundraising. As one relative opined, the school fees are already five million shillings a year, and they ask for more money?

After the fundraising the head boy and head girl cut the impressive graduation cake. This was a confected masterpiece: a sponge cake one meter long and half a meter wide, covered in thick white sugar icing and decorated with the school motto piped in the school's colors, a tablet bearing the names of all the graduating students in piping, and a large book and a mortar board. Once this was done, at around three in the afternoon, all of the guests were invited to the self-service buffet lunch, a huge feast that consisted of high-status foods including pilau, chicken, beef, cooked bananas, potatoes, salads, avocadoes, watermelon, and cake. After people had eaten, they began drifting home at around four o'clock. Some parents had planned private parties in their homes directly after the school ceremony. At Clara's house the family and some uncles, aunts, and cousins were in attendance for a small family gathering to mark Joseph's achievements. Clara's domestic

FIGURE 10. A secondary school graduation cake. Photo by author, August 2017.

worker, who had been working at the house throughout the day while we attended the graduation ceremony, had prepared a large amount of celebratory food. There was also a special graduation cake, commissioned from a local bakery, replete with personalized inscription and sugar icing mortar board.

The private English-medium primary school graduation ceremony provides a new space for the practice of middle-class distinction. Familiar tropes of Tanzanian middle-classness are evident: in the discourse that success is a matter of self-control and hard work, and in the public celebration of the school's achievements in national exams. The new forms of middle-class boundary work practiced at the graduation ceremony—such as the consumption of the professionally baked graduation cake and the presence of headteachers from high-performing secondary schools—locates the private English-medium primary school as a significant node in the archipelago of middle-class sites and services on the suburban frontier.

THE BAR AND THE MEN'S SOCIAL GROUP

On a typical Saturday morning between nine and ten, a dozen members of Wazo Social Group (WSG) could be found doing a step aerobics class on the covered concrete patio of Wazo Bar in full view of the tarmac road that ran through Kilimahewa.[19] WSG hired a personal trainer from one of the upscale hotels in the city center to run the weekly class for them. This was a social group for middle-class men who lived in the neighborhood and who knew each other through extended family and hometown ties, school and professional networks, and neighborly connections. Members were mostly married and were aged between their late thirties and sixties. They worked in the public and private sectors and included among their members civil servants, businessmen, accountants, engineers, export/importers, management consultants, and financial officers. They had all built a house in the neighborhood. Once the exercise class was over, the plastic tables and chairs were pulled back onto the bar's concrete floor, and sodas, beers, and meat soup were served from the bar's kitchen. Some members peeled off to run errands or go to the office while others made plans for the afternoon's socializing. This took place at a bar in another nearby neighborhood, and on this particular day WSG members had been invited by the members of Kunduchi Social Group (KSG) to join them to celebrate the latter's first anniversary as an organized entity. WSG and KSG were two of a series of interconnected men's social groups that included Wazo North Social Group and Morogoro Old Boys, which was a northern Kinondoni branch of the alumni group of a nationally renowned government secondary school. As one man who was a member of both WSG and KSG explained, "We are all friends, neighbors, business partners, relatives . . . All the members of the groups are interlinked."

At the bar that afternoon, KSG members were wearing KSG T-shirts, sitting at clusters of outdoor tables, and socializing with WSG members and girlfriends. The group members drank beer, took turns DJing on the bar's sound system, and talked. Beyond the concrete slab of the bar, the group members' four-by-four-wheel-drive cars were lined up.

WSG was a men's social network, a club, an investment vehicle, a registered company, and an NGO. It was established in 2012 at a time when more houses were being built and inhabited in the neighborhood around Kilimahewa. At that time the area was relatively insecure. There was no local police post (the nearest were in Mtongani, Kawe, Wazo, and Tegeta) and the newly built houses were interspersed with large areas of land covered in trees and grasses. Security was therefore the group members' first priority. As the WSG chairman explained, this was a new area where "80 percent of the people are new residents. We realized we needed something, because we could not depend on government, and security was our first concern. This was a new settlement, and it was vital . . . We made this a calm area, and it even encouraged some people to come back—they had left because of robberies."[20] The focus on security also partly explained the all-male membership. As the chairman explained, in 2012 the area suffered threats from bandits who came to steal during the day when homeowners were at work, apparently even kidnapping servants and killing some homeowners. Local businesses were also routinely targeted. As we saw in chapter 3, the first members of WSG took it upon themselves to patrol their streets at night in their cars and to check who passed along their roads and paths.

The group started in 2011 with around twenty members and had grown to around sixty-five members by 2016, when they applied for NGO status. At first the joining fee was TSh250,000 (US$161) plus a monthly contribution of TSh20,000 (US$13). They then raised the joining fee to TSh500,000 (US$313), and by 2016 it was TSh1,000,000 (US$459). As the chairman explained, they raised the entrance fee to reflect the group's investments and to limit membership to those they deemed had something to offer, or as another member explained, to prevent the group from growing too large and making discipline and coordination difficult. Membership applicants had to have two current members to act as guarantors, and their application forms were passed to a membership committee who decided "whether the person is going to be valuable to us, whether they are credible."[21] The group also contributed to members' wedding and burial obligations, as is common among social groups in Tanzania.

WSG had developed good relations with the local government office in Kilima-hewa, having helped to construct the office buildings "because we need an office to resemble the houses in the area."[22] As another member noted, "We have to help our local government. It's not their fault that they have no money. Say there is one million shillings for a project . . . so it comes to the Regional Commissioner, and then there is this and this and this . . . and when it comes to Salasala there is 200,000 shillings left! We have to help them." The group had hired a caterpillar to level an open sports ground in the neighborhood, repaired roads, and planted over three thousand trees in the streets around members' houses for environ-mental protection and beautification purposes. In so doing, they had improved their immediate environment but could also claim legitimacy by working with local government in order to support the community. Other activities were more tightly focused on the area of Kilimahewa, in which many group members had built their houses rather than spread across the whole neighborhood. As noted in chapter 4, road repairs, particularly after the rainy season, were necessary if people were to continue to be able to drive their cars on local untarmacked roads. As one member noted, WSG members contributed to hire a road grader because "if we wait for government to do it they will never come."[23] The graders were paid to repair the roads on which members lived, rather than the entire neigh-borhood. Another member opined, "We were damaging our cars." Yet the focus on the broader community was a recurrent theme in members' descriptions of the group's work. A third member pointed out, "We want our grandchildren to find roads here. We want a government secondary school because we are a com-munity group, we have to support the community. Those children, if they are successful enough and if they become big, they will be the future members of WSG . . . and we want there to be a hospital. Yes, we use Aga Khan but in your area you have to make sure these things are there."[24]

In 2015 WSG and its members acquired two hundred acres of agricultural land in Bagamoyo Region, sixty-five miles to the northwest of Kilimahewa. The long-term plan was to develop the land for agricultural and residential development. As the chairman explained:

> Someone was selling a small parcel of land [in Bagamoyo], and our Financial and Economic Committee said "Why don't we buy that land?" The seller was selling quickly for an emergency. We discussed on WhatsApp—why don't we go large? Someone said "I know someone who is selling land along the river" . . . so the members agreed, this was an opportunity. We used the group's money to buy the land and members are paying back, for twenty, ten, five, three acres; and there is eighty acres reserved for the group. It's an economic project, for the group and for individuals . . . It's about economies of scale . . . We hired a farmworker. You know Dar es Salaam is growing very fast. In twenty years' time this place will be full and we will be *wazee* [elders]. So we are going to go and live that side. But for now, we use the land as investment *mashamba* [farms]. One member is developing a business plan for modern farming, we will do it together. We have an SUA [Sokoine University of Agriculture] graduate who is looking at the soils. We got our [land] titles two weeks ago. We will have godowns there to keep our produce. The land is along the river so we will have irrigation, we're not depending on rain.[25]

Other members enthusiastically explained their vision for the WSG land in Bagamoyo; one anticipated the residential development would include a shopping center and a nursery as well as individuals' houses: "It will be a WSG village!"[26] Another pointed out, "We have a lot of expertise in the group . . . we have a vision!"

. . .

In private homes and new exclusive social amenities, a distinctive middle-class lifestyle has been taking shape on Dar es Salaam's suburban frontier. Ideas about how and what to build, how to use one's time and money, how to improve the self, how to manage daily life, how to celebrate existing and new lifecycle events, and with whom, are being established in the new neighborhoods and businesses that have been built by and for the middle classes. Liberalization may have benefited the elite,[27] but it has also provided myriad smaller opportunities for the middle classes to invest in land, housing, and new businesses on the suburban frontier that enable their material and cultural reproduction. Yet what is emerging is not quite a middle-class enclave. Middle-class investments and lifestyle practices have produced an archipelago of sites and services across the suburbs, many of which are porous rather than rigidly exclusive.[28] Homes are attended to by domestic workers and sometimes by neighbors, weddings include kin of different social classes, and the bars frequented by WSG are open to the public. What makes these nodes in archipelagic space exclusive is rather the economic and cultural capital necessary to successfully navigate them.

Conclusion

Returning to Salasala in 2022, I was struck by two developments. The first seemed to confirm that Salasala had "arrived": a mall development attached to a ten-storey tower block was under construction along the main tarmac road through Salasala, apparently being built with South African money. It was the tallest structure in Salasala by a considerable margin. Across northern Kinondoni only the private Rabininsia Hospital and the Wazo Hill cement factory, both a few kilometers away in Tegeta, were taller. Within a decade, the retail space along this road had developed from a string of disparate small concrete block "frames" constructed by local residents to rent out to small businesses selling soft drinks, fresh food, and small groceries into a more upscale collection of retail shops and service businesses. Aside from the mall, by 2022 there were two new petrol stations, two large expensive-looking private pharmacies, and several new bars arranged with matching furniture in landscaped gardens that had been built as local investments to serve a more affluent local clientele. The second development suggested something else: that just as Salasala was reaching "peak development," residents were looking for opportunities to buy plots to build houses and small businesses further out, in places that had yet to fully "arrive."

When I arranged to visit Rosemary, who had been living in a rapidly densifying neighborhood in Salasala, she invited me to her newly constructed frames in Mabwepande, ten kilometers to the north of Salasala near the border with neighboring Coast Region. To get there, I took a bus to Tegeta, then switched to a shared bajaj (three-wheel motorized transport), which took me several kilometers along earth roads through a half-built landscape of modest newly constructed houses, pieces of land enclosed by makeshift fence posts, and lots of trees, to a small cluster of local shops, beyond which the road disintegrated into several small paths. From there a motorcycle taxi took me the final kilometer, along a sandy riverbed, to Rosemary's new place. Along the main path through this emerging neighborhood and opposite the only other nearby shop, which sold building materials, Rosemary had constructed a row of five frames. She ran a small grocery business from two of the frames and was in the process of completing the other three for business rentals. She had just moved into a newly constructed, three-bedroom house nearby; the Salasala house was now being rented to tenants. Rosemary explained that it had become too congested there, whereas here in Mabwepande she and her husband had managed to buy the land—from someone who was subdividing a larger piece of land—before prices had started to rise, and there was an opportunity to expand her business as other newcomers arrived. She anticipated that the suburban frontier would come to Mabwepande.

THE MIDDLE CLASSES, PROPERTY, AND THE COLONIALITY OF SPACE

Middle-class formation in Dar es Salaam is driven by the shared class project of constructing the suburban frontier. It is a project of making property, landscape, and lifestyle. In Salasala aspirant house-builders bought plots of land and engaged in various practices to secure them: they erected fences, walls and gates, negotiated boundaries and access paths with neighbors, had their plots surveyed, attempted to navigate government bureaucracy to obtain land titles, and contested pieces of land in the local courts. These house-builders accelerated the long, slow process of dispossessing Zaramo farmers through the market that had begun in the 1980s. They transformed the formerly periurban zone that had been dominated by small-scale farms and shifting cultivators into a desirable residential landscape characterized by relatively low-density buildings with sufficient space for a three-bedroom house and a yard for infrastructure such as a water storage tank or a well, a septic tank and soak pit, equipment such as a pickup or a home-based enterprise such as rearing livestock, or a small shop. This shared class project was not only driven by dispossession, commodification, and enclosure on the city's former periurban fringe: it was also an aesthetic project in which ideas about desirable urban space and who deserved to live where in the city were put into practice. The suburban ideal in and around Salasala was to build differently from *uswahilini*, which the middle classes saw as a place of cramped living quarters, constant noise, and a lack of privacy. On the suburban frontier, the middle classes could build what they considered to be good-quality houses, even if most of the streets in Salasala lacked state-provided paving, piped water, electricity, and sanitation. These were not the big, ostentatious houses of the elite, but they were large enough to be distinguished from the homes of the poor.

Modest houses were designed as a variation on the bungalow model, which had been the architectural basis of most residential buildings constructed with permanent materials since the colonial period, and distinguished by the incorporation of new architectural features and modern materials. They were built with imported reflective glass windows or expensive, locally made hardwood window frames, colored roofing sheets, imported decorative tiles, and domestically produced paints, and internally furnished with a carefully curated mix of locally made and imported furniture and soft furnishings that nodded to a globalized middle-class aesthetic. Beyond their homes, the middle classes invested in small local businesses to suit their tastes and lifestyles. Bars, hair and nail salons, and shops selling livestock feed, fresh food, and groceries lined the main streets through the suburbs, punctuated by a new church or mosque, an English-medium primary school or nursery, or a private-hire hall, creating an archipelago of middle-class sites and services held together on the suburban frontier by the private car. The suburban frontier became a place of middle-class formation where material and cultural capital could be slowly accumulated.

In foregrounding property as material and cultural capital, this book has developed an approach to understanding Africa's middle classes that pays attention to the multidimensional nature of social class. Such an approach takes seriously the new aspirations and experiences, as well as the cultural politics and modes of wealth creation that characterize this emerging social group.[1] Middle-class formation on Dar es Salaam's suburban frontier has gone hand-in-hand with the making of property as land has been commodified and enclosed, houses have been built, and landscapes and lifestyles have taken shape. As they have fenced in their plots, installed gates and grilles, and invested in a landscape that meets their aesthetic aspirations, suburban house-builders have developed a distinctive repertoire of property-based class practices that have mutually constituted the suburban frontier *and* the middle class.

As scholars of property Nick Blomley and Carol Rose have pointed out, property is material, spatial, and social, and requires constant work.[2] In Dar es Salaam this work is similar to the shared "state of mind" that E. P. Thompson identified as the driving force behind the ruling classes' introduction of the Black Act in early eighteenth-century England.[3] Thompson demonstrated that a shared disposition towards property and the law developed among the English ruling class in response to relatively minor threats to their private property from villagers and foresters who claimed agrarian use-rights. The move to protect private property inscribed in the Black Act of 1723 served to dignify the violence of class struggle. In Dar es Salaam, the middle classes have developed a similar disposition towards the property and the landscape they have constructed. This shared "state of mind" in relation to property and landscape channels their class anxieties in apparently neutral ways—"this place will become congested"—rather than in terms that are explicitly exclusionary or violent towards the urban poor. It is true that there is a difference in the class interests that are being protected in these two cases, for the houses and landscapes of the middle classes in contemporary Dar es Salaam are not equivalent to the properties of the landed gentry in early eighteenth-century England. The land on which the houses were built in Dar es Salaam is a store of value that can be used as savings, income, speculation, or inheritance, but the houses themselves currently have little exchange value, as most people build rather than buy, not least because of the lack, or undesirability, of affordable credit. In addition, houses are not widely used to leverage formal finance due to a combination of the lack of formal property titles and affordable finance options, and a widespread unwillingness to risk a significant asset by using it as collateral. Yet in both cases property held aesthetic value that was central to class positions, and that value was perceived as under threat from class others. In Dar es Salaam, middle-classness was partly characterized by the anxiety that the aesthetic value of the houses and landscapes that had been constructed would be diminished if land continued to be subdivided into smaller plots and sold to lower-income urbanites. The fear of *uswahilini*, of densely arranged, lower-quality housing, was widespread among the middle classes. The property of the suburban frontier—the self-built houses and landscapes that have been explored in this book—is a store of aesthetic value that is central to classed relations on the suburban frontier.

The value judgments attached to different kinds of built environment in Dar es Salaam are a symptom of the coloniality of space. The syntax of the postcolonial city, the coloniality of space, is a mode of making space that draws on and reworks colonial forms of building, imagining, and living in the built environment. The coloniality of space has been assembled by colonial and postcolonial governments and urban dwellers over decades as ideas accrete about who belongs where in the city even though the city itself has changed. This is not to suggest that space is in some way ossified, forever trapped by its colonial enframing, but rather to draw attention to the way that many urban residents continue to make sense of social differentiation in urban space in part through reference to the colonial past.[4] The coloniality of space throws light on the dynamics of urban space as it is made and experienced by the middle classes on the suburban frontier who are anxious to maintain social and spatial distance from the urban poor. This was the very purpose of the original suburbs built by and for Europeans during the colonial period. In the contemporary city the coloniality of space is evident in the choices that the middle classes make about where to live in the city, in ideas about what a good house looks like, in the continued salience of *uzunguni* and *uswahilini* to refer to rich and poor neighborhoods respectively, and the increasing exclusivity of venues for leisure and celebration. It is also evident in the continued uncertainty over land tenure on the suburban frontier, where the apparently neat colonial bifurcation between native/rural/customary and nonnative/urban/statutory broke down long ago as the city grew into its former hinterland and the state failed to clarify the nature of land tenure there. The coloniality of space is therefore central to the contemporary middle-class urban experience—in both shaping the conditions in which many middle-class urbanites were able to access urban land and also condemning that land to insecurity. It also goes straight to the central con-tradiction at the heart of middle-class construction on the suburban frontier, for the porosity of land and landscape there threatens its very existence. The middle classes are, in effect, victims of their own success, since their investment in land and housing on the suburban frontier has made it a more attractive place for other aspiring house-builders. That has increased congestion and reduced exclusivity. The middle classes will move on, and the suburban frontier will move with them.

THE MIDDLE CLASSES AND THE STATE IN TANZANIA

Across much of Africa, a large proportion of the middle classes are state employ-ees.[5] This is true in Tanzania, although not all middle classes are employed by the state, and neither are all state employees middle class. Yet the conditions for mid-dle-class formation have been created by the state. State employees have received salaries, perquisites, allowances, and (some access to) subsidized housing, during the colonial, socialist, and the postsocialist periods. Others made the most of their social relations, knowledge, and other opportunities to tap state or other resources in order to improve their living conditions. The fruits of these efforts have been particularly evident in the case of property. While many urbanites—not only the middle classes—took part in the slow enclosure of periurban land on the sub-urban frontier in the wake of the state *ujamaa* and food production campaigns of the 1970s and 1980s, the middle classes and the elite were better placed to capitalize on the ambiguous nature of postcolonial periurban land tenure as land com-modification accelerated after the 1990s. They were also instrumental in extend-ing the party-state to the suburban frontier, establishing branches of the CCM and acting as *balozi* (the ten-cell leaders) and, after the shift to multipartyism in the mid-1990s, subward governments. They benefited from the wider circulation of cash in the economy under presidents Mwinyi, Mkapa, and Kikwete. While much attention has rightly focused on the ways in which the country's postcolo-nial political and economic elite have availed themselves of the resources of the state in "grand corruption" schemes,[6] "the state" nevertheless encompasses a wide range of people who do very different kinds of work across different "scales."[7] As Jon Schubert has noted in Angola, many people developed their own ways of "working the system."[8] Constructing middle-classness on the suburban frontier has been a project of slow, quiet accumulation of material and cultural assets in a contradictory context where the state has both enabled and disavowed middle-class formation over decades.

In contrast to middle-class formation in countries such as Angola, India, Mozambique, and South Africa,[9] the Tanzanian state has never publicly champi-oned the middle classes as ideal national citizens, even if they embody national visions of progress such as those embedded in the Tanzania Development Vision 2025.[10] During the socialist period the state actively sought to undermine them, and the same could be said for the recent government of John Magufuli (2015–21). In the postsocialist period, the middle classes have been mostly invisible, unnamed in official government discourse or policy programming, and uncelebrated when the country ascended to the World Bank income classification of Lower Middle Income status in July 2020. As one commentator opined, the middle class in Tanzania has had to "fend for itself" in a postsocialist country that has not fully turned its back on its socialist past.[11]

The state's ambivalence towards the middle class was particularly evident during the presidency of John Magufuli, who styled himself after Nyerere as the defender of the nation's poor and downtrodden against a cast of exploiters, both domestic and foreign. National development was now to be pursued via state investment in large infrastructure projects and factories, and the middle classes were expected to play their part by contributing to the domestic tax base. His public pronouncements excoriated the lifestyle and consumption habits of the elite and he pursued those accused of "grand corruption" in the courts, to much public satisfaction. But he also targeted mid-level government officials whose petty corruption was castigated for hampering national progress and frustrating ordinary citizens. Many were fired, as for example in land administration, but he also cut public servants' allowances and clamped down on absenteeism and various kinds of fraud (including, for example, relating to educational credentials). Magufuli's tenure heralded a new political economic landscape for the middle classes in which business, property, and land taxes were aggressively pursued and government workers came under significant scrutiny. Many opined that money was "not circulating" or that democratic space was shrinking; or they viewed Magufuli's economic and political program as parochial or antibusiness; but most just wanted things to go back to the conditions of the Kikwete period when they were left alone to pursue their various *miradi* ("projects"). All the while, houses continued to be built on the suburban frontier during Magufuli's presidency and the government launched a drive across the country to encourage people to formalize their land ownership, including on the suburban frontier, where the coloniality of space had long rendered tenurial rights uncertain. Middle-class formation did not come to a halt during the Magufuli era, even if the middle classes had to lie low for a while in order not to draw too much attention to themselves. Hidden in plain sight, their houses on the suburban frontier announced middle-class formation even while they did not seem to officially exist.

In this context the middle classes have quietly positioned themselves as the bearers of legitimate culture sandwiched between what they consider to be a parasitic and immoral elite, who are thought to accumulate wealth through dubious means, and the uneducated poor, who are cast as the subjects of "development."[12] The middle classes see themselves as having earned their position through a combination of hard work and education, despite the fact that the structural barriers to education success in Tanzania are substantial.[13] Earlier modes of class distinction continue to reverberate in the present. The connection between education and cultural capital has existed since the colonial period, when an emerging elite, most of whom came from up-country Christian areas and had been to mission or government schools, considered themselves natural leaders on the national stage.[14] The reference to hard work is also a familiar claim to legitimate national, and urban, citizenship from the socialist period. It distances the middle classes from the accusation of exploitation, particularly via the labor of others. In the contemporary period the middle classes consider their social and economic position as the legitimate reward for their educational success, personal capacity for industry, and skill in making the most of available opportunities, while the poor are considered to suffer from a lack of education, or the wrong "mindset."[15] These classed relations can be witnessed in multiple settings from the development workshop in which middle-class NGO workers proceed with a natural right to instruct the poor on "development" to everyday interactions in which those lower down the social hierarchy wait for instructions to run errands or undertake labor for those higher up, often for the latter's income generation projects.[16] The flipside is that the nature of these social relations means that there are multiple claims on the incomes of the middle classes, and the redistribution of cash through kin and other social relationships is part of everyday life.[17]

URBAN ACCRETION IN "CITIES OF CASH"

Cities accrete.[18] Their built form takes shape slowly over time as urban residents, businesses, governments, investors and many others construct them piece by piece. This book has shown that the South African shopping mall and Rosemary's shop frames were among the most recent developments on Dar es Salaam's northern suburban frontier in a long period of slow transformation stretching back to at least the late nineteenth century. Since then, the land in and around Salasala was settled by Zaramo shifting cultivators and then Shomvi and Arab plantations; it was alienated by colonial powers and then sold to Greek plantation owners; it was nationalized and then cleared of subsistence cultivators during the *ujamaa* campaign of the postcolonial state; and most recently it has been enclosed, commodified, subdivided, and built on by urbanites who have transformed the landscape into a frontier of middle-class suburban living.

This book has proposed a way of thinking of the city as an accretion of land and property that is produced in a dialectical relationship with society—the suburb and the middle classes construct each other. As a particular form of urban accretion, the suburban frontier captures one dynamic of contemporary social and spatial change in postcolonial cities where the majority of urban residents build their own houses. The suburban frontier is a dynamic zone created by layers of dispossession, commodification, risk, aspiration, construction, experimentation, and accumulation. As the middle classes have acquired land and built houses, landscapes, and lifestyles, the suburban frontier has emerged as *the* place where the middle classes are shaped. We need to look more closely at how urban residents are investing in their cities and beyond, to better understand how social class is spatially reproduced in contemporary Africa.

Domestic investment on Dar es Salaam's suburban frontier may not match universalized assumptions about what counts as productive property, value, or surplus, and putting cash into urban property may not offer much in terms of capital accumulation. In economies dominated by cash, land and houses are important stores of material and aesthetic value. Urban residents' investments in land and housing drive opportunities for land value capture and urban rents in African cities.[19] My aim in this book has been to demonstrate the social and spatial significance of the small, yet widely repeated, investments of the middle classes, which mostly take place outside of global circuits of finance capital as cash is put directly into property. As Jane Guyer and Sara Berry have shown in West Africa, everyday cash transactions and domestic investments in houses, cocoa farms, and teak trees reap "marginal gains" over time and drive social class formation.[20]

This does not mean that African cities and their residents exist outside of global financial markets. The ways in which different financial circuits and systems are interconnected in people's everyday lives would repay further research.[21] Some money that goes into housing comes from remittances that might be sent as cash or through a money transfer operator or mobile money app,[22] though this is not yet a major contributor to the financial landscape in Dar es Salaam.[23] Better understanding the dynamics of urban land is key. The "land grab" literature in Africa has made a recent welcome urban turn and has drawn attention to large-scale investments of elite and international capital in African cities.[24] There have been a few such developments in Dar es Salaam, such as the (now stalled) gated communities at Dege Village and Kawe, though compared to other cities Dar es Salaam has yet to become a favored site for gated community developments.[25] But there is much to learn about how Africa's urban residents are themselves investing in cities, intermediate towns, and rural areas in less immediately visible but no less significant ways.[26]

The most common use of land in African towns and cities is for housing. Yet the question of how most housing is produced in urban Africa has fallen off most governments' and researchers' agendas. In Accra, Addis Ababa, Kigali, and Lagos, international companies and elite members of the diaspora have invested in high-end real estate, or are building "world class" city appendages.[27] In Addis Ababa and Luanda, governments have decided to redesign urban living space or to tackle the housing crisis from the supply side. Yet in most urban areas across the continent, urban residents fashion their own living space.[28] The majority of urban residents make urban space through the everyday practices of saving, building, investing, and renting. This is a form of urban space-making that is small-scale and cash-based, yet widely repeated across time and space. As I have shown for

Dar es Salaam's middle classes in this book, they acquire, buy, occupy, use, enclose, or lend land, and they build, rent, extend, and improve their domestic space. In so doing the middle classes make property, raise land values, produce rental opportunities, and slowly accumulate material and cultural assets that reproduce middle-classness. In the process, they make urban space that works for them.

GLOSSARY OF SWAHILI WORDS

amani	peace
balozi	ten-household cell leader
bodaboda	motorcycle taxi
bomoa	demolish
bwanyenye	bourgeoisie
dalali (sg.; madalali pl.)	broker
duka	shop
deiwaka	day laborer
hapa kazi tu	only work here
kabwela	exploited poor person
Kila mtu afanye kazi	Every Able-Bodied Person Must Work (a government campaign)
kiongozi wa wanyonge	leader of the downtrodden
kipindi cha Magufuli	the Magufuli era
kuku wa kisasa	Broilers (chickens)
Kilimo cha kufa na kupona	Farming for Survival (a government campaign)
kiwanja (sg.; viwanja pl.)	plot of land
kupika data	to cook data
kutumbua majipu	to burst the boils
mtaa (sg,; pl mitaa)	subward
mapazi	Zaramo leaders

makupe	ticks
makabaila	landlords
maendeleo	development
maeneo yasiopangwa	unplanned areas
makazi yasio rasmi	unofficial residences or residential areas
matajiri	rich people
mazagazaga	haphazard
mradi (sg.; miradi pl.)	project
mageuzi	reforms
miguu	legs or steps/strides
mjumbe (sg.; wajumbe pl.)	representative member of subward governments
mlinzi	guard or caretaker
mzee (sg.; wazee pl.)	male elder
Nguvu kazi	Labour (a government campaign)
njaa	hunger
naizisheni	nationalization
naizi	shortened version of naizisheni
nyumba hii haiuzwi	this house is not for sale
nyumba nzuri	a good house
ogopa matapeli	beware conmen
ondoa	remove
ovyo	disorderly, reckless, or valueless
pori	wilderness or scrub land
pombe	alcohol
simama	stop
shamba	farm
serikali ya mtaa	subward government
sungusungu	community police
tamaa	desire, temptation
ukumbi	private hire hall
ulinzi shirikishi	participatory policing
upendo	love
uwezo	capacity, capability, authority or power
uhindini	the place of the Indian
uswahilini	the place of the Swahili or African
uzunguni	the place of the European

uzaramo	the place of the Zaramo
ujamaa	literally "familyhood"; also the cornerstone of Julius Nyerere's approach to African socialism based on collective villagization
vigogo	a euphemism for the elite (lit. tree trunks)
wakubwa	big shots
wanyonge	the oppressed
wabenzi	a euphemism for the elite (lit. those who drive Mercedes Benz)
walalahoi	a euphemism for the poor (lit. those who sleep heavily after hard labor)
ushenzi	uncivilized
wafanyakazi	workers
wahuni	un- and underemployed people in urban areas
wakulima	farmers
wananchi	citizens
wanyonyaji	exploiters
wavamizi	invaders (of land; occupiers)

NOTES

INTRODUCTION: MIDDLE-CLASS CONSTRUCTION ON DAR ES SALAAM'S SUBURBAN FRONTIER

1. Six a.m. is *saa kumi na mbili*, or twelve in the morning, in Swahili time, but I am using English time here for ease of understanding.

2. Mwamfupe 1994.

3. Fishman 1987.

4. Soja 1980; Lefebvre 1991; Massey 1994; Harvey 2006; Sheppard 2008; Hart 2018.

5. Keil 2018.

6. UNDESA 2019.

7. Rao et al. 2010: 28.

8. Andreasen 2013.

9. Gough et al. 2003.

10. Meth et al. 2021.

11. Roy 2003; Holston 2008; Perlman 2010; Sawyer 2014; Caldeira 2017; Simone 2019; Karaman et al. 2020; Streule et al. 2020; Massive Urbanisation Collective 2020.

12. Simone 2004.

13. Kombe and Kreibich 2010; Napier et al. 2013; Landau 2017; C. Marx 2020.

14. Watson 2013; Steel et al. 2017; Gillespie 2020; Goodfellow 2022.

15. Rakodi and Leduka 2003; A. Lupala 2002; Jenkins 2013; de Boeck and Baloji 2016; Elliot 2016.

16. Roy 2015; Harms 2016; Levien 2018; Ghertner 2020; Lund 2021; Cowan 2023.

17. Berry 2002, 2009; Peters 2004, 2009; Chimhowu and Woodhouse 2006; Boone 2007; Sikor and Lund 2009; B. White et al. 2012; Lund and Boone 2013; Murray Li 2014; Greco 2015; Lund 2016; Chimhowu 2019; Sunjo and Page 2022.

18. Myers 2003; Freund 2007.

19. T. Mitchell 1991.

20. Fanon 1963; wa Thiong'o 1986; Njoh 2008; Quayson 2014; Bhandar 2018; Kimari 2021.

21. On other modes of space-making, see L. White 1986; Myers 2003; de Boeck and Plissart 2004; Simone 2004. On the persistence of the colonial, see Quijano 2000; Stoler 2008; Ndlovu-Gatsheni 2013; Chitonge 2019.

22. Burton 2005.

23. Lugalla 1989; Degani 2022.

24. Smiley 2009.

25. Brennan 2012.

26. Kironde 1991; Simson 2020.

27. Lugalla 1989: 187.

28. *Ujamaa*, the translation of which from Swahili means "familyhood," was the cornerstone of Julius Nyerere's approach to "African socialism." It was a strategy for postindependence nation-building and development, in which *ujamaa vijijini*, or collective villagization, would become the basis of rural agricultural production and governance (Chachage and Cassam 2010; Schneider 2014; Lal 2015).

29. Swantz 1996.

30. G. Owens 2010.

31. Briggs and Mwamfupe 2000.

32. Murray Li 2014; Tsing 2004; Watts 2018.

33. Yiftachel 2009.

34. Ghertner 2015; Archambault 2018; Gastrow 2020; Sumich and Nielsen 2020; Page and Sunjo 2018; Page 2019.

35. Kopytoff 1989; de Boeck 2000; Cons and Eilenberg 2019; Auerbach 2020.

36. Ncube et al. 2011.

37. Ncube and Lufumpa 2015.

38. Ncube et al. 2011. They also estimated that 87.6 percent of the population of Tanzania fell into the "poor class." This would suggest that 0.3 percent of the population falls into their "rich class" category (with a daily per capita expenditure over US$20).

39. URT 2019.

40. Chande 2021.

41. The national basic needs poverty line in 2018 was TSh49,320 per adult per month. The national food poverty line in 2018 was TSh33,748 (Ministry of Finance and Planning, 2019).

42. Rizzo 2017.

43. World Bank 2019.

44. Ministry of Finance and Planning 2019.

45. Green 2017; Brockington 2019; Ponte and Brockington 2020; Howland et al. 2021.

46. Ministry of Finance and Planning 2020.

47. World Bank 2016.

48. National Bureau of Statistics 2014a.

49. Jayne et al. 2016.

50. Banerjee and Duflo 2008; Birdsall 2010; Shimeles and Ncube 2015; Resnick 2015; Therborn 2020; Lentz 2015, Melber 2016; Kroeker et al. 2018; Sumich 2018.

51. Kalb 2015; Melber 2016; Southall 2016, 2018; Darbon 2018; Neubert 2019.

52. TANU (Tanganyika African National Union) came to power in the first free elections in 1961. In 1976 it merged with the Zanzibari Afro-Shirazi Party to become the *Chama Cha Mapinduzi* (Party of the Revolution). Between 1965 and 1995 Tanzania was a one-party state. CCM has won every multiparty election to date since 1995.

53. Shivji 1976, 1986; Hydén 1980; Chachage 1986; Aminzade 2013; Coulson 2013; Lofchie 2014; Gray 2015; Kelsall 2018.

54. Cliffe 1977; Raikes 1978; Samoff 1979a.

55. Coulson 2013.

56. Iliffe 1979: 387.

57. Molohan 1959: 49, in Brennan and Burton 2007: 44.

58. Rodney 2022.

59. Shivji 1976.

60. Simson 2020.

61. Kironde 1994; Brennan 2012.

62. Brennan 2012: 9.

63. von Freyhold 1977; Ivaska 2011.

64. Callaci 2017.

65. Lewinson 2006.

66. Simson 2020.

67. Lugalla 1995.

68. Kombe and Kreibich 2000; Moyer 2003: 49; Degani 2022.

69. Moyer 2003: 61.

70. Moyer 2003; Sanders 2008.

71. Mercer 2002; Sheuya 2007; Green 2017; Brockington 2019.

72. Edmondson 2007: 44.

73. Mercer and Green 2013; Green 2021.

74. Employment here means paid employees, self-employed persons, and unpaid family workers in family businesses (National Bureau of Statistics 2022).

75. National Bureau of Statistics 2022; see also Rizzo 2017.

76. K. Marx (1867) 1977, (1885) 1978, (1894) 1981; Weber (1922) 1978; Bourdieu (1984) 2010.

77. Thompson 1963: 8.

78. Liechty 2003; Fernandes 2006; Zhang 2010; López and Weinstein 2012; Spronk 2012, 2014; Fehérváry 2013; Freeman 2014; Heiman 2015; Noret 2020; Dejung et al. 2019.

79. Heiman et al. 2012.

80. Bourdieu (1984) 2010; Skeggs 2004.

81. West 2002; Budniok and Noll 2018; Spronk 2020; Lentz and Noll 2021.

82. Liechty 2012: 274; Spronk 2020: 471.

83. Comaroff and Comaroff 1990; Juul and Lund 2002.

84. Berry 1985; Peters 2004. On the land question in Africa see Kitching 1980; Moyo 1995; Mafeje 2003.

85. Lund 2002; Sikor and Lund 2009; Boone 2014; Hammar 2017; Bolt 2021.

86. Mabandla 2013.

87. Ndjio 2009; Page 2019; Durham 2020; Gastrow 2020.

88. Bhandar 2018: 2.

89. Njoh 2008.

90. Myers 2003.

91. Blomley 2004.

92. Thompson 1975: 197.

93. *Mitaa* translates as "streets," lower local government administrative territories in urban areas.

94. Manara 2022; Manara and Pani 2023.

95. T. Mitchell 1991.

1. GROUNDWORK: THE COLONIALITY OF SPACE

1. Brennan 2018: 47.

2. There is a longer history to urban property on the Swahili coast, particularly at Pangani (Glassman 1995) and Bagamoyo (Fabian 2019). A discussion of the continent-wide history of property-making beyond the colonial period is beyond the scope of this chapter.

3. Njoh 2004, 2008; Freund 2007; Home 2013; Coquery-Vidrovitch 2014.

4. Cooper 1987; Myers 1993; Penvenne 1995; Konadu-Agyemang 2001; Hay and Harris 2007; Dalberto et al. 2013; Beeckmans and Lagae 2015.

5. G. Owens 2004.

6. G. Owens 2004; Bryceson 2009.

7. Glassman 1995: 40.

8. Glassman 1995; G. Owens 2004; Fabian 2019.

9. Bryceson 2009; G. Owens 2004.

10. G. Owens 2004.

11. URT 1994; Shivji 1998.

12. URT 1994.

13. *Native* was a German legal category that included Africans, Arabs, and Indians. During the British colonial period, *native* generally meant African, while the new term *nonnative* generally referred to Indian and European settlers. The British administration did not provide a constitutional definition of who was a native, preferring to deal with individual cases on the basis of descent or social class (Brennan 2012). I use *native* and *nonnative* here according to their use in sources to avoid confusion. For example, a discussion of "nonnative" landlords might relate to European, Indian, or in some cases Arab individuals: since it is not always possible to know the individuals concerned in each case, I have opted to remain with the colonial terminology.

14. At the end of the German colonial period, 1,300,000 acres (equivalent to 0.5 percent of the landmass) were held in freehold mostly by settlers, concentrated in areas where some of the most valuable land in the country was located (Tanga, Lushoto, Kilimanjaro, and Meru; R. James 1971). On native urban property see Kironde 1994; Shivji 1998.

15. Kironde 1994.

16. Fimbo 1992; R. James 1971; Kironde 1994.

17. Kironde 1994.

18. Brennan 2012.

19. G. Owens 2004.

20. Brennan 2012.

21. Brennan 2012: 43.

22. URT 1994.

23. G. Owens 2004.

24. Following the First World War, the League of Nations placed Tanganyika under British mandate.

25. Tanganyika 1923: 2.

26. Kironde 1994; Ally 2015.

27. Mamdani 1996.

28. Iliffe 1979.

29. Burton 2005.

30. R. James 1971; Fimbo 1992.

31. Kironde 1994.

32. Kironde 1994; Burton 2005.

33. Brennan and Burton 2007.

34. Burton 2005; Brennan 2012.

35. Burton 2005.

36. Brennan 2012.

37. Burton 2005.

38. Bryceson 1985.

39. Burton 2005.

40. Burton 2005.

41. Burton 2005.

42. Kironde 1994.

43. Brennan 2012.

44. Burton 2005; Kironde 1994.

45. Burton 2005: 68.

46. Iliffe 1979; Brennan and Burton 2007.

47. Brennan 2012.

48. Burton 2005.

49. Cooper 1983; Brownell 2020.

50. Kironde 1994.

51. Iliffe 1979.

52. Hunter 2019.

53. Coulson 2013.

54. Iliffe 1979.

55. Iliffe 1979: 267–68.

56. Iliffe 1979.

57. Fair 2018.

58. Burton 2005.

59. Hunter 2019.

60. Mbilinyi 1985: 94.

61. Kironde 1994.

62. Major items of expenditure included water supply (£3.5 million), European housing (£3 million), railways and ports (£2 million) the new airport (£880,000), a hospital (£690,000), a central sewage system (£450,000), a technical college (£280,000), a medical

training center (£190,000), roads and surface drainage (£140,000), industrial site development (£100,000), and antimalarial drainage of Msimbazi Creek (£40,000). Kironde 1994.

63. Kironde 1994.

64. Molohan 1959.

65. Kironde 1994.

66. Leslie 1963; Iliffe 1979.

67. Kironde 1994.

68. Brennan 2012.

69. Leslie 1963.

70. Iliffe 1979: 387.

71. Unless they have obtained a CRO (Certificate of Right of Occupancy) as part of a regularization scheme in recent years; see chapter 3.

72. Kironde 1994.

73. McCleery 1939; Brennan 2012.

74. Shivji 1976.

75. Tanganyika and Zanzibar united in 1964 to form the United Republic of Tanzania.

76. URT 1994.

77. In a series of writings in which he developed his ideas about African socialism, Tanzania's first president, Julius Nyerere, resisted recommendations to adopt a freehold tenure system similar to that which had been introduced in Kenya on the grounds that it would constrain the government's ability to control land, would likely lead to great inequality in landholdings, and reduce the majority of the population to tenants (Nyerere 1967).

78. Gastorn 2010.

79. Gray 2018.

80. Shivji 1976; Coulson 2013; Gray 2018.

81. Gray 2018.

82. Coulson 2013; Eckert 2014.

83. Samoff 1979b; Lofchie 2014.

84. South Africa had around seventy segregated drive-in cinemas by the 1960s. Kenya had a drive-in from the 1950s, Uganda's opened just before Tanzania did, and by the late 1970s Namibia, Zambia, and Rhodesia had also opened drive-in cinemas (Fair 2018).

85. Fair 2018.

86. Fair 2018: 234.

87. Brownell 2020.

88. Fair 2018: 234.

89. Grace 2021.

90. Brownell 2020.

91. Nyerere 1968.

92. Brennan 2012.

93. Jennings 2003; Ivaska 2011.

94. Brennan 2012.

95. Ivaska 2011; Brennan 2012.

96. Brennan 2012; Brownell 2020.

97. Nyerere 1962; Pratt 1976.

98. Tripp 1997.

99. Brennan 2012.

100. Brennan 2012.

101. Green 2014; Callaci 2017.

102. Lewinson 2006; Ivaska 2011; Callaci 2017.

103. Kironde 1994.

104. Myers 1993: 404.

105. If a six-room Swahili house cost around TSh10,000 to build in the mid-1970s (Burton 2007), the Revolving Loan Fund was loaning on average seven times that per borrower; Kironde 1994.

106. Kironde 1994.

107. Kironde 1994; Brownell 2020.

108. Stren 1975a.

109. Kironde 1994.

110. Burton 2007.

111. Kironde 1991.

112. Stren 1982.

113. Kironde 1994.

114. Stren 1975b.

115. Brownell (2020) notes that the lack of available good quality housing led some of Dar es Salaam's factories to provide housing to employees, and at others employees started housing cooperatives.

116. Brownell 2020.

117. Stren 1975a.

118. Stren 1982: 80.

119. Mgullu 1978, in Stren 1982: 82.

120. Stren 1982.

121. Stren 1975a: 47.

122. Burton 2007.

123. Burton 2007: 131.

124. Kironde 1994.

125. Kironde 1994: 368.

126. Kironde 1994.

127. Havnevik 1993; Tripp 1997.

128. Lal 2015.

129. Havnevik 1993; Dar es Salaam's experience is discussed in chapter 2.

130. Havnevik 1993.

131. Tripp 1997.

132. Bryceson 1985.

133. Mwamfupe 1994.

134. Lugalla 1989.

135. Lofchie 2014.

136. Bryceson 1985.

137. Kironde 1994: 325.

138. Armstrong 1986.

139. Brownell 2020.

2. THE SUBURBAN FRONTIER

1. Campbell and Stein 1992; Gibbon 1995; Ponte 2002; Shivji 2006; Weiss 2009.

2. Kelsall 2002; Degani 2022.

3. Tripp 1997.

4. Dar es Salaam City Council had only a third of the two hundred surveying staff it required in 1992 (Kombe and Kreibich 2000).

5. Lugalla 1989; Kironde 1997; Kombe and Kreibich 2000.

6. URT 1994.

7. Kombe 1995: 66, in Kombe and Kreibich 2000: 21.

8. Msangi 2011, 2014; Ally 2015.

9. Gastorn 2010.

10. Yiftachel 2009.

11. The new legislation consisted of the Land Act of 1999 pertaining to general lands and land administration, the Village Land Act of 1999 pertaining to village lands, and the Land Disputes Courts Act of 2002.

12. Tenga and Mramba 2015.

13. Stein and Askew (2009) point out that despite the legal recognition of villagers' land rights in domestic legislation donors have nevertheless pushed formal individual land titling.

14. Burton 2005.

15. Brownell 2020.

16. Brownell 2020.

17. Molohan 1959; Leslie 1963.

18. Swantz 1996.

19. Kironde 1994. The villages included Boko Maji, Kigamboni, Kunduchi, Kunduchi Mtongani, Mabibo Kidete, Mbagala, Mbezi Juu, Mtoni Kijichi, Radio Tanzania, Segerea, Tabata, Tegeta, Ununio, Wazo Hill, and Yombo Vituka.

20. Government circular no. 4 of 1953, in Fimbo 1992: 78.

21. Fimbo 1992; URT 1994.

22. A. Lupala 2002; Kombe and Kreibich 2006.

23. Fimbo 1992; URT 1994.

24. G. Owens 2004.

25. Mwamfupe 1994; A. Lupala 2002; Brownell 2020.

26. Swantz 1996.

27. McCleery 1939.

28. Kombe and Kreibich 2000.

29. Msangi 2014.

30. Swantz 1996; G. Owens 2004.

31. Chimhowu and Woodhouse 2006.

32. Lugalla 1989.

33. Tripp 1997.

34. Mwamfupe 1994; Swantz 1996; G. Owens 2004.

35. Kombe and Kriebich 2000: 67.

36. G. Owens 2004: 240.

37. Mwamfupe 1994.

38. Kombe 2005.

39. Msangi 2014.

40. A. Lupala 2002.

41. Msangi 2014.

42. Msangi 2014.

43. Mwamfupe 1994.

44. Sheuya 2007, 2009.

45. Mwamfupe 1994.

46. Kombe and Kreibich 2000.

47. Briggs and Mwamfupe 2000.

48. G. Owens 2010.

49. Mwamfupe 1994.

50. A. Lupala (2002). The minimum salary was TSh30,000 per month; the average income in Lupala's survey was TSh125,050.

51. Kombe 1995; A. Lupala 2002.

52. The subward chair is a voluntary post. They are elected in nationally organized elections on a party political ticket. They are responsible for local administrative issues, including chairing the subward assembly, and they represent their subward to the ward council. Below the chairperson are the *wajumbe*, who represent a group of households (up to the hundreds) within the subward.

53. Mwamfupe 1994; Kombe 1995; Kombe and Kreibich 2000; A. Lupala 2002.

54. Kombe and Kreibich 2000: 33.

55. URT 1981.

56. Swantz 1996; G. Owens 2004.

57. The *balozi* position originated in the ten-cell unit under the single party system, in which one *balozi* per ten households connected the mass of the population to the party hierarchy. Since the shift to multipartyism in the early 1990s, the position of *balozi* has been replaced by the *mjumbe* (sg.; *wajumbe* pl.), who represents neighborhoods in subwards. They are elected positions on party political tickets. In everyday parlance people tend to use *balozi* and *mjumbe* interchangeably. These days the *balozi/mjumbe* in urban areas can have hundreds of households in their neighborhood. In Salasala, eight or nine of them were supposed to work with the subward office on everyday urban governance issues such as government directives (e.g., around ID card registration, rubbish disposal) and land disputes, among other things. The extent to which they were active in these roles varied between individuals.

58. At the time, the Salasala area was administered from Mtongani village; subwards came later.

59. Interview, Kilimahewa, April 8, 2016.

60. The population of Kunduchi Rural Ward in 1978, which consisted of the villages of Mtongani, Tegeta, Kunduchi Pwani (containing Salasala), Ununio, and "Institution," was 11,761; by 1988 it had doubled in size to 22,743 (URT 1981; Kironde 1994).

61. Personal communication, Dar es Salaam, September 5, 2022.

62. *Jeshi la Kujenga Taifa*, the National Service Army.

63. Malele 2009.

64. URT 1997.

65. Solomon 2011.

66. URT 1997.

67. Degani 2022.

68. The IPTL plant at Salasala was built by a partnership between Malaysian firm Mechmar and Tanzanian firm VIP Engineering and Marketing with a loan from Malaysian banks. The plant is the material manifestation of a grand corruption case (Cooksey 2017; Gray 2018; Degani 2022).

69. Kilimahewa was further divided into two *mitaa* in 2014 (Kiliimahewa and Kilimahewa Juu). Population data for the 2022 census was only available for the ward (Wazo) rather than subward when this book went to press. The population of Wazo Ward increased from 90,825 in 2012 (URT 2013) to 153,013 in 2022 (URT 2022).

70. Interview, *Jumuiya Watumiaji Maji Salasala* (Salasala Water Users' Association), April 5, 2016.

71. Shivji 2006.

72. Fanon (1952) 2017, 1963.

73. Buire 2017; Pitcher 2017; Croese and Pitcher 2019; Meth et al. 2021; Nielsen et al. 2021; Goodfellow 2022.

74. Mercer 2014; Wolff et al. 2018; Andreasen et al. 2021; Nielsen and Jenkins 2021.

3. LAND

1. "Quasi-customary" tenure is discussed in chapter 2. It refers to formerly customary land that has been transacted for cash rather than loaned, inherited, or gifted according to the customary law of the indigenous group. It means the owners are not bound by customary law in using or disposing of the land; in effect, they treat it as their private property despite not having formal title (granted right of occupancy) to the land, and despite the fact that it is not legally their private property (because all land is vested in the state).

2. Swantz 1996; Owens 2004.

3. Msangi 2014.

4. Interview, Klimahewa, August 10, 2017.

5. Interview, Salasala, August 8, 2017. The Makonde are an ethnic group from southern Tanzania.

6. Kombe 1995, in Kombe 2000: 170.

7. Interview, Kilimahewa Juu, August 9, 2017.

8. The Subward Executive Officer (*Afisa Mtendaji wa Mtaa*) is an appointed government position in lower local government urban administration.

9. Beacons are used to demarcate official boundaries on a surveyed plot. Official beacons are geo-coded iron pins encased in concrete and buried in the ground. Improvised beacons are also used to claim land in the absence of a survey or property title, often fashioned out of concrete pillars.

10. The lowest tier of the formal legal system, dealing with disputes relating to immovable property valued at TSh40–50 million. In fiscal year 2020–21 DLHTs across the country had a caseload of 49,638; 25,711 existing cases and 23,927 new cases. Of those cases 22,711 were resolved that year, taking forward 26,927 to the next fiscal year (URT 2021b).

11. Ministry of Lands, Housing and Human Settlements Development, personal communication, August 2018.

12. Dancer 2015. Ward tribunals mediated and attempted to solve disputes on the basis of customary principles of mediation, natural justice if customary principles did not apply (as in the case of Salasala), or any mediation practices in which ward tribunal members were trained (Section 13 (3) of the Land Disputes Courts Act No.2 of 2002).

13. Interview, Wazo Ward tribunal, April 11, 2016.

14. When people discuss the size of a plot in Swahili, the default measurement is *miguu* ("legs" or "feet") or *hatua* ("pace"), both of which refer to the length of a stride and reflect a common method for estimating the size of a plot without the use of digital surveying technology. This can create confusion as official measurements and documents use meters. M can therefore stand for *miguu* or for meters.

15. Ward tribunals do not have the authority to summon witnesses, as they are designed to facilitate mediation rather than to enforce law.

16. Msangi 2011, 2014.

17. Askew et al. 2013; Ally 2015.

18. Interview, Kilimahewa, July 23, 2015.

19. The homes were demolished as part of a road-widening project. See "Ongoing Demolition along Morogoro Road Causes Havoc to the Citizenry," IPPMedia, August 29, 2017, www.ippmedia.com/en/news/ongoing-demolition-along-morogoro-road-causes-havoc -citizenry; and "Bomoabomoa ya Kimara imezika zaidi ya Sh60 bilioni," *Daily Nation*, September 21, 2017, www.mwananchi.co.tz/mw/habari/makala/biashara/bomoabomoa-ya -kimara-imezika-zaidi-ya-sh60-bilioni-2867242.

20. Though there was also some sympathy on Twitter for those whose houses were demolished (#KimaraNiSisi).

21. "Opposition MP in Anguish After His House Is Demolished in Dar," IPPMedia, October 2, 2017, www.ippmedia.com/en/news/opposition-mp-anguish-after-his-house -demolished-dar.

22. John et al. 2019.

23. DAWASCO is the Dar es Salaam Water and Sewerage Corporation, a public parastatal body responsible for water and sewerage infrastructure. Water supply is managed by a separate, part-privatized company, Dar es Salaam Water and Sewerage Authority (DAWASA).

24. A unit in the national police force responsible for public order.

25. Interview, Salasala, April 11, 2016.

26. Kombe and Kreibich 2000.

27. Interview, Salasala, March 31, 2015.

28. A. Lupala 2002.

29. Kironde 1994; Msangi 2014.

30. Conducting his PhD fieldwork in neighboring Kimara in 2010, Fortunatus Bahendwa found that just 7 percent of a random sample of residents had managed to obtain formal title on unplanned land (Bahendwa 2013).

31. Nationwide, Kinondoni reported among the highest numbers for armed robbery, robbery with violence, break-ins, and theft of motorbikes and cars between 2016 and 2020 (URT 2017, 2021a).

32. Interview, Salasala, April 7, 2016.

33. Interview, Salasala, April 4, 2016.

34. Cross 2014, 2016.

35. Walwa 2017.

36. The Salasala Water Users' Association, discussed in chapter 2.

37. "Govt to Seize, Redistribute All Idle Land," *The Citizen*, February 19, 2016, www .thecitizen.co.tz/tanzania/news/national/govt-to-seize-redistribute-all-idle-land-2547942.

38. Sumaye claimed that the seizure of two of his farms, one in Mabwepande and the other in Morogoro Region, was politically motivated as he had defected from CCM to Chadema. See "Sumaye: Confiscation of My Farms Is a Political Game," *The Citizen*, August 22, 2017, www.thecitizen.co.tz/tanzania/news/national/sumaye-confiscation-of-my-farms -is-a-political-game-2601174.

39. *Wizara ya Ardhi* (Ministry of Land) 2016.

40. Croese et al. 2023.

41. With the wider move towards decentralization from the 1990s, property tax collection was decentralized to and controlled by local governments, constituting a substantial proportion of their budgets. In 2008 property tax collection was centralized in the TRA; between 2014 and 2016 it was decentralized again, and then recentralized after 2016 (Fjeldstad et al. 2017).

42. Formalization refers to the recognition and registration of property. Regularization involves planning land use and surveying or demarcating plot boundaries at the community scale, demarcating space for roads and basic services, and issuing rights of occupancy. The Land Act of 1999 and the Urban Planning Act of 2007 laid out guidance for surveying unplanned land.

43. Owens et al. (2018) provide a detailed discussion of the different government, donor, and NGO land-titling programs that have been implemented in rural areas.

44. Owens et al. 2018.

45. Kusiluka and Chiwambo 2018.

46. URT 2021b.

47. Manara 2022. See "Project Information Document—Land Tenure Improvement Project—P164906 (English)," World Bank, May 20, 2020, https://documents.worldbank .org/en/publication/documents-reports/documentdetail/934461589985643361/project -information-document-land-tenure-improvement-project-p164906; and "Tanzania: New World Bank Financing to Secure Land Rights for Up to Two Million Citizens," World Bank, December 21, 2021, www.worldbank.org/en/news/press-release/2021/12/21/tanzania-new -world-bank-financing-to-secure-land-rights-for-up-to-two-million-citizens.

48. See, for example, "Tanzania's Lands Minister Sacks Registrar over Title Deed Fraud," *The Citizen*, July 31, 2019, www.thecitizen.co.tz/tanzania/news/national/tanzania-s-lands -minister-sacks-registrar-over-title-deed-fraud-2688216.

49. "Councils Banned from Surveying Land," *The Citizen*, April 7, 2016, https://www .thecitizen.co.tz/tanzania/news/national/councils-banned-from-surveying-land-2552094.

50. Minister of Lands William Lukuvi claimed that any title deed issued by the City Council was invalid as the council had no jurisdiction over land. See "Minister Disbands Dar City Lands Unit," *The Citizen*, November 30, 2018, www.thecitizen.co.tz/tanzania /news/national/minister-disbands-dar-city-lands-unit-2663340.

51. Paget 2021.

52. Collord 2018.

53. Paget 2021.

54. In 2016, 16,127 ghost workers were removed (Rweyemamu 2016) and a further 10,000 workers were dismissed for having fake certificates (Njoji 2018). See "Maagizo sita ya Magufuli," *Mwananchi*, March 16, 2016, www.mwananchi.co.tz/mw/habari/kitaifa/maagizo-sita-ya-magufuli-2803546; and "Magufuli: Wenye vyeti feki ni majambazi, majizi," *Mwananchi*, April 28, 2017, www.mwananchi.co.tz/mw/habari/kitaifa/magufuli-wenye-vyeti-feki-ni-majambazi-majizi-2846582.

55. Collord 2018; Pedersen and Jacob 2019.

56. Tundu Lissu, the leader of the opposition party Chadema, suffered an assassination attempt in September 2017. See also "Magufuli Criticised as Tanzania Bans Rallies," *The East African*, June 11, 2016, www.theeastafrican.co.ke/tea/news/east-africa/magufuli-criticised-as-tanzania-bans-rallies-1351138; and "Uproar over Blogger Tax," IPPMedia, April 14, 2018, www.ippmedia.com/en/news/uproar-over-blogger-tax.

57. McLellan 2020.

58. "Tanzania's Main Opposition Party, Chadema, Boycotts Local Government Polls," *The Citizen*, November 8, 2019, www.thecitizen.co.tz/tanzania/news/national/tanzania-s-main-opposition-party-chadema-boycotts-local-government-polls-2696418.

59. "Gharama ya urasimishaji Tsh.130,000-Lukuvi," Uhuru Media Group, August 17, 2021, https://umg.co.tz/gharama-za-urasimishaji-tsh-130000-lukuvi/. This was a substantial reduction: in July 2018 Minister for Lands William Lukuvi had advised that surveys should not cost more than TSh250,000; see "Getting Land Title Deeds in Tanzania Has Just Become Cheaper, Here Is How Much," *The Citizen*, July 13, 2018, www.thecitizen.co.tz/tanzania/news/national/getting-land-title-deeds-in-tanzania-has-just-become-cheaper-here-is-how-much-2646722.

60. Wakongere and Alanganga 2020; Nuhu and Kombe 2021; Manara 2022.

61. Owens et al 2018; Boone 2019.

62. Sundet 1997; Lofchie 2014; Fjeldstad 2017.

4. LANDSCAPE

1. Lentz 2020; Mercer 2020.

2. Cosgrove 1984; D. Mitchell 1996; Duncan 1999; Duncan and Duncan 2004.

3. Zhang 2010; Donner 2013; Fehérváry 2013; Heiman 2015.

4. Neumann 2002; Beinart and McGregor 2003; McGregor 2009; Fontein 2015.

5. Myers 2003; de Boeck and Baloji 2016; Hoffman 2017; Smith 2019; Tomás 2022; Gastrow 2024.

6. Roque 2012; Lazzarini 2017; Morton 2019; Tomás 2022; Gastrow 2024.

7. Gastrow 2017.

8. Caldeira 2000; Brosius 2010; Centner 2010; Zhang 2010; Murray 2011; Harms 2016.

9. Bissell 2011: 176.

10. Frenkel and Western 1988; Njoh 2008; Home 2013.

11. T. Mitchell 1991.

12. Myers 2003.

13. Said 1978.

14. T. Mitchell 1991.

15. Fanon 1963; wa Thiong'o 1986; see also Mbembe 2012.

16. Fanon 1963: 39.

17. Fanon 1963.

18. wa Thiong'o 1986: 16.

19. Kipfer 2007.

20. Lugalla 1995; Tripp 1997; Brennan 2012; Rizzo 2017; Brownell 2020; Degani 2022.

21. Brownell 2020.

22. Táíwò 2022.

23. Raimbault 2010.

24. Sutton 1970: 11.

25. Raimbault 2010. The rebellion, led by Bushiri bin Salim, was launched in November 1888 against the Germans in Bagamoyo in protest at the Germans' failure to properly consult local leaders on the introduction of customs duties at all of the coastal ports from Tanga to Lindi. They were eventually defeated by the German imperial government, using hundreds of soldiers from Sudan and Mozambique (Fabian 2007).

26. Kironde 1994.

27. Burton 2005; Raimbault 2010.

28. J. Lupala 2002.

29. Brennan 2012.

30. Smiley 2010.

31. Brennan and Burton 2007.

32. Brennan and Burton 2007.

33. Brennan 2012.

34. Brennan and Burton 2007.

35. Kironde (1994) argues that the Germans separated the Indian and African zones to keep Africans out of the Indian and European business area. They were less motivated to separate the European and Indian zones because they did not want to leave the commercial zone to Indians alone.

36. Burton 2005.

37. Kironde 1994.

38. In Smiley 2009: 186.

39. Mabogunje 1990; Njoh 2008; Bissell 2011.

40. Brennan 2012.

41. Kironde 1994: 97–98; Myers 2003.

42. In Brennan 2012: 170.

43. Brennan and Burton 2007; Kironde 2007.

44. Lugalla 1989; Kelly 2018.

45. Moyer 2003; Lekule 2004.

46. Lewinson 2008; Kerr 2018; Kirby 2020.

47. Bongo Flava is a popular musical genre in Tanzania mixing rap, ragga, and R&B (Perullo 2011). See also Moyer 2003; Perullo 2005; Sanga 2013.

48. Degani 2022.

49. Wazo Ward Councilor, April 5, 2018.

50. Interview, Kilimahewa, April 7, 2016.

51. Interview, Kilimahewa, June 26, 2018.

52. Interview, Kilimahewa, April 5, 2015.

53. Interview, August 7, 2017.

54. Gastorn 2010.

55. Gastorn 2010; Rwegasira 2012.

56. Garth Myers (1993) noted that colonial officials in Zanzibar used the same terminology to describe "unplanned" residential areas on the edge of Zanzibar Town.

57. Interview, April 5, 2015.

58. Nielsen 2011.

59. Interview, August 10, 2017.

60. Owens 2010.

61. Tanzania Electric Supply Company.

62. This was before the naming of all streets for the 2022 census.

63. Myers 2016.

64. Interview, April 12, 2015. Mtongani was the site of a former *ujamaa* village located a few kilometers away.

65. Brownell 2020; Gastrow 2024.

5. DOMESTIC ARCHITECTURE

1. This changed after 2019, when the piped water distribution was improved in Salasala as a result of the upgrading of the water infrastructure serving the city by the Dar es Salaam Water and Sanitation Authority (DAWASA).

2. Rex and Moore 1967; Savage et al. 1992; Hamnett 2003; Piketty 2014.

3. Davidoff and Hall 1987.

4. Fishman 1987; Archer 2008.

5. Ley 1994; Hamnett 1995; Savage 2010.

6. Buchli 2013: 1.

7. Zhang 2010; Fehérváry 2013; Srivastava 2014; Harms 2016.

8. Donner 2013; Page 2019; Durham 2020; Gastrow 2020.

9. Kusno 2000; King 2004; Klaufus 2012; Ortega 2016.

10. Pellow 2015; Morton 2019; Hammar 2020; Gastrow 2024.

11. Brownell 2020.

12. Lewinson 2006: 476.

13. Callaci 2017.

14. Brownell 2020.

15. *Uwezo* signals capability, authority, and power. *Ana uwezo* is an oft-heard phrase meaning "s/he has the capacity" (to do something, usually in the context of marshaling material resources to meet an individual or family need). Also in relation to houses, Garth Myers (1993) describes the "*uwezo* continuum" on Zanzibar, denoting the extent to which houses incorporated new architectural features and building materials.

16. Turner 1972; Holston 2008.

17. Adjaye 2011.

18. See also Elleh 2014; Makachia 2021; Myers 2021; Perzyna et al. 2021.

19. Miller 2010.

6. LIFESTYLE

1. Lewinson 1999.

2. Lentz 2020.

3. Mercer 2017.

4. Interview, Salasala, March 29, 2015. The Chagga are the most numerous ethnic group in Kilimanjaro Region. *Pombe* is the locally brewed beer on the mountain, made from bananas.

5. Archambault 2021.

6. Mayige et al. 2011.

7. Lewinson 2008: 210.

8. Green 2015.

9. Funerals, on the other hand, were held throughout the week.

10. Kanga are colorful pieces of decorated cloth, usually worn by women, with a decorated border inscribed with an idiom, slogan, or message that might have meaning for the wearer (Yahya-Othman 1997).

11. Pauli 2019.

12. Hansen 1997: 113 and passim.

13. Lewinson 2008.

14. Lewinson 1999.

15. Lewinson 1999.

16. Lewinson 1999.

17. Interview, Salasala, August 13, 2017.

18. Interview, Wazo Ward Executive Officer, April 2015.

19. All of the names of the social groups referred to in this section are pseudonyms.

20. Interview, WSG chairman, Kilimahewa, April 7, 2016.

21. Interview, WSG chairman, Kilimahewa, April 7, 2016.

22. Interview, WSG chairman, Kilimahewa, April 7, 2016.

23. Interview, WSG member, Kilimahewa, August 12, 2017.

24. Interview, WSG member, April 4, 2016. Aga Khan is the large private multispeciality hospital in the city center.

25. Interview, WSG chairman, Kilimahewa, April 7, 2016.

26. Interview, WSG member, Kiimahewa, April 2, 2016.

27. Kelsall 2002; Gray 2015; Cooksey 2017; Degani 2022.

28. Durham 2020.

CONCLUSION

1. Noret 2017; Werbner 2017. On aspirations and lifestyles see Spronk 2012; D. James 2015, 2019; Auerbach 2020; on cultural politics see Schubert 2017; Sumich 2018; Gastrow 2024; on wealth creation see Southall 2018.

2. Rose 1994; Blomley 2003, 2004.

3. The Black Act of 1723 introduced the death penalty for hundreds of petty crimes against private property, including deer hunting grounds and parks. Poachers were referred to as "Blacks" because of their mode of disguise.

4. Kimari 2021; Okoye 2021.

5. Sumich 2018; Bolt and Schubert 2022.

6. Kelsall 2013; Lofchie 2014; Gray 2015, 2018.

7. Ferguson and Gupta 2002; Gupta 2012; Bierschenk and Olivier de Sardan 2014.

8. Schubert 2017.

9. Fernandes 2006; Southall 2016; Schubert 2017; Sumich 2018.

10. URT 1999.

11. Mgahemera 2012.

12. Green 2015; Degani 2022.

13. Mosha 2012.

14. Coulson 2013.

15. Green 2021.

16. Mercer and Green 2013; Green 2021.

17. Durham 2020; D. James 2021.

18. I am paraphrasing Nihkil Anand's "infrastructures accrete" (2015). The subhead refers to Sarah Nuttall and Achille Mbembe's characterization of African urban economies as "cities of cash" (2005: 194).

19. Brennan 2018; Goodfellow 2020, 2022; Obeng-Odoom 2020, 2021.

20. Berry 1985; Guyer 2014.

21. Guyer 2014; Breckenridge and James 2021; Joelson 2021.

22. Page and Mercer 2012; Bloch 2015; Guermond 2022.

23. Mercer et al. 2008.

24. Mbiba 2017; Steel et al. 2017, 2019; Gillespie 2020; Robinson et al. 2021; Goodfellow 2022.

25. See Wolff 2018 on Dege Village; see Owens 2014 on redevelopment in the city center.

26. de Boeck 2020; Green 2015.

27. Watson 2013; Arthur 2018; Grant et al. 2019; Olajide and Lawanson 2021; Goodfellow 2022.

28. Croese and Pitcher 2019; Weldeghebrael 2022. On building for rental, see Cadstedt 2006; Jenkins 2013; Amoako and Boamah 2017; Asante et al. 2018; Page and Sunjo 2018; Andreasen et al. 2021.

REFERENCES

Adjaye, David. 2011. *Africa Architecture: A Photographic Survey of Metropolitan Architecture.* London: Thames and Hudson.

Ally, Bashiru. 2015. "State and Market in Urban Land Conflicts: The Case of Dar es Salaam City, Tanzania, 1995–2015." PhD diss., University of Dar es Salaam.

Aminzade, Ronald. 2013. *Race, Nation and Citizenship in Post-Colonial Africa: The Case of Tanzania.* New York: Cambridge University Press.

Amoako, Cllifford, and Emmanuel Frimpong Boamah. 2017. "Build as You Earn and Learn: Informal Urbanism and Incremental Housing Finance in Kumasi, Ghana." *Journal of Housing and the Built Environment* 32: 429–48.

Anand, Nikhil. 2015. "Accretion." *Theorizing the Contemporary, Fieldsights*, September 24, 2015. https://culanth.org/fieldsights/accretion.

Andreasen, Manja Hoppe. 2013. "Population Growth and Spatial Expansion of Dar es Salaam." Rurban Africa Working Paper 1, Department of Geosciences and Natural Resource Management, University of Copenhagen.

Andreasen, Manja Hoppe, Gordon McGranahan, Griet Steel, and Sadaf Khan. 2021. "Self-Builder Landlordism: Exploring the Supply and Production of Private Rental Housing in Dar es Salaam and Mwanza." *Journal of Housing and Built Environment* 36, 1011–31.

Archambault, Julie Soleil. 2018. "'One Beer, One Block': Concrete Aspiration and the Stuff of Transformation in a Mozambican Suburb." *Journal of the Royal Anthropological Institute* 24: 692–708.

Archer, John. 2008. *Architecture and Suburbia: From English Villa to American Dream House, 1690–2000.* Minneapolis: University of Minnesota Press.

Armstrong, Allen. 1986. "Colonial and Neocolonial Urban Planning: Three Generations of Master Plans for Dar es Salaam Tanzania." *Utafiti* 8, no. 1: 43–66.

Arthur, Isaac Kwamena. 2018. "Exploring the Development Prospects of Accra Airport City, Ghana." *Area Development and Policy* 3, no. 2: 258–73.

Asante, Lewis Abedi, Emmanuel Kofi Gawu, Dennis Papa Odenyi Quansah, and Derek Osei Tutu. 2018. "The Difficult Combination of Renting and Building a House in Urban Ghana: Analysing the Perception of Low and Middle Income Earners in Accra." *GeoJournal* 83: 1223–37.

Askew, Kelly, Faustin Maganga, and Rie Odgaard. 2013. "Of Land and Legitimacy: A Tale of Two Lawsuits." *Africa* 83, no. 1: 120–41.

Auerbach, Jess. 2020. *From Water to Wine: Becoming Middle Class in Angola*. Toronto: University of Toronto Press.

Bahendwa, Fortunatus. 2013. "Urban Form through Residents' Practices: The Unconventional Transformation Processes in Suburban Areas in DSM, Tanzania." PhD diss., Oslo School of Architecture and Design.

Banerjee, Abhijit V., and Esther Duflo. 2008. "What Is Middle Class about the Middle Classes around the World?" *Journal of Economic Perspectives* 22, no. 2: 3–28.

Beeckmans, Luce, and Johan Lagae. 2015. "Kinshasa's Syndrome-Planning in Historical Perspective: From Belgian Colonial Capital to Self-Constructed Megalopolis." In *Urban Planning in Sub-Saharan Africa: Colonial and Post-Colonial Planning Cultures*, edited by Carlos Nunes Silva, 201–24. New York: Routledge.

Beinart, William, and JoAnn McGregor, eds. 2003. *Social History and African Environments*. Oxford: James Currey; Athens: Ohio University Press; Cape Town: David Philip.

Berry, Sara. 1985. *Fathers Work for Their Sons: Accumulation, Mobility and Class Formation in an Extended Yoruba Community*. London: University of California Press.

———. 2002. "Debating the Land Question in Africa." *Comparative Studies in Society and History* 44, no. 4: 638–68.

———. 2009. "Building for the Future? Investment, Land Reform and the Contingencies of Ownership in Contemporary Ghana." *World Development* 37, no. 8: 1370–78.

Bhandar, Brenna. 2018. *Colonial Lives of Property: Law, Land, and Racial Regimes of Ownership*. Durham, NC: Duke University Press.

Bierschenk, Thomas, and Jean-Pierre Olivier de Sardan, eds. 2014. *States at Work: Dynamics of African Bureaucracies*. Leiden: Brill.

Birdsall, Nancy. 2010. "The (Indispensable) Middle Class in Developing Countries; or the Rich and the Rest, not the Poor and the Rest." Washington, DC: Center for Global Development, Working Paper 207.

Bissell, William Cunningham. 2011. *Urban Design, Chaos, and Colonial Power in Zanzibar*. Bloomington: Indiana University Press.

Bloch, Robin. 2015. "Africa's New Suburbs." In *Suburban Governance: A Global View*, edited by Pierre Hamel and Roger Keil, 253–77. Toronto: University of Toronto Press.

Blomley, Nicholas. 2003. "Law, Property, and the Geography of Violence: The Frontier, the Survey and the Grid." *Annals of the Association of American Geographers* 93, no. 1: 121–41.

———. 2004. *Unsettling the City: Urban Land and the Politics of Property*. London: Routledge.

Bolt, Maxim. 2021. "Homeownership, Legal Administration and the Uncertainties of Inheritance in South Africa's Townships: Apartheid's Legal Shadows." *African Affairs* 120, no. 479: 219–41.

Bolt, Maxim, and Jon Schubert. 2022. "Engineering the Middle Classes: State Institutions and the Aspirations of Citizenship." *Critique of Anthropology* 42, no. 2: 347–58.

Boone, Catherine. 2007. "Property and Constitutional Order: Land Tenure Reform and the Future of the African State." *African Affairs* 106, no. 425: 557–86.

———. 2014. *Property and Political Order in Africa: Land Rights and the Structure of Politics.* Cambridge: Cambridge University Press.

———. 2019. "Legal Empowerment of the Poor through Property Rights Reform: Tensions and Trade-offs of Land Registration and Titling in Sub-Saharan Africa." *Journal of Development Studies* 55, no. 3: 384–400.

Bourdieu, Pierre. (1984) 2010. *Distinction: A Social Critique of the Judgment of Taste.* London: Routledge.

Breckenridge, Keith, and Deborah James. 2021. "Recentring the Margins: Theorizing African Capitalism after 50 Years." *Economy and Society* 50, no. 1: 1–8.

Brennan, James. 2012. *Taifa: Making Nation and Race in Urban Tanzania.* Athens: Ohio University Press.

———. 2018. "The Rents of the Dead: Growth and Entropy in African Cities." *Afrika Focus* 31, no. 2: 47–60.

Brennan, James, and Andrew Burton. 2007. "The Emerging Metropolis: A History of Dar es Salaam, Circa 1862–2000." In *Dar es Salaam: Histories from an Emerging African Metropolis*, edited by James Brennan, Andrew Burton, and Yusuf Lawi, 13–75. Nairobi: Mkuki na Nyota Publishers, in association with the British Institute in Eastern Africa.

Briggs, John, and Davis Mwamfupe. 2000. "Peri-Urban Development in an Era of Structural Adjustment in Africa: The City of Dar es Salaam, Tanzania." *Urban Studies* 37, no. 4: 797–809.

Brockington, Dan. 2019. "Persistent Peasant Poverty and Assets: Exploring Dynamics of New Forms of Wealth and Poverty in Tanzania 1999–2018." *The Journal of Peasant Studies* 48, no. 1: 201–20.

Brosius, Christiane. 2010. *India's Middle Class: New Forms of Urban Leisure, Consumption and Prosperity.* London: Routledge.

Brownell, Emily. 2020. *Gone to Ground: A History of Environment and Infrastructure in Dar es Salaam.* Pittsburgh: University of Pittsburgh Press.

Bryceson, Deborah Fahy. 1985. "Food and Urban Purchasing Power: The Case of Dar es Salaam, Tanzania." *African Affairs* 84, no. 337: 499–522.

———. 2009. "The Urban Melting Pot in East Africa: Ethnicity and Urban Growth in Kampala and Dar es Salaam." In *African Cities: Competing Claims on Urban Spaces*, edited by Francesca Locatelli and Paul Nugent, 241–60. Leiden: Brill.

Buchli, Victor. 2013. *An Anthropology of Architecture.* London: Routledge.

Budniok, Jan, and Andrea Noll. 2018. "The Ghanaian Middle Class, Social Stratification, and Long-Term Dynamics of Upward and Downward Mobility of Lawyers and Teachers." In *Middle Classes in Africa: Changing Lives and Conceptual Challenges*, edited by Lena Kroeker, David O'Kane, and Tabea Scharrer, 109–34. London: Palgrave Macmillan.

Buire, Chloe. 2017. "New City, New Citizens? A Lefebvrian Exploration of State-Led Housing and Political Identities in Luanda, Angola." *Transformation: Critical Perspectives on Southern Africa* 93: 13–40.

Burton, Andrew. 2005. *African Underclass: Urbanisation, Crime and Colonial Order in Dar es Salaam.* Nairobi: British Institute in Eastern Africa, in association with Oxford: James Currey; Dar es Salaam: Mkuki na Nyota; and Athens: Ohio University Press.

———. 2007. "Haven of Peace Purged: Tackling the Undesirable and Unproductive Poor in Dar es Salaam, ca. 1950s–1980s." *International Journal of African Historical Studies* 40, no. 1: 119–51.

Cadstedt, Jenny. 2006. *Influence and Invisibility: Tenants in Housing Provision in Mwanza City, Tanzania*. Department of Human Geography, Stockholm University.

Caldeira, Teresa. 2000. *City of Walls: Crime, Segregation and Citizenship in São Paulo*. Berkeley: University of California Press.

———. 2017. "Peripheral Urbanization: Autoconstruction, Transversal Logics, and Politics in Cities of the Global South." *Environment and Planning D: Society and Space* 35, no. 1: 3–20.

Callaci, Emily. 2017. *Street Archives and City Life: Popular Intellectuals in Postcolonial Tanzania*. Durham, NC: Duke University Press.

Campbell, Horace, and Howard Stein, eds. 1992. *Tanzania and the IMF: The Dynamics of Liberalization*. Oxford: Westview Press.

Centner, Ryan. 2010. "Spatializing Distinction in Cities of the Global South: Volatile Terrains of Morality and Citizenship." *Political Power and Social Theory* 21: 281–98.

Chachage, Chachage Seithy Loth. 1986. "Socialist Ideology and Reality in Tanzania." PhD diss., Glasgow University.

Chachage, Chambi, and Anar Cassam, eds. 2010. *Africa's Liberation: The Legacy of Nyerere*. Oxford: Pambazuka Press.

Chande, Faustina. 2021. "Raising the Bar—Achieving Tanzania's Development Vision." Washington, DC: World Bank Group, Tanzania Economic Update, no. 15. http://docu ments.worldbank.org/curated/en/803171614697018449/Tanzania-Economic-Update -Raising-the-Bar-Achieving-Tanzania-s-Development-Vision.

Chimhowu, Admos. 2019. "The 'New' African Customary Land Tenure: Characteristics, Features and Policy Implications of a New Paradigm." *Land Use Policy* 81: 897–903.

Chimhowu, Admos, and Phil Woodhouse. 2006. "Customary vs Private Property Rights? Dynamics and Trajectories of Vernacular Land Markets in Sub-Saharan Africa." *Journal of Agrarian Change* 6, no. 3: 346–71.

Chitonge, Horman. 2019. "The Land Question and the Economy: Cues of an Incomplete Decolonisation Project in Africa." In *Land, the State and the Unfinished Decolonisation Project in Africa: Essays in Honour of Professor Sam Moyo*, edited by Horman Chitonge and Yoichi Mine, 21–53. Bamenda, Cameroon: Langaa Research and Publishing CIG.

Cliffe, Lionel. 1977. "Rural Class Formation in East Africa." *The Journal of Peasant Studies* 4, no. 2: 195–224.

Collord, Michaela. 2018. "Tanzania—The 'New' CCM, Same as the Old CCM? Continuity and Change in Authoritarian Parties." *Presidential Power* (blog), last modified September 26, 2018. https://presidential-power.net/.

Comaroff, Jean, and John L Comaroff. 1990. "Goodly Beasts, Beastly Goods: Cattle and Commodities in a South African Context." *American Ethnologist* 17, no. 2: 195–216.

Cons, Jason, and Michael Eilenberg, eds. 2019. *Frontier Assemblages: The Emergent Politics of Resource Frontiers in Asia*. Oxford: Wiley.

Cooksey, Brian. 2017. "IPTL, Richmond and 'Escrow': The Price of Private Power Procurement in Tanzania." Africa Research Institute Briefing Note 1702, November 2017.

Cooper, Frederick, ed. 1983. *Struggle for the City: Migrant Labor, Capital, and the State in Urban Africa*. Beverly Hills: Sage Publications.

———. 1987. *On the African Waterfront: Urban Disorder and the Transformation of Work in Colonial Mombasa*. New Haven: Yale University Press.

Coquery-Vidrovitch, Catherine. 2014. "From Residential Segregation to African Urban Centres: City Planning and the Modalities of Change in Africa South of the Sahara." *Journal of Contemporary African Studies* 32, no. 1: 1–12.

Cosgrove, Denis. 1984. *Social Formation and Symbolic Landscape*. London: Croom Helm.

Coulson, Andrew. 2013. *Tanzania: A Political Economy*. 2nd ed. Oxford: Oxford University Press.

Cowan, Thomas. 2023. *Subaltern Frontiers: Agrarian City-Making in Gurgaon*. Cambridge: Cambridge University Press.

Croese, Sylvia, M., and Anne Pitcher. 2019. "Ordering Power? The Politics of State-Led Housing Delivery under Authoritarianism—the Case of Luanda, Angola." *Urban Studies* 56, no. 2: 401–18.

Croese, Sylvia, Jennifer Robinson, Kofi Kekeli Amedzro, Philip Harrison, Wilbard Kombe, Evance Mwathunga, and George Owusu. 2023. "Persistent, Pragmatic and Prolific: Urban Master Planning in Accra, Dar es Salaam and Lilongwe." *Land Use Policy* 133, https://doi.org/10.1016/j.landusepol.2023.106832.

Cross, Charlotte. 2014 "Community Policing and the Politics of Local Development in Tanzania." *Journal of Modern African Studies* 52, no. 4: 517–40.

———. 2016. "Ulinzi Shirikishi: Popular Experiences of Hybrid Security Governance in Tanzania." *Development and Change* 47, no. 5: 1102–24.

Dalberto, Séverine Awenengo, Hélène Charton, and Odile Goerg. 2013. "Urban Planning, Housing and the Making of 'Responsible Citizens' in the Late Colonial Period: Dakar, Nairobi and Conakry.'" In *Politics and Policies: Governing Cities in Africa*, edited by Simon Bekker and Laurent Fourchard, 43–66. Cape Town: HSRC Press.

Dancer, Helen. 2015. *Women, Land and Justice in Tanzania*. Suffolk: Eastern Africa Series, James Currey.

Darbon, Dominique. 2018. "Turning the Poor into Something More Inspiring: The Creation of the African Middle Class Controversy." In *Middle Classes in Africa: Changing Lives and Conceptual Challenges*, edited by Lena Kroeker, Tabea Scharrer, and David O'Kane, 35–56. Cham, Switzerland: Palgrave Macmillan.

Davidoff, Leonore, and Catherine Hall. 1987. *Family Fortunes: Men and Women of the English Middle Class, 1780–1850*. Chicago: University of Chicago Press.

de Boeck, Filip. 2000. "Borderland Breccia: The Mutant Hero in the Historical Imagination of a Central African Diamond Frontier." *Journal of Colonialism and Colonial History* 1, no. 2.

———. 2020. "Urban Expansion, the Politics of Land and Occupation as Infrastructure in Kinshasa." *Land Use Policy* 93.

de Boeck, Filip, and Sammy Baloji. 2016. *Suturing the City: Living Together in Congo's Urban Worlds*. London: Autograph ABP.

de Boeck, Filip, and Marie-Francoise Plissart. 2004. *Kinshasa: Tales of the Invisible City*. Leuven: Leuven University Press.

Degani, Michael. 2022. *The City Electric: Infrastructure and Ingenuity in Postsocialist Tanzania*. Durham, NC: Duke University Press.

Dejung, Christof, David Motadel, and Jürgen Osterhammel, eds. *The Global Bourgeoisie: The Rise of the Middle Classes in the Age of Empire*. Princeton: Princeton University Press, 2019.

Donner, Henrike, ed. 2013. *Being Middle Class in India: A Way of Life*. London: Routledge.

Duncan, James. 1999. "Elite Landscapes as Cultural (Re)productions: The Case of Shaughnessy Heights." In *Cultural Geographies*, edited by Kay Anderson and Fay Gale, 53–70. Melbourne: Addison Wesley Longman.

Duncan, James, and Nancy Duncan. 2004. *Landscapes of Privilege: The Politics of the Aesthetic in an American Suburb*. London: Routledge.

Durham, Deborah. 2020. "Morality in the Middle: Choosing Cars or Houses in Botswana." *Africa* 90, no. 3: 489–508.

Eckert, Andreas. 2014. "'We Must Run While Others Walk': African Civil Servants, State Ideologies and Bureaucratic Practices in Tanzania, from the 1950s to the 1970s." In *States at Work: Dynamics of African Bureaucracies*, edited by Thomas Bierschenk and Jean-Pierre Olivier de Sardan. Leiden: Brill.

Edmondson, Laura. 2007. *Performance and Politics in Tanzania: The Nation on Stage*. Bloomington: Indiana University Press.

Elleh, Nnamdi, ed. 2014. *Reading the Architecture of the Underprivileged Classes: A Perspective on the Protests and Upheavals in Our Cities*. Surrey: Ashgate.

Elliot, Hannah. 2016. "Planning, Property and Plots at the Gateway to Kenya's 'New Frontier.'" *Journal of Eastern African Studies* 10, no. 3: 511–29.

Fabian, Steven. 2007. "Curing the Cancer of the Colony: Bagamoyo, Dar es Salaam, and Socioeconomic Struggle in German East Africa. *International Journal of African Historical Studies* 40, no. 3: 441–69.

———. 2019. *Making Identity on the Swahili Coast: Urban Life, Community and Belonging in Bagamoyo*. Cambridge: Cambridge University Press.

Fair, Laura. 2018. *Reel Pleasures: Cinema Audiences and Entrepreneurs in Twentieth-Century Urban Tanzania*. Athens: Ohio University Press.

Fanon, Frantz. (1952) 2017. *Black Skin, White Masks*. London: Pluto Press.

———. 1963. *The Wretched of the Earth*. New York: Grove Weidenfeld.

Fehérváry, Krisztina. 2013. *Politics in Color and Concrete: Socialist Materialities and the Middle Class in Hungary*. Bloomington: Indiana University Press.

Ferguson, James, and Akil Gupta. 2002. "Spatializing States: Toward an Ethnography of Neoliberal Governmentality." *American Ethnologist* 29, no. 4: 981–1992.

Fernandes, Leela. 2006. *India's New Middle Class: Democratic Politics in an Era of Economic Reform*. Minneapolis: University of Minnesota Press.

Fimbo, Gamaliel Mgongo. 1992. *Essays in Land Law, Tanzania*. Dar es Salaam: Dar es Salaam University Press.

Fishman, Robert. 1987. *Bourgeois Utopias: The Rise and Fall of Suburbia*. New York: Basic Books.

Fjeldstad, Odd-Helge, Merima Ali, and Lucas Katera. 2017. *Taxing the Urban Boom in Tanzania: Central Versus Local Government Property Tax Collection*. Bergen, Norway: CMI Insight No. 3.

Fontein, Joost. 2015. *Remaking Mutirikwi: Landscape, Water and Belonging in Southern Zimbabwe*. Oxford: BIEA/James Currey.

Freeman, Carla. 2014. *Entrepreneurial Selves: Neoliberal Respectability and the Making of a Caribbean Middle Class*. Durham, NC: Duke University Press.

Frenkel, Steven, and John Western. 1988. "Pretext or Policy? Racial Segregation and Malarial Mosquitoes in a British Tropical Colony: Sierra Leone." *Annals of the Association of American Geographers* 78: 211–28.

Freund, Bill. 2007. *The African City: A History*. Cambridge: Cambridge University Press.

Gastorn, Kennedy. 2010. "Squatters' Rights and the Land Laws in Tanzania." *Verfassung und Recht in Übersee (Law and Politics in Africa, Asia and Latin America)* 3, no. 43: 349–65.

Gastrow, Claudia. 2017. "Cement Citizens: Housing, Demolition and Political Belonging in Luanda, Angola." *Citizenship Studies* 21, no. 2: 224–39.

———. 2020. "Housing Middle Classness: Formality and the Making of Distinction in Luanda." *Africa* 90, no. 3: 509–28.

———. 2024. *The Aesthetics of Belonging: Indigenous Urbanism and City Building in Oil Boom Luanda.* Chapel Hill: University of North Carolina Press.

Ghertner, Asher. 2015. *Rule by Aesthetics: World-Class City Making in Delhi.* Oxford: Oxford University Press.

———. 2020. "Lively Lands: The Spatial Reproduction Squeeze and the Failure of the Urban Imaginary." *International Journal of Urban and Regional Research* 44, no. 4: 561–81.

Gibbon, Peter, ed. 1995. *Liberalised Development in Tanzania: Studies on Accumulation Processes and Local Institutions.* Uppsala: Nordiska Afrikainstitutet.

Gillespie, Tom. 2020. "The Real Estate Frontier." *International Journal of Urban and Regional Research* 44, no. 4: 599–616.

Glassman, Jonathan. 1995. *Feasts and Riot: Revelry, Rebellion and Popular Consciousness on the Swahili Coast, 1856–1888.* Portsmouth: Heinemann.

Goodfellow, Tom. 2020. "Finance, Infrastructure and Urban Capital: The Political Economy of African 'Gap-filling.'" *Review of African Political Economy* 47, no. 164: 256–74.

———. 2022. *Politics and the Urban Frontier: Transformation and Divergence in Late Urbanizing East Africa.* Oxford: Oxford University Press.

Gough, Kate, Graham Tipple, and Mark Napier. 2003. "Making a Living in African Cities: The Role of Home-Based Enterprises in Accra and Pretoria." *International Planning Studies* 8, no. 4: 253–77.

Grace, Joshua. 2021. *African Motors: Technology, Gender and the History of Development.* Durham, NC: Duke University Press.

Grant, Richard, Martin Oteng-Ababio, and Jessy Sivilien. 2019. "Greater Accra's New Urban Extension at Ningo-Prampram: Urban Promise or Urban Peril?" *International Planning Studies* 24, no. 3–4: 325.

Gray, Hazel. 2015. "The Political Economy of Grand Corruption in Tanzania." *African Affairs* 114, no. 456: 382–403.

———. 2018. *Turbulence and Order in Economic Development: Institutions and Economic Transformation in Tanzania and Vietnam.* Oxford: Oxford University Press.

Greco, Elisa. 2015. "Landlords in the Making: Class Dynamics of the Land Grab in Mbarali, Tanzania." *Review of African Political Economy* 42, no. 144: 225–44.

Green, Maia. 2014. *The Development State: Aid, Culture and Civil Society in Tanzania.* Suffolk: James Currey.

———. 2015. "Making Africa Middle Class: From Poverty Reduction to the Production of Inequality in Tanzania." *Economic Anthropology* 2, no. 2: 295–309.

———. 2017. "Dairying as Development: Caring for 'Modern' Cows in Tanzania." *Human Organization* 76, no. 2: 109–20.

———. 2021. "The Work of Class: Cash Transfers and Community Development in Tanzania." *Economic Anthropology* 8, no. 2: 273–86.

Guermond, Vincent. 2022. "Contesting the Financialisation of Remittances: Repertoires of Reluctance, Refusal and Dissent in Ghana and Senegal." *Environment and Planning A* 54, no. 4: 800–21.

Gupta, Akil. 2012. *Red Tape: Bureaucracy Structural Violence and Poverty in India.* Durham, NC: Duke University Press.

Guyer, Jane. 2014. *Marginal Gains: Monetary Transactions in Atlantic Africa.* Chicago: University of Chicago Press.

Hammar, Amanda. 2017. "Urban Displacement and Resettlement in Zimbabwe: The Paradoxes of Propertied Citizenship." *African Studies Review* 60, no. 3: 81–104.

———. 2020. "Speaking through Houses: Interweaving Biography, Property and Personhood in Urban Zimbabwe." JJ Bachhofen Lecture No. 5, Institute of Social Anthropology, University of Basel.

Hamnett, Chris. 1995. "Home-ownership and the Middle Classes." In *Social Change and the Middle Classes*, edited by Tim Butler and Mike Savage, 257–272. London: UCL Press.

———. 2023. *Unequal City: London in the Global Arena.* London: Routledge.

Hansen, Karen Tranberg. 1997. *Keeping House in Lusaka.* New York: Columbia University Press.

Harms, Erik. 2016. *Luxury and Rubble: Civility and Dispossession in the New Saigon.* Oakland: University of California Press.

Hart, Gillian. 2018. "Relational Comparison Revisited: Marxist Postcolonial Geographies in Practice." *Progress in Human Geography* 42, no. 3: 371–94.

Harvey, David. 2006. "Space as Keyword." In *David Harvey: A Critical Reader*, edited by Noel Castree and Derek Gregory, 270–93. Oxford: Blackwell.

Havnevik, Kjell J. 1993. *Tanzania: The Limits to Development from Above.* Uppsala: Nordiksa Afrikainstitute.

Hay, Alison, and Richard Harris. 2007. "'Shauri ya sera kali': The Colonial Regime of Urban Housing in Kenya to 1939." *Urban History* 34, no. 4: 504–30.

Heiman, Rachel. 2015. *Driving after Class: Anxious Times in an American Suburb.* Oakland: University of California Press.

Heiman, Rachel, Carla Freeman, and Mark Liechty, eds. 2012. *The Global Middle Classes: Theorizing through Ethnography.* Santa Fe: School for Advanced Research Press.

Hoffman, Danny. 2017. *Monrovia Modern: Urban Form and Political Imagination in Liberia.* Durham, NC: Duke University Press.

Holston, James. 2008. *Insurgent Citizenship: Disjunctions of Democracy and Modernity in Brazil.* Princeton: Princeton University Press.

Home, Robert. 2012. "Colonial Township Laws and Urban Governance in Kenya." *Journal of African Law* 56, no. 2: 175–93.

———. 2013. *Of Planting and Planning: The Making of British Colonial Cities.* 2nd ed. Abingdon: Routledge.

Howland, Olivia, Dan Brockington, and Christine Noe. 2021. "The Multiple Meanings of Prosperity and Poverty: A Cross-Site Comparison from Tanzania." *Journal of Peasant Studies* 48, no. 1: 180–200.

Hunter, Emma. 2019. "Modernity, Print Media and the Middle Class in Colonial East Africa." In *The Global Bourgeoisie: The Rise of the Middle Classes in the Age of Empire*, edited by Christ of Dejung, David Motadel, and Jürgen Osterhammel, 105–22. Princeton: Princeton University Press.

Hydén, Goran. 1980. *Beyond Ujamaa in Tanzania: Underdevelopment and an Uncaptured Peasantry.* London: Heinemann.

Iliffe, John. 1979. *A Modern History of Tanganyika*. Cambridge: Cambridge University Press.

Ivaska, Andrew. 2011. *Cultured States: Youth, Gender and Modern Style in 1960s Dar es Salaam*. Durham, NC: Duke University Press.

James, Deborah. 2015. *Money from Nothing: Indebtedness and Aspiration in South Africa*. Stanford: Stanford University Press.

———. 2019. "New Subjectivities: Aspiration, Prosperity and the New Middle Class." *African Studies* 78, no. 1: 33–50.

———. 2021. "Life and Debt: A View from the South." *Economy and Society* 50, no. 1: 36–56.

James, R. W. 1971. *Land Tenure and Policy in Tanzania*. Nairobi: East African Literature Bureau.

Jayne, T. S, Jordan Chamberlin, Lulama Traub, Nicholas Sitko, Milu Muyanga, Felix K. Yeboah, Ward Anseeuw, Antony Chapoto, Ayala Wineman, Chewe Nkonde, and Richard Kachule. 2016. "Africa's Changing Farm Size Distribution Patterns: The Rise of Medium-Scale Farms." *Agricultural Economics* 47: 197–214.

Jenkins, Paul. 2013. *Urbanization, Urbanism, and Urbanity in an African City: Home Spaces and House Cultures*. New York: Palgrave Macmillan.

Jennings, Michael. 2003. "'We Must Run While Others Walk': Popular Participation and Development Crisis in Tanzania, 1961–69." *Journal of Modern African Studies* 41, no. 2: 163–187.

Joelson, Irmelin. 2021. "Risky Urban Futures: The Bridge, the Fund and Insurance in Dar es Salaam." In *African Cities and Collaborative Futures: Urban Platforms and Metropolitan Logistics*, edited by Michael Keith and Andreza Aruska de Souza Santos, 143–65. Manchester: Manchester University Press.

John, Regina, Fredrick Bwire Magina, and Emmanuel Fares Kemwita. 2019. "From Msimbazi River Valley to Mabwepande Settlement: The Resettlement Process and Its Challenges." *Current Urban Studies* 7, no. 3: 399–426.

Juul, Kristine, and Christian Lund, eds. 2002. *Negotiating Property in Africa*. Portsmouth, NH: Heinemann.

Kalb, Don. "Introduction: Class and the New Anthropological Holism." In *Anthropologies of Class: Power, Practice and Inequality*, edited by James G Carrier and Don Kalb, 1–27. Cambridge: Cambridge University Press, 2015.

Karaman, Ozan, Lindsay Sawyer, Christian Schmid, and Kit Ping Wong. 2020. "Plot by Plot: Plotting Urbanism as an Ordinary Process of Urbanisation." *Antipode* 52, no. 4: 1122–51.

Keil, Roger. 2018. *Suburban Planet: Making the World Urban from the Outside In*. Cambridge: Polity Press.

Kelly, Chau Johnsen. 2018. "'A Pleasant and Tidy Arrangement': Housing Development and Economies of Segregation in Mtwara, Tanganyika, 1949–1954." *Journal of Urban History* 44, no. 4: 713–35.

Kelsall, Tim. 2002. "Shop-Windows and Smoke-filled Rooms: Governance and the Re-politicisation of Tanzania." *Journal of Modern African Studies* 40, no. 4: 597–619.

———. 2013. *Business, Politics and the State in Africa: Challenging Orthodoxies on Growth and Transformation*. London: Zed Books.

———. 2018. "Thinking and Working with Political Settlements: The Case of Tanzania." Working Paper 541, London: Overseas Development Institute.

Kerr, David. 2018. "From the Margins to the Mainstream: Making and Remaking an Alternative Music Economy in Dar es Salaam." *Journal of African Cultural Studies* 30, no. 1: 65–80.

Kimari, Wangui. 2021. "The Story of a Pump: Life, Death and Afterlives within an Urban Planning of 'Divide and Rule' in Nairobi, Kenya." *Urban Geography* 42, no. 2: 141–60.

King, Anthony. 2004. *Spaces of Global Cultures: Architecture, Urbanism, Identity*. London: Routledge.

Kipfer, Stefan. 2007. "Fanon and Space: Colonization, Urbanization, and Liberation from the Colonial to the Global City." *Environment and Planning D: Society and Space* 25: 701–26.

Kirby, Benjamin. 2020. "Flags and Shields: Muslim Socialities and Informal Livelihoods in Dar es Salaam." *City and Society* 32, no. 3: 556–78.

Kironde, Joseph M. Lusugga. 1991. "Sites and Services in Tanzania: The Case of Sinza, Kijitonyama and Mikocheni Areas in Dar es Salaam." *Habitat International* 15, no. 1/2: 27–38.

———. 1992. "Rent Control Legislation and the National Housing Corporation in Tanzania, 1985–1990." *Canadian Journal of African Studies* 26, no. 2: 306–27.

———. 1994. "The Evolution of the Land Use Structure of Dar es Salaam 1890–1990: A Study in the Effects of Land Policy." PhD diss., University of Nairobi.

———. 1997. "Land Policy Options for Urban Tanzania." *Land Use Policy* 14, no. 2: 99–117.

———. 2007. "Race, Class and Housing in Dar es Salaam: The Colonial Impact on Land Use Structure, 1891–1961." In *Dar es Salaam: Histories from an Emerging African Metropolis*, edited by James Brennan, Andrew Burton, and Usuf Lawi, 97–117. Nairobi: Mkuki na Nyota Publishers, in association with the British Institute in Eastern Africa.

Kitching, Gavin. 1980. *Class and Economic Change in Kenya: The Making of an African Petite Bourgeoisie, 1905–1970*. New Haven: Yale University Press.

Klaufus, Christien. 2012. *Urban Residence: Housing and Social Transformations in Globalizing Ecuador*. New York: Berghahn Books.

Kombe, Wilbard J. 1995. "Formal and Informal Land Management in Tanzania: The Case of Dar es Salaam City." Dortmund: SPRING Research Series 13.

———. 2000. "Regularizing Housing Land Development during the Transition to Market-Led Supply in Tanzania." *Habitat International* 24: 167–84.

———. 2005. "Land Use Dynamics in Peri-urban Areas and their Implications on the Urban Growth and Form: The Case of Dar es Salaam, Tanzania." *Habitat International*, 29: 113–35.

———. 2010. "Land Conflicts in Dar es Salaam: Who Gains? Who Loses?" Crisis States Working Papers Series no. 2. London: London School of Economics.

Kombe, Wilbard J., and Volker Kreibich. 2000. *Informal Land Management in Tanzania*. Dortmund: SPRING Centre, Faculty of Spatial Planning, University of Dortmund.

———. 2006. *Governance of Informal Urbanisation in Tanzania*. Dar es Salaam: Mkuki na Nyota.

Konadu-Agymang, Kwadwo. 2001. *The Political Economy of Housing and Urban Development in Africa: Ghana's Experience from Colonial Times to 1998*. Westport, CT: Praeger.

Kopytoff, Igor. 1989. "The Internal African Frontier: The Making of African Political Culture." In *The African Frontier: The Reproduction of Traditional African Societies*, edited by Igor Kopytoff, 3–84. Bloomington: Indiana University Press.

Kroeker, Lena, David O'Kane, and Tabea Scharrer, eds. 2018. *Middle Classes in Africa: Changing Lives and Conceptual Challenges*. London: Palgrave Macmillan.

Kusiluka, Moses, and Dorice Chiwambo. 2018. "Accessing Land Titles Application and Uptake in Regularised Informal Settlements in Tanzania." *International Journal of Urban Sustainable Development* 10, no. 3: 279–91.

Kusno, Abidin. 2000. *Behind the Postcolonial: Architecture, Urban Space and Political Cultures in Indonesia*. London: Routledge.

Lal, Priya. 2015. *African Socialism in Tanzania: Between the Village and the World*. Cambridge: Cambridge University Press.

Landau, Loren. 2017. "Friendship Fears and Communities of Convenience in Africa's Urban Estuaries: Connection as Measure of Urban Condition." *Urban Studies* 55, no. 3: 505–21.

Lazzarini, Alicia. 2017. "Açúcar nem sempre doce (Sugar Isn't Always Sweet): Reinvestment, Land and Gendered Labor in a 'New' Mozambique." PhD diss., University of Minnesota.

Lefebvre, Henri. 1991. *The Production of Space*. Oxford: Blackwell.

Lekule, Camillus Thomas. 2004. "Place Dynamics: Meanings of Urban Space to Residents in Keko Magurumbasi Informal Settlement, Dar es Salaam, Tanzania." PhD diss., School of Architecture, Royal Danish Academy of Fine Arts, Copenhagen.

Lentz, Carola. 2015. "Elites or Middle Classes? Lessons from Transnational Research for the Study of Social Stratification in Africa." Working Paper 161, Johannes Gutenberg Universität Mainz.

———. 2020. "Doing Being Middle Class in the Global South: Comparative Perspectives and Conceptual Challenges." *Africa* 90, no. 3: 439–69.

Lentz, Carola, and Andrea Noll. 2021. "Across Regional Disparities and Beyond Family Ties: A Ghanaian Middle Class in the Making." *History and Anthropology* 34, no. 3: 455–72.

Leslie, J. A. K. 1963. *A Survey of Dar es Salaam*. London: Oxford University Press.

Levien, Michael. 2018. *Dispossession without Development: Land Grabs in Neoliberal India*. Oxford: Oxford University Press.

Lewinson, Anne. 1999. "Going with the Times: Transforming Visions of Urbanism and Modernity among Professionals in Dar es Salaam, Tanzania." PhD diss., University of Wisconsin-Madison.

———. 2006. "Domestic Realms, Social Bonds, and Class: Ideologies and Indigenizing Modernity in Dar es Salaam, Tanzania." *Canadian Journal of African Studies* 40, no. 3: 462–95.

———. 2008. "Viewing Postcolonial Dar es Salaam, Tanzania through Civic Spaces: A Question of Class." *African Identities* 5, no. 2: 199–215.

Ley, David. 1994. "Gentrification and the Politics of the New Middle Class." *Environment and Planning D: Society and Space* 12, no. 1: 53–74.

Liechty, Mark. 2003. *Suitably Modern: Making Middle-Class Culture in a New Consumer Society*. Princeton: Princeton University Press.

———. 2012. "Middle Class Deja Vu: Conditions of Possibility, from Victorian England to Contemporary Kathmandu." In *The Global Middle Classes: Theorizing through Ethnography*, edited by Rachel Heiman, Carla Freeman, and Mark Liechty, 271–300. Santa Fe: School for Advanced Research Press.

Lofchie, Michael. 2014. *The Political Economy of Tanzania: Decline and Recovery*. Philadelphia: University of Pennsylvania Press.

López, A. Ricardo, and Barbara Weinstein, eds. 2012. *The Making of the Middle Class: Toward a Transnational History*. Durham, NC: Duke University Press.

Lugalla, Joe. 1989. "Conflicts and Politics in Urban Planning in Tanzania." *African Study Monographs* 9, no. 4: 181–90.

———. 1995. *Crisis, Urbanization, and Urban Poverty in Tanzania*. Lanham, MD: University Press of America.

Lund, Christian. 2002. *Local Politics and the Dynamics of Property in Africa*. Cambridge: Cambridge University Press.

———. 2016. "Rule and Rupture: State Formation through the Production of Property and Citizenship." *Development and Change* 47, no. 6: 1199–228.

———. 2021. *Nine-Tenths of the Law: Enduring Dispossession in Indonesia*. London: Yale University Press.

Lund, Christian, and Catherine Boone. 2013. "Introduction: Land Politics in Africa— Constituting Authority over Territory, Property and Persons." *Africa* 83, no. 1: 1–13.

Lupala, Aldo. 2002. "Peri-urban Land Management for Rapid Urbanisation: The Case of Dar es Salaam." Dortmund: Spring Research Series No. 32.

Lupala, John M. 2002. *Urban Types in Rapidly Urbanising Cities: Analysis of Formal and Informal Settlements in DSM, Tanzania*. Department of Infrastructure and Planning, Division of Urban Studies, Royal Institute of Technology, Sweden.

Mabandla, Nkululeko. 2013. *Lahla Ngubo: The Continuities and Discontinuities of a South African Black Middle Class*. Leiden: African Studies Centre.

Mabogunje, Akin L. 1990. "Urban Planning and the Post-colonial State in Africa: A Research Overview." *African Studies Review* 33, no. 2: 121–203.

Mafeje, Archie. 2003. "The Agrarian Question, Access to Land, and Peasant Responses in Sub-Saharan Africa." Civil Society and Social Movements Programme Paper no. 6, United Nations Research Institute for Social Development.

Makachia, Peter. 2021. "Modern Vernacular: Theorising Popular Architecture." In *Architectural Guide: Sub-Saharan Africa*, vol. 1, *Introduction to the History and Theory of Sub-Saharan Architecture*, edited by Philipp Meuser and Adil Dalbai, 190–93. Berlin: DOM Publishers.

Malele, Benedict F. 2009. "The Contribution of Ineffective Urban Planning Practices to Disaster and Disaster Risks Accumulation in Urban Areas: The Case of Former Kunduchi Quarry Site in Dar es Salaam, Tanzania." *JAMBA: Journal of Disaster Risk Studies* 2, no. 1: 28–52.

Mamdani, Mahmood. 1996. *Citizen and Subject: Contemporary Africa and the Legacy of Late Colonialism*. Princeton, NJ: Princeton University Press.

Manara, Martina. 2022. "From Policy to Institution: Implementing Land Reform in Dar es Salaam's Unplanned Settlements." *Environment and Planning A* 54, no. 7: 1368–90.

Manara, Martina, and Erica Pani. 2023. "Incremental Land Tenure Formalisation: A Reflection on Interim Property Rights in Urban Tanzania." *Land Use Policy* 129.

Marx, Colin. 2020. "Urban Land Markets in Africa: Multiplying Possibilities via a Diverse Economy Reading." In *The Handbook of Diverse Economies*, edited by J.K. Gibson-Graham and Kelly Dombroski, 300–307. Cheltenham: Edward Elgar.

Marx, Karl. (1867) 1977. *Capital*. Vol. 1. Translated by B. Fowkes. New York: Vintage Books.

———. (1885) 1978. *Capital*. Vol. 2. Translated by D. Fernbach. London: Pelican Books.

———. (1894) 1981. *Capital*. Vol. 3. Translated by Fernbach D. London: Pelican Books.

Massey, Doreen. 1994. *Space, Place and Gender*. Minneapolis: University of Minnesota.

Massive Urbanisation Collective. 2020. "The Time of the 'Maybe' in Massive Urbanization: Reflections from a Collective of Southern Urban Scholars." *Society and Space*, March 24, 2021. www.societyandspace.org/forums/massive-urbanization-forum.

Mayige, Mary, Gibson Kagaruki, Kaushik Ramaiya, and Andrew Swai. 2011. "Non Communicable Diseases in Tanzania: A Call for Urgent Action." *Tanzanian Journal of Health Research* 13, no. 5 (Supplement 1): 378–86.

Mbembe, Achille. 2012. "Metamorphic Thought: The Works of Frantz Fanon." *African Studies* 71, no. 1: 19–28.

Mbiba, Beacon. 2017. "Idioms of Accumulation: Corporate Accumulation by Dispossession in Urban Zimbabwe." *International Journal of Urban and Regional Research* 41, no. 2: 213–34.

Mbilinyi, Marjorie. 1985. "'City' and 'Countryside' in Colonial Tanganyika." *Economic and Political Weekly* 26, no. 43: WS88–96.

McCleery, H. H. 1939. "Report of an Enquiry into Landownership in Dar es Salaam." Typescript, Rhodes House MSS Afr.s.870.

McGregor, JoAnn. 2009. *Crossing the Zambezi: The Politics of Landscape on a Central African Frontier*. Suffolk: James Currey; Harare: Weaver Press.

McLellan, Rachael. 2020. "The Politics of Local Control in Electoral Autocracies." PhD diss., Princeton University.

Melber, Henning, ed. 2016. *The Rise of Africa's Middle Class: Myths, Realities and Critical Engagements*. London: Zed Books.

Mercer, Claire. 2002. "Deconstructing Development: The Discourse of Maendeleo and the Politics of Women's Participation on Mount Kilimanjaro." *Development and Change* 33, no. 1: 101–27.

———. 2014. "Middle Class Construction: Domestic Architecture, Aesthetics and Anxieties in Tanzania." *Journal of Modern African Studies* 52, no. 2: 227–50.

———. 2017. "Landscapes of Extended Ruralisation: Postcolonial Suburbs in Dar es Salaam, Tanzania." *Transactions of the Institute of British Geographers* 42, no. 1: 72–83.

———. 2020. "Boundary Work: Becoming Middle Class in Suburban Dar es Salaam." *International Journal of Urban and Regional Research* 44, no. 3: 521–36.

Mercer, Claire, and Maia Green. 2013. "Making Civil Society Work: Contracting, Cosmopolitanism and Community Development in Tanzania." *Geoforum* 45: 106–15.

Mercer, Claire, Ben Page, and Martin Evans. 2008. *Development and the African Diaspora: Place and the Politics of Home*. London: Zed Books.

Meth, Paula, Tom Goodfellow, Alison Todes, and Sarah Charlton. 2021. "Conceptualizing African Urban Peripheries." *International Journal of Urban and Regional Research* 45, no. 6: 985–1007.

Mgahemera, Shermarx. 2012. "Tanzania Suppresses Middle Class Growth." *The African*, Dar es Salaam, August 31, 2012.

Mgullu, Francis Peter. 1978. "Housing: A Study of Tanzania's National Sites and Services Schemes." LIM diss., University of Dar es Salaam.

Miller, Daniel. 2010. *Stuff*. Cambridge: Polity Press.

Ministry of Finance and Planning—Poverty Eradication Division (MoFP-PED) [Tanzania Mainland] and National Bureau of Statistics (NBS). 2019. *Tanzania Mainland Household Budget Survey 2017–18, Key Indicators Report*. Dodoma: Tanzania.

Ministry of Finance and Planning—Poverty Eradication Division (MoFP-PED) [Tanzania Mainland], National Bureau of Statistics (NBS) and the World Bank. 2020. *Tanzania Mainland Household Budget Survey 2017/18. Final Report.* Dodoma: Tanzania.

Mitchell, Donald. 1996. *The Lie of the Land: Migrant Workers and the California Landscape.* Minneapolis: University of Minneapolis Press.

Mitchell, Timothy. 1991. *Colonising Egypt.* Berkeley: University of California Press.

Molohan, M. J. B. 1959. *Detribalization.* Dar es Salaam: Government Printer.

Morton, David. 2019. *Age of Concrete: Housing and the Shape of Aspiration in the Capital of Mozambique.* Athens: Ohio University Press.

Mosha, Herme. 2012. "The State and Quality of Education in Tanzania: A Reflection." *Papers in Education and Development* 31, no. 2.

Moyer, Eileen. 2003. "In the Shadow of the Sheraton: Imagining Localities in Global Spaces in Dar es Salaam, Tanzania." PhD diss., University of Amsterdam.

Moyo, Sam. 1995. *The Land Question in Zimbabwe.* Harare: SAPES Books.

Msangi, Daniel Eliwaha. 2011. "Land Acquisition for Urban Expansion: Process and Impacts on Livelihoods of Peri-urban Households, Dar es Salaam, Tanzania." Licentiate thesis, Faculty of Natural Sciences and Agricultural Sciences, Swedish University of Agricultural Sciences.

———. 2014. "Organic Urban Expansion: Processes and Impacts on Livelihoods of Peri-urban Households in Dar es Salaam, Tanzania." PhD diss., Ardhi University, Dar es Salaam.

Murray, Martin. 2011. *City of Extremes: The Spatial Politics of Johannesburg.* Durham, NC: Duke University Press.

Murray Li, Tanya. 2014. *Land's End: Capitalist Relations on an Indigenous Frontier.* Durham, NC: Duke University Press.

Mwamfupe, Davis. 1994. "Changes in Agricultural Land Use in the Peri-urban Zone of Dar es Salaam, Tanzania." PhD diss., University of Glasgow.

Myers, Garth Andrew. 1993. "Reconstructing Ng'ambo: Town Planning and Development on the Other Side of Zanzibar." PhD diss., University of California Los Angeles.

———. 2003. *Verandahs of Power: Colonialism and Space in Urban Africa.* Syracuse, NY: Syracuse University Press.

———. 2016. *Urban Environments in Africa: A Critical Analysis of Environmental Politics.* Bristol: Policy Press.

———. 2021. "Theorising Complexity: Five Commonalities in African Architecture." In *Architectural Guide Sub-Saharan Africa*, vol. 1, *Introduction to the History and Theory of Sub-Saharan Architecture*, edited by Philipp Meuser and Adil Dalbai, 144–45. Berlin: DOM.

Napier, Mark, Stephen Berrisford, Caroline Wanjiku Kihato, Rob McGaffin, and Lauren Royston. 2013. *Trading Places: Accessing Land in African Cities.* South Africa: African Minds for Urban LandMark.

National Bureau of Statistics (Tanzania). 2014a. *Household Budget Survey Main Report, 2011/12.* Dar es Salaam, Tanzania.

———. 2014b. *Tanzania Integrated Labour Force Survey, 2014.* Dar es Salaam, Tanzania.

———. 2022. *Tanzania Integrated Labour Force Survey 2020/21.* Dodoma, Tanzania.

National Bureau of Statistics and Ministry of Finance and Planning. 2019. *Key Indicators Report: 2017–18 Household Budget Survey.* Dodoma: Tanzania.

Ncube, Mthuli, and Charles Leyeka Lufumpa, eds. 2015. *The Emerging Middle Class in Africa*. London: Routledge.

Ncube, Mthuli, Charles Leyeka Lufumpa, and Steve Kayizzi-Mugerwa. 2011. "The Middle of the Pyramid: Dynamics of the Middle Class in Africa." Market brief, African Development Bank.

Ndjio, Basile. 2009. "Migration, Architecture, and the Transformation of the Landscape in the Bamileke Grassfields of West Cameroon." *African Diaspora* 2: 73–100.

Ndlovu-Gatsheni, Sabelo. 2013. *Coloniality of Power in Postcolonial Africa: Myths of Decolonization*. Dakar: CODESRIA.

Neubert, Dieter. 2019. *Inequality, Socio-cultural Differentiation and Social Structures in Africa*. Cham, Switzerland: Palgrave Macmillan.

Neumann, Roderick. 2002. *Imposing Wilderness: Struggles over Livelihood and Nature Preservation in Africa*. Berkeley: University of California Press.

Nielsen, Morten. 2011. "Inverse Governmentality: The Paradoxical Production of Peri-urban Planning in Maputo, Mozambique." *Critique of Anthropology* 31, no. 4: 329–58.

———. 2021. "Speculative Cities: Housing and Value Conversions in Maputo, Mozambique." *Housing Studies* 37, no. 6: 889–909.

Nielsen, Morten, and Paul Jenkins. 2021. "Insurgent Aspirations? Weak Middle-Class Utopias in Maputo, Mozambique." *Critical African Studies* 13, no. 2: 162–82.

Nielsen, Morten, Jason Sumich, and Bjørn Bertelson. 2021. "Enclaving: Spatial Detachment as an Aesthetics of Imagination in an Urban Sub-Saharan African Context." *Urban Studies* 58, no. 5: 881–902.

Njoh, Ambe J. 2004. "The Experience and Legacy of French Colonial Urban Planning in Sub-Saharan Africa." *Planning Perspectives* 19, no. 4: 435–54.

———. 2008. "Colonial Philosophies, Urban Space, and Racial Segregation in British and French Colonial Africa." *Journal of Black Studies* 38, no. 4: 579–99.

Njoji, Augusta. 2018. "Hatima mafao wenye vyeti feki yatajwa." *Nipashe*, Dar es Salaam, February 13, 2018.

Noret, Joël. 2017. "For a Multidimensional Class Analysis in Africa." *Review of African Political Economy* 44, no. 154: 654–61.

———, ed. 2019. *Social Im/mobilities in Africa: Ethnographic Approaches*. New York: Berghahn Books.

Nuhu, Said, and Wilbard Jackson Kombe. 2021. "Experiences of Private Firms in Delivering Land Services in Peri-urban Areas in Tanzania." *International Planning Studies* 26, no. 2: 101–16.

Nuttall, Sarah, and Achille Mbembe. 2005. "A Blasé Attitude: A Response to Michael Watts." *Public Culture* 17, no. 1: 193–201.

Nyerere, Julius Kambarage. 1962. *Ujamaa: The Basis of African Socialism*. Dar es Salaam: Tanganyika Standard.

———. 1967. *Freedom and Unity / Uhuru na Umoja: A Selection from Writings and Speeches, 1952–1965*. Dar es Salaam: Oxford University Press.

———. 1968. *Freedom and Socialism / Uhuru na Ujamaa: A Selection from Writings and Speeches, 1965–1967*. Dar es Salaam: Oxford University Press.

Obeng-Odoom, Franklin. 2020. *Property, Institutions, and Social Stratification in Africa*. Cambridge: Cambridge University Press.

———. 2021. *The Commons in an Age of Uncertainty: Decolonizing Nature, Economy and Society*. Toronto: University of Toronto Press.

Okoye, Victoria Ogoegbunam. 2021. "The Colonial Afterlife of Encroachment." *L'internationale Online*, December 11, 2021. www.internationaleonline.org/research/decolonising_practices/207_the_colonial_afterlife_of_encroachment/.

Olajide, Oluwafemi, and Taibat Lawanson. 2021. "Urban Paradox and the Rise of the Neoliberal City: Case Study of Lagos, Nigeria." *Urban Studies* 59, no. 9: 1763–81.

Ortega, Arnisson Andre. 2016. *Neoliberalizing Spaces in the Philippines: Suburbanization, Transnational Migration, and Dispossession*. London: Lexington Books.

Owens, Geoffrey Ross. 2004. "On the Edge of a City: An Historical Ethnography of Urban Identity in the Northwestern Suburbs of Dar es Salaam, Tanzania." PhD diss., University of Wisconsin–Madison.

———. 2010. "Post-Colonial Migration: Virtual Culture, Urban Farming and New Periurban Growth in Dar es Salaam, Tanzania, 1975–2000." *Africa* 80, no. 2: 249–74.

Owens, Kathryn E. 2014. "Negotiating the City: Urban Development in Tanzania." PhD diss., University of Michigan.

Owens, Kathryn E., Kelly Askew, Rie Odgaard, Howard Stein, and Faustin Maganga. 2018. "Fetishizing the Formal: Institutional Pluralism and Land Titling in Tanzania." *Tanzania Journal of Development Studies* 16, no. 1: 39–86.

Page, Ben. 2019. "Domestic Dramas: Class, Taste and Home Decoration in Buea, Cameroon." In *Social Im/mobilities in Africa: Ethnographic Approaches*, edited by Joël Noret, 178–98. New York: Berghahn Books.

Page, Ben, and Claire Mercer. 2012. "Why Do People Do Stuff? Reconceptualizing Remittance Behaviour in Diaspora-Development Research and Policy." *Progress in Development Studies* 12, no. 1: 1–18.

Page, Ben, and Emile Sunjo. 2018. "Africa's Middle Classes: Building Houses and Constructing Identities in the Small Town of Buea, Cameroon." *Urban Geography* 39, no. 1: 75–103.

Paget, Dan. 2021. "Mistaken for Populism: Magufuli, Ambiguity and Elitist Plebeianism in Tanzania." *Journal of Political Ideologies* 26, no. 2: 121–41.

Pauli, Julia. 2019. *The Decline of Marriage in Namibia: Kinship and Social Class in a Rural Community*. Bielefeld: Transcript Verlag.

Pedersen, Rasmus Hundsbæk, and Thabit Jacob. 2019. "Political Settlement and the Politics of Legitimation in Countries Undergoing Democratization: Insights from Tanzania, Effective States and Inclusive Development." Working Paper no. 124, University of Manchester.

Pellow, Deborah. 2015. "Multiple Modernities." *Home Cultures* 12, no. 1: 55–81.

Penvenne, Jeanne. 1995. *African Workers and Colonial Racism: Mozambican Strategies and Struggles in Lourenço Marques, 1877–1962*. London: James Currey.

Perlman, Janice. 2010. *Favela: Four Decades of Living on the Edge in Rio de Janeiro*. Oxford: Oxford University Press.

Perullo, Alex. 2005. "Hooligans and Heroes: Youth Identity and Hip-hop in Dar es Salaam, Tanzania." *Africa Today* 51, no. 4: 75–101.

———. 2011. *Live from Dar es Salaam: Popular Music and Tanzania's Music Economy*. Bloomington: Indiana University Press.

Perzyna, Iga, Marie Morel, Berend van der Lans, and Antoni Fokers. 2021. "Everyday Originals: Between Iconic and Vernacular Architecture." In *Architectural Guide: Sub-Saharan*

Africa, vol. 1, *Introduction to the History and Theory of Sub-Saharan Architecture*, edited by Philipp Meuser and Adil Dalbai, 202–5. Berlin: DOM Publishers.

Peters, Pauline. 2004. "Inequality and Social Conflict over Land in Africa." *Journal of Agrarian Change* 4, no. 3: 269–314.

———. 2009. "Challenges in Land Tenure and Land Reform in Africa: Anthropological Contributions." *World Development* 37, no. 8: 1317–25.

Piketty, Thomas. 2014. *Capital in the Twenty-First Century*. Cambridge: Harvard University Press.

Pitcher, M. Anne. 2017. "Varieties of Residential Capitalism in Africa: Urban Housing Provision in Luanda and Nairobi." *African Affairs* 116 (464): 365–90.

Ponte, Stefano. 2002. *Farmers and Markets in Tanzania: How Policy Reforms Affect Rural Livelihoods in Africa*. Oxford: James Currey.

Ponte, Stefano, and Dan Brockington. 2020. "From Pyramid to Pointed Egg? A 20-year Perspective on Poverty, Prosperity, and Rural Transformation in Tanzania." *African Affairs* 119, no. 475: 203–23.

Pratt, Cranford. 1976. *The Critical Phase in Tanzania, 1945–1968: Nyerere and the Emergence of a Socialist Strategy*. Cambridge: Cambridge University Press.

Quayson, Ato. 2014. *Oxford Street, Accra: City Life and the Itineraries of Transnationalism*. Durham, NC: Duke University Press.

Quijano, Annibal. 2000. "Coloniality of Power, Eurocentrism and Latin America." *Nepantla: Views from the South* 1, no. 3: 533–80.

Raikes, Phil. 1978. "Rural Differentiation and Class-Formation in Tanzania." *Journal of Peasant Studies* 5, no. 3: 285–325.

Raimbault, Franck. 2010. "The Evolution of Dar es Salaam's Peri-urban Space during the Period of German Colonisation (1890–1914)." In *From Dar es Salaam to Bongoland: Urban Mutations in Tanzania*, edited by Bernard Calas, 23–97. Dar es Salaam: Mkuki na Nyota Publishers.

Rakodi, Carole, and Clement Leduka. 2003. "Informal Land Delivery Processes and Access to Land for the Poor: A Comparative Study of Six African Cities." Policy Brief 6, International Development Department, University of Birmingham.

Rao, Vyjayanthi, Filip de Boeck, and AbdouMaliq Simone. 2010. "Urbanism beyond Architecture: African Cities as Infrastructure." In *African Cities Reader 01*, edited by Ntone Edjabe and Edgar Pieterse, 23–40. Cape Town: African Centre for Cities and Chimurenga.

Resnick, Danielle. 2015. "The Political Economy of Africa's Emergent Middle Class: Retrospect and Prospects." *Journal of International Development* 27: 573–87.

Rex, John, and Robert Moore. 1967. *Race, Community and Conflict*. Oxford: Oxford University Press.

Rizzo, Matteo. 2017. *Taken for a Ride: Grounding Neoliberalism, Precarious Labour, and Public Transport in an African Metropolis*. Oxford: Oxford University Press.

Robinson, Jennifer, Philip Harrison, Jie Shen, and Fulong Wu. 2021. "Financing Urban Development, Three Business Models: Johannesburg, Shanghai and London." *Progress in Planning*, 154, https://doi.org/10.1016/j.progress.2020.100513.

Rodney, Walter. 2022. "Class Contradictions in Tanzania." In *Decolonial Marxism: Essays from the Pan-African Revolution*, edited by Asha Rodney, Patricia Rodney, Ben Mabie, and Jesse Benjamin, 246–75. London: Verso.

Roque, Sandra. 2012. "Cidade and Bairro: Classification, Constitution and Experience of Urban Space in Angola." *Social Dynamics: A Journal of African Studies* 37, no. 3: 332–48.

Rose, Carol. 1994. *Property as Persuasion: Essays on the History, Theory and Rhetoric of Ownership*. Boulder, CO: Westview Press.

Roy, Ananya. 2003. *City Requiem, Calcutta: Gender and the Politics of Poverty*. Minneapolis: University of Minnesota Press.

———. 2015. "What Is Urban about Critical Urban Theory?" *Urban Geography* 37, no. 6: 810–23.

Rwegasira, Abdon. 2012. *Land as a Human Right: A History of Land Law and Practice in Tanzania*. Dar es Salaam: Mkuki na Nyota Publishers.

Rweyemamu, Aisa. 2016. "Over Sh193bn Lost Annually to Ghost Workers." *Guardian on Sunday*, Dar es Salaam, August 21, 2016.

Said, Edward W. 1978. *Orientalism*. London: Routledge and Kegan Paul.

Samoff Joel. 1979a. "The Bureaucracy and the Bourgeoisie: Decentralization and Class Structure in Tanzania." *Comparative Studies in Society and History* 21, no. 1: 30–62.

———. 1979b. "Education in Tanzania: Class Formation and Reproduction." *Journal of Modern African Studies* 17, no. 1: 47–69.

Sanders, Todd. 2008. "Buses in Bongoland: Seductive Analytics and the Occult." *Anthropological Theory* 8, no. 2: 107–32.

Sanga, Imani. 2013. "Musical Figuring of Postcolonial Urban Segmentarity and Marginality in Selected 'Bongo Fleva' Songs in Dar es Salaam, Tanzania." *International Review of the Aesthetics and Sociology of Music* 44, no. 2: 385–405.

Savage, Mike. 2010. "The Politics of Elective Belonging." *Housing, Theory and Society* 27, no. 2: 115–61.

Savage, Mike, James Barlow, Peter Dickens, and Tony Fielding. 1992. *Property, Bureaucracy and Culture: Middle-Class Formation in Contemporary Britain*. London: Routledge.

Sawyer, Lindsay. 2014. "Piecemeal Urbanisation at the Peripheries of Lagos." *African Studies* 73, no. 2: 271–89.

Schneider, Leander. 2014. *Government of Development: Peasants and Politicians in Postcolonial Tanzania*. Bloomington: Indiana University Press.

Schubert, Jon. 2017. *Working the System: A Political Ethnography of the New Angola*. Ithaca, NY: Cornell University Press.

Sheppard, Eric. 2008. "Geographic Dialectics?" *Environment and Planning A* 40: 2603–12.

Sheuya, Shaaban. 2007. "Reconceptualizing Housing Finance in Informal Settlements: The Case of Dar es Salaam, Tanzania." *Environment and Urbanization* 19, no. 2: 441–56.

———. 2009. "Urban Poverty and Housing Transformations in Informal Settlements: The Case of Dar es Salaam, Tanzania." *International Development Planning Review* 31, no. 1: 81–108.

Shimeles, Abebe, and Mthuli Ncube. 2015. "The Making of the Middle Class in Africa: Evidence From DHS Data." *Journal of Development Studies* 51, no. 2: 178–93.

Shivji, Issa G. 1976. *Class Struggles in Tanzania*. London: Heinemann.

———, ed. 1986. *The State and the Working People in Tanzania*. Dakar: CODESRIA.

———. 1998. *Not Yet Democracy: Reforming Land Tenure in Tanzania*. International Institute for Environment and Development, HAKIARDHI and Faculty of Law, University of Dar es Salaam.

————. 2006. *Let the People Speak: Tanzania Down the Road to Neo-liberalism*. Senegal: CODESRIA.

Sikor, Thomas, and Christian Lund. 2009. "Access and Property: A Question of Power and Authority." *Development and Change* 40, no. 1: 1–22.

Simone, AbdouMaliq. 2004. *For the City Yet to Come: Changing African Life in Four Cities*. Durham, NC: Duke University Press.

————. 2019. "Maximum Exposure: Making Sense in the Background of Extensive Urbanization." *Environment and Society D: Society and Space* 37, no. 6: 990–1006.

Simson, Rebecca. 2020. "The Rise and Fall of the Bureaucratic Bourgeoisie: Public Sector Employees and Economic Privilege in Postcolonial Kenya and Tanzania." *Journal of International Development* 32, no. 5: 607–35.

Skeggs, Beverley. 2004. "Exchange, Value and Affect: Bourdieu and 'the Self.'" *Sociological Review* 52, no. 2: 75–95.

Smiley, Sarah. 2009. "The City of Three Colors: Segregation in Colonial Dar es Salaam, 1891–1961." *Historical Geography* 37: 178–96.

————. 2010. "Expatriate Everyday Life in Dar es Salaam, Tanzania: Colonial Origins and Contemporary Legacies." *Social and Cultural Geography* 11, no. 4: 327–42.

Smith, Constance. 2019. *Nairobi in the Making: Landscapes of Time and Urban Belonging*. Oxford: James Currey.

Soja, Edward. 1980. "The Socio-spatial Dialectic." *Annals of the Association of American Geographers* 70, no. 2: 207–25.

Solomon, Aisa Oberlin. 2011. *The Role of Households in Solid Waste Management in East Africa Capital Cities*. Environmental Policy Series, vol. 4. Wageningen: Wageningen Academic Publishers.

Southall, Roger. 2016. *The New Black Middle Class in South Africa*. Suffolk: James Currey.

————. 2018. "(Middle-) Class Analysis in Africa: Does It Work?" *Review of African Political Economy*, 45, no. 157: 467–77.

Spronk, Rachel. 2012. *Ambiguous Pleasures: Sexuality and Middle Class Self-Perceptions in Nairobi*. New York: Berghahn Books.

————. 2014. "Exploring the Middle Classes in Nairobi: From Modes of Production to Modes of Sophistication." *African Studies Review* 57, no. 1: 93–114.

————. 2020. "Structures, Feelings and Savoir Faire: Ghana's Middle Classes in the Making." *Africa* 90, no. 3: 470–88.

Srivastava, Sanjay. 2014. *Entangled Urbanism: Slum, Gated Community and Shopping Mall in Delhi and Gurgaon*. Oxford: Oxford University Press.

Steel, Griet, Femke van Noorloos, and Christien Klaufus. 2017. "The Urban Land Debate in the Global South: New Avenues for Research." *Geoforum* 83: 133–41.

Steel, Griet, Femke van Noorloos, and Kei Otsuki. 2019. "Urban Land Grabs in Africa?" *Built Environment* 44, no. 4: 389–96.

Stein, Howard, and Kelly Askew. 2009. "Embedded Institutions and Rural Transformation in Tanzania: Privatizing Rural Property and Markets." Paper prepared for the Fourth Meeting of the Africa Task Force, Initiative for Policy Dialogue (Columbia University), Pretoria, South Africa, 9–10 July, 2009.

Stoler, Ann Laura. 2008. "Imperial Debris: Reflections on Ruins and Ruination." *Cultural Anthropology* 23, no. 2: 191–219.

Streule, Monika, Ozan Karaman, Lindsay Sawyer, and Christian Schmid. 2020. "Popular Urbanization: Conceptualizing Urbanization Processes beyond Informality." *International Journal of Urban and Regional Research* 44, no. 4: 652–72.

Stren, Richard. 1975a. *Urban Inequality and Housing Policy in Tanzania: The Problem of Squatting*. Berkeley: Institute of International Studies, University of California Berkeley.

———. 1975b. "Urban Policy and Performance in Kenya and Tanzania." *Journal of Modern African Studies* 13, no. 2: 267–94.

———. 1982. "Underdevelopment, Urban Squatting, and the State Bureaucracy: A Case Study of Tanzania." *Canadian Journal of African Studies* 16, no. 1: 67–91.

Sumich, Jason. 2018. *The Middle Class in Mozambique: The State and the Politics of Transformation in Southern Africa*. Cambridge: Cambridge University Press.

Sumich, Jason, and Morten Nielsen. 2020. "The Political Aesthetics of Middle Class Housing in (not so) Neoliberal Mozambique." *Antipode* 52, no. 4: 1216–34.

Sundet, Gier. 1997. "The Politics of Land in Tanzania." DPhil diss., Oxford University.

Sunjo, Emile, and Ben Page. 2022. "Land Restitution and Conflict in Cameroon: The Case of the Bakweri." *African Affairs* 121, no. 485: 623–48.

Sutton, John E. G. 1970. "Dar es Salaam: A Sketch of a Hundred Years." *Tanzania Notes and Records* 71: 1–20.

Swantz, Marja-Liisa. 1996. "Village Development: on Whose Conditions?" In *What Went Right in Tanzania: People's Response to Directed Development*, edited by Marja-Liisa Swantz and Aili Mari Tripp. Dar es Salaam: Dar es Salaam University Press.

Táíwò, Olúfémi. 2022. *Against Decolonisation: Taking African Agency Seriously*. London: International African Institute, Hurst and Company.

Tanganyika. 1923. *Land Ordinance, 1923. Ordinance No. 3 of 1923*. Dar es Salaam: Government Printer.

Tenga, Ringo Willy, and Sist J. Mramba. 2015. *Tanzania LGAF Synthesis Report*. Washington, DC: World Bank, 2015. https://openknowledge.worldbank.org/handle/10986/28512.

Therborn, Göran. 2020. "Dreams and Nightmares of the World's Middle Classes." *New Left Review*, July/August: 63–87.

Thompson, E. P. 1963. *The Making of the English Working Class*. London: Penguin.

———. 1975. *Whigs and Hunters: The Origins of the Black Act*. London: Penguin.

Tomás, Antonio. 2022. *In the Skin of the City: Spatial Transformation in Luanda*. Durham, NC: Duke University Press.

Tripp, Aili Mari. 1997. *Changing the Rules: The Politics of Liberalization and the Urban Informal Economy in Tanzania*. Berkeley: University of California Press.

Tsing, Anna Lowenhaupt. 2004. *Friction: An Ethnography of Global Connection*. Princeton: Princeton University Press.

Turner, John. 1972. *Freedom to Build: Dweller Control of the Housing Process*. New York: Macmillan.

UNDESA (United Nations Department of Economic and Social Affairs) 2019. *World Urbanization Prospects: The 2018 Revision*. New York: United Nations.

URT (United Republic of Tanzania). 1981. *1978 Population Census*, vol. 2, *Population by Age and Sex for Villages/Wards and Urban Areas*. Dar es Salaam: Bureau of Statistics, Ministry of Planning and Economic Affairs.

———. 1994. *Report of the Presidential Commission of Inquiry into Land Matters*, vol. 1, *Land Policy and Land Tenure Structure*. Ministry of Lands, Housing and Urban

Development, in cooperation with the Scandinavian Institute of African Studies, Uppsala, Sweden.

———. 1997. *Songo Songo Gas to Electricity Project Resettlement Programme and Plan.* December 1997. http://documents1.worldbank.org/curated/en/331161468117561160/pdf /multi-page.pdf.

———. 1999. *The Tanzania Development Vision 2025.* Planning Commission.

———. 2013. *2012 Population and Housing Census: Population Distribution by Administrative Areas.* Dar es Salaam: National Bureau of Statistics and Ministry of Finance.

———. 2017. *Crime and Traffic Incidents Statistics Report, January to December 2016.* Dodoma: Tanzania Police Force and National Bureau of Statistics.

———. 2019. *The Economic Survey 2018.* Dodoma, Tanzania: Ministry of Finance and Planning.

———. 2021a. *Crime and Traffic Incidents Statistics Report, January to December 2020.* Dodoma: Tanzania Police Force and National Bureau of Statistics.

———. 2021b. Speech of the Minister of Land, Housing and Human Settlements Development, The Honourable William V. Lukuvi MP, Presenting to Parliament the Ministry's Estimates of Income and Expenditure for Financial Year 2021/22. Accessed 21 July 2022. www.lands.go.tz/speeches.

URT (United Republic of Tanzania), Ministry of Finance and Planning, Tanzania National Bureau of Statistics and President's Office—Finance and Planning, Office of the Chief Government Statistician, Zanzibar. 2022. *The 2022 Population and Housing Census: Administrative Units Population Distribution Report; Tanzania Mainland.* Dodoma: December 2022.

Von Freyhold, Michaela. 1977. "The Post-Colonial State and Its Tanzanian Version." *Review of African Political Economy* 4, no. 8: 75–89.

Wakongere, Simon Daudi, and Samwel Sanga Alanganga. 2020. "Factors Affecting Land Titling during Regularization of Informal Settlements in Dar es Salaam Tanzania." *International Journal of Real Estate Studies* 14, no. 2: 73–97.

Walwa, William J. 2017. "Governing Security at the Grassroots Level: Effectiveness of Community-Led Security Mechanisms in Dar es Salaam." *African Review* 44, no. 1: 99–137.

wa Thiong'o, Ngũgĩ. 1986. *Decolonising the Mind: The Politics of Language in African Literature.* Rochester, NY: Boydell and Brewer.

Watson, Vanessa. 2013. "African Urban Fantasies: Dreams or Nightmares?" *Environment and Urbanization* 26, no. 1: 215–31.

Watts, Michael. 2018. "Frontiers: Authority, Precarity and Insurgency at the Edge of the State." *World Development* 101: 477–88.

Weber, Max. (1922) 1978. *Economy and Society: An Outline of Interpretive Sociology.* Berkeley: University of California Press.

Weiss, Brad. 2009. *Street Dreams and Hip Hop Barbershops: Global Fantasy in Urban Tanzania.* Bloomington: Indiana University Press.

Weldeghebrael, Ezana Haddis. 2022. "The Framing of Inner-City Slum Redevelopment by an Aspiring Developmental State: The Case of Addis Ababa, Ethiopia." *Cities* 125.

Werbner, Pnina. 2018. "Rethinking Class and Culture in Africa: Between E. P. Thompson and Pierre Bourdieu." *Review of African Political Economy* 45, no. 155: 7–24.

West, Michael O. 2002. *The Rise of an African Middle Class: Colonial Zimbabwe, 1898–1965.* Bloomington: Indiana University Press, 2002.

White, Ben, Saturnino M Borras Jr, Ruth Hall, Ian Scoones, and Wendy Wolford. 2012. "The New Enclosures: Critical Perspectives on Corporate Land Deals." *The Journal of Peasant Studies* 39, no. 3–4: 619–47.

White, Luise. 1986. "Prostitution, Identity and Class Consciousness in Nairobi during World War II." *Signs* 11, no. 2: 255–73.

Wizara ya Ardhi, Nyumba na Maendeleo ya Makazi (Ministry of Land, Housing and Human Settlements Development). 2016. *Toleo No.7, Mei 2016–Oktoba 2016*. Dodoma, Tanzania.

Wolff, Stina Møldrup, Amelia Kuch, and Joshua Chipman. 2018. "Urban Land Governance in Dar es Salaam: Actors, Processes and Ownership Documentation." *International Growth Centre Working Paper* no. C-40412-TZA-1.

World Bank. 2016. *Measuring Living Standards within Cities*. Washington, DC: World Bank.

——. 2019. *Tanzania Mainland Poverty Assessment*. Washington, DC: World Bank. https://openknowledge.worldbank.org/handle/10986/33031.

Yahya-Othman, Saida. 1997. "If the Cap Fits: Kanga Names and Women's Voice in Swahili Society." *Afrikanistische Arbeitspapiere* 51: 135–49.

Yiftachel, Oren. 2009. "Theoretical Notes on 'Gray Cities': The Coming of Urban Apartheid." *Planning Theory* 8, no. 1: 88–100.

Zhang, Li. 2010. *In Search of Paradise: Middle-Class Living in a Chinese Metropolis*. Ithaca, NY: Cornell University Press.

INDEX

Founded in 1893,
UNIVERSITY OF CALIFORNIA PRESS
publishes bold, progressive books and journals
on topics in the arts, humanities, social sciences,
and natural sciences—with a focus on social
justice issues—that inspire thought and action
among readers worldwide.

The UC PRESS FOUNDATION
raises funds to uphold the press's vital role
as an independent, nonprofit publisher, and
receives philanthropic support from a wide
range of individuals and institutions—and from
committed readers like you. To learn more, visit
ucpress.edu/supportus.